W9-AEF-383

WITHDRAWN

Gramley Library
Salem Academy and College
Winston-Salem, N.C. 27108

WITHDRA...

The Republic
of Burma
Shave

Books by Richard Katrovas

Dithyrambs
Prague, USA (Stories)
The Book of Complaints
The Public Mirror
Snug Harbor
Green Dragons

The Republic of Burma Shave

Richard Katrovas

Gramley Library
Salem Academy and College
~~ton-Salem, N.C. 27108

Carnegie Mellon University Press
Pittsburgh 2001

Acknowledgments

Sections of this book, in different versions, appeared in *California Childhood* (Berkeley: Creative Arts Books, ed. Gary Soto), *New Virginia Review*, and *Telescope: A Journal of Literature and Thought*; I thank the editors. I thank the essential American poet Gerald Stern for the right encouragement at the right time, and I thank Susan Tete and Susan Gebhardt for their critical comments. I thank my colleagues in the English Department of the University of New Orleans for numerous acts of friendship and several invigorating battles, all of which have informed my understanding of the social role of the poet.

This book is dedicated to the memory of the scholar Mary FitzGerald, who loved poetry and poets much more than either deserve.

Library of Congress Control Number 99-72506
ISBN 0-88748-328-3 (Pbk.)
Copyright © 2001 by Richard Katrovas
All rights reserved
Printed and bound in the United States of America

10 9 8 7 6 5 4 3 2 1

All of the epigraphs herein are from *Plato's Republic*, translated by G.M.A. Grube (Indianapolis: Hackett Publishing Company, 1974).

The Republic of Burma Shave

> Then we must first of all, it seems,
> control the story tellers.
>
> Book II 377 C

At mid-life, I'm compelled to consider why, were I not a "poet," I'd not be much of anything. And yet I hate the sound of the word "poet," and am embarrassed to be one. I assume I have, if not a talent, at least a knack, a compulsion to marshal it, and a love for the art that turns to loathing and back to love and back and back and back with greater rapidity as I age. Do I belabor the obvious to observe that poetic ambition is a disease whose primary symptom is self-aggrandizing foolishness?

I have known and felt affection for many other poets, hundreds, and I have met no more than four or five who did not desire every waking moment to stand before crowds and declaim their latest hearts' issue, fully aware that any poetry "audience" is comprised primarily of individuals who, if they had their druthers, would themselves be standing at the podium. Concert goers may fantasize standing on the stage sawing at an electric guitar, or bellowing the lead in *Don Giovani,* but few, I imagine, would actually, if given the opportunity, spring from their seats and trot to the stage ecstatic. Yet I've rarely met an audience member of a poetry reading who wasn't ready to supplant the evening's entertainment (one can see such a desire smoldering in the eyes). Every poetry reading is attended primarily by understudies praying that the lead takes deathly ill.

As a member of the poetry community, I have over the years witnessed the most outrageous displays of egotism, and as a younger man was often guilty of such displays. I'd stand on a stage or in whatever performance space had been afforded me, and speak my early published poems as though I knew the secret to breaking hearts. I was probably quite sexy because, Lord, I sure wanted to be! Sexy or not, I was certainly an incredible asshole, and I now find it so easy to admit that I was— twenty, fifteen, even twelve years ago—a narcissistic asshole because at present I stand among so many other confirmed and reformed narcissistic assholes in this far-flung, contentious tribe of poets.

Poor Keats. . . one night he and that asshole Hunt exchanged laurels, and I imagine that broad-shouldered, squat man-child at first thrilling to the occasion, but later feeling the profoundest shame. Keats could not have achieved greatness had he not felt that shame, which he wrote about in letters and even in verses, and which seemed to have been his turning point out of prodigious mediocrity.

I've come to realize that when I manage to write a few good lines of verse, the occasion is as much a matter of dumb luck as will. I can't say how many times I've gotten lucky, but those few occasions are afloat on a quaint pond of mere competence, the murky bottom of which is littered with hideous shapes. The knowledge of how difficult it is to write good verse weighs more heavily on me each year, and each year I'm amazed at how many people I meet who are in so many ways smarter, wiser and more erudite than I and yet seem unaware that writing good verse is difficult. Keats knew it; his soul was crushed by the knowledge that his ambition, over which he, like the rest of us over our own, had no control, was a slippery slope to giddy despair.

But the kind of ambition John Keats was driven by few feel anymore. Poetic ambition in the old sense—propelled by an other-worldly passion for the Sublime—few, outside of mental hospitals, are even capable of feeling. Poetic ambition in the old sense has given way to an ambition akin to that of movie actors, pop singers and, more to the point, stand-up comics. If only poets, especially the young ones, worked as hard as stand-up comics! If only they were as sensitive to audiences.

I recently snapped at a poetry reading, went a little nuts. We were finishing the second of the four weeks of the Prague Summer Seminars, a study-abroad program primarily for creative writers I founded with Dominika, my wife, and for which I serve as director. Each Friday night is reserved for "student readings," a tedious but extremely important aspect of the program. I sat in the front row, as I usually do, sipping Becherovka—a delicious herbal liquor concocted in Karlovy Vary—trying to appear focused. I compose and deliver six formal introductions, each week of the program, for the fine "established" writers who serve as faculty, but on Friday nights my only job is to be present and seem engaged after five consecutive twelve-hour workdays.

No matter how much I would rather be at home watching M*A*S*H dubbed in Czech, I am always charmed and surprised at these events. The hit of this past program was a woman in her eighties who seemed over the course of the program to be barely fending off dementia; she had that wild gaze of the very old, and needed assistance with almost everything, the phones, municipal transportation, even getting to and from her room sometimes. But then one Friday night she mounted the stage, as gingerly as. . . an eighty-something year-old person mounts anything, and transformed into a lucid, funny, engaging chanter of the story of her life, the most compelling aspect of which was that she'd been a pilot during World War II, dragging training targets behind her single-engine something-or-other. She read a charming, very moving poem dedicated to Amelia Earhart, and the subtext of her performance of course had to do with being a woman and dreaming— and acting— beyond gender biases. The young women in the audience were particularly moved. Her verse was not spectacular, but its occasion was transcendent, and hearing that old woman speak her life brought tears to my eyes.

But later I snapped when a twenty-something beautiful boy with an obvious loving nature, but one which engaged primarily itself, assumed the stage. He'd read his naively sexy poems the previous Friday, yet had not attended (I can't help but keep track of such silly things) a single event of the program in between. I wanted to wag my finger at him like the old schoolmarm I sometimes am, or just slap him up 'side the head. Which is to say I'd taken one too many pulls off the Becherovka, and sat through one too many readings. I actually heckled him— hardly behavior becoming a program director. His performance was melodramatic and his verse ill-conceived and naive, and he enjoyed himself, despite my heckling, much too much. The audience was there for him, not the other way around; and though, unfortunately, such is usually the case at literary readings, the fellow was so tightly entombed in his own phony voice that for me, at that moment, he became the symbol of everything I hate about myself and about the community which grants me my social identity.

After his ghastly performance, during a break, I approached him and, in an even voice, asked if he'd attended a single event that week; he nonchalantly said no, to which I responded by further inquiring as to what in his mind justified his performing on consecutive Friday nights having not bothered to attend the three readings that week at which six very good "established" writers had given splendid, professional performances, not to mention the Czech Lecture Series in which several of the Czech Republic's leading literary figures had also performed brilliantly.

First he assured me he was every day out among the Czechs "learning their culture" (I have myself learned nothing about the culture from having sex with my Czech wife or drinking Czech-produced alcohol products, but that I haven't may simply mean I lack the necessary sensitivity) and therefore did not need to attend any other program readings or events. Then he babbled something insulting; I responded in kind but more to the point, then patted his cheek, smiled sardonically (I hope it appeared sardonic), and suggested that he grow up. He screamed that Robert Creeley loves his work, which I'm certain meant that Creeley on some occasion glanced at a few lines and didn't pronounce them horrible.

Who was the bigger ass? I was, of course. The guy had paid for the program, wasn't seeking academic credit, and if that meant he'd spend Saturday through Thursday bonking pretty Czech girls or pretty Czech boys or both and using a captured audience for his own onanistic pleasure on consecutive Fridays, well, that should have been just fine with me. That it wasn't was my problem, not his. I apologized to him later, but it didn't matter. Between my heckling and my apology he'd experienced enough additional unfettered sex, alcohol, and God-knows-what else, that he'd Rimbauded his life leagues beyond me and my quaint judgments, and had probably spewed many reams more of such stuff as that for which I'd heckled him. Such as he are blissfully numb to criticism, though one day, in his late thirties, if he lives that long, he will awaken one dark morning, alone, and weep, convulsively and inexplicably, for the fool he was as a younger man. I did.

Gramley Library
Salem Academy and College
Winston-Salem, N.C. 27108

Plato was concerned with the power of poetry, particularly but not exclusively, in terms of performance. He wanted poetry to have certain— what he considered— positive effects so that citizens of his ideal state, particularly his theoretical leaders-in-training, would be appropriately influenced. Of course, if Plato crawled out of the dust to do an updated edition of his *Republic*, he would focus on electronic media exclusively, though his argument would, I fancy, remain relatively unchanged. Poetry, or anything printed that doesn't sell in supermarkets, would be irrelevant to his argument. We who call ourselves and each other poets have absolutely no effect on the social order in terms of the quality and nature of what we make; we may, though, have some quirky collective effect. That is, the mere fact that there are so many thousands of people today calling themselves poets surely creates some resonance through the population, a low sustained humming so innocuous most folks don't even bother seeking the source of it. And this is only perhaps because, unlike skateboarding, ballooning, or ballroom dancing, poetry, as an idea, continues to have some cultural heft, even if the specific products are largely irrelevant. Poetry remains a powerful idea, or ideal, even as poems have been supplanted by music videos, TV commercials, and billboards. The community of poets, as it continues to swell by virtue of its insular activities, reinforces what most non-poets assume: that poetry is irrelevant yet transcendent. That something as integral to the origin of all human society should be thus regarded is poetry's, albeit paradoxical, authority. I'm convinced that under social circumstances in which poetry may say whatever the poet wishes it to, that is, may regard any subject matter and express any sentiment, this paradoxical authority is the necessary lot of poets and the art. Only when political power is duped into thinking that poetry is not irrelevant, as was true, for example, in Prague before '89, do poets and what they make achieve a moral authority whose aesthetic dimension is integral.

Well, the fact of the matter is, for whatever reasons, I am a poet, and being one has afforded me a livelihood (teaching, of course) and even a little dubious prestige. If I were not a poet I don't know what I'd be, maybe dead. Poetry and the community of poets saved my life and gave me a life. I was encouraged to sing my oddness, have even been celebrated a little for doing so. I'm an American poet, one literally of thousands, but I didn't grow up in America, nor in any other country, under any other authority than the spastic whim of my insane young father. I grew up in cars on American highways, the oldest child of two outlaws, Dick and Joan, who made five children on their journey to nowhere, and in the loveless care of the welfare system for those years my father was in prison. I knew despair as a child, and hunger and debilitating loneliness and rootlessness, though as an adult I have known joy and wonder. I have lived, like so many, through the hell of divorce, in my case from a person who is more beautiful and decent and wise than what anyone such as I could ever deserve, only to marry someone more beautiful and decent and wise than anyone such as I could ever deserve, and by this final union I have been blessed with two children who are all I need to know of redemption. Somehow, being a poet, I believe, has granted me my joy, my blessed life, and for all my grousing about the silliness of American poetry—and, Lord, it is hugely silly—I love it, embrace it, owe it my life.

I am the son of a pathological liar, and because I am so desperate not to be like him my strongest compulsion in all discourses is to tell the truth, though I have lied on occasion to protect myself and to maintain privacy. I shall continue to lie herein, though to protect others and their privacy; I've changed a few names and details in the hope that certain individuals will not be tempted to take contracts out on my life. I cannot, alas, spare some people possible embarrassment, my ex-wife and wife most notably. That is, they will probably be quite embarrassed for some folks to note here that they put up with my shilly-shallying as long as they did. Luckily, my wife doesn't read anything I write unless it gets translated into Czech, and my ex-wife is emotionally so far beyond the events here recounted she will simply call or write me to point out all the details I screwed up. The hardest aspect of summing up my little life has, in fact, been determining what I may get away with leaving out. I have, finally, not felt compelled to display all of my dull trophies of shame, but there are two or three which, if I'd not displayed them herein, this entire enterprise, in my own heart, would have been false to the core. And I will admit here, with no pride, that I wrote this book to satisfy myself, not exclusively, but first, to heal myself to the extent it is possible to do so, and to force myself to face my own foolishness and self-deceptions, particularly as these qualities determine my social roles as teacher, artist, father, husband, son, brother, colleague, political ally, political enemy, citizen. If I hadn't threatened myself with publication of such a book as this, its making would have been mere therapy. My self-regard occurs here in the midst of much damning and praising, cultural stock-taking, stuff I've wanted to say out loud for a while.

All of my little crimes have been crimes of the heart, and few who read this will not be reminded of similar, if more discrete, crimes they have committed. Love makes us goofy, and if we come to love having not accounted for a profound loss adequately or at all, that goofiness can become something dark and psychically dangerous; for that which is unmourned remains unburied, and so, in the ancient sense, corrupt and corrupting.

What follows is as much reverie as memory. The organizing principle here, I suppose, may be simply the thousands of hours I stared out of car windows as a child.

What about the verbal lie? When
and to whom is it useful and not
deserving hatred? Is it not useful
against one's enemies and those of
one's so-called friends who, through
madness or ignorance, are attempting
to do some wrong. . . ? The lie then
becomes useful, like a drug.

Book II 382 c

Dick beat me, I recall, quite savagely. I wept a long time in a bed-room of some dump where we were hiding out. And then after an hour he entered the room, weeping, holding a black sock filled with pennies. It was thus he sought forgiveness. That dark wad hangs still over my life. I was, I think, three or four, maybe five. He, my father, was twenty-two or -three or -four, and, if he was not then, he would soon be wanted, I'm told, in over forty states by various authorities. Joan was a beautiful, bright, funny and mysteriously passive woman a year younger than he. There were already one, two or three kids besides me, the oldest. I had a dream in that place, the day of the beating, a lucid afternoon nap-time dream of a large lidded white box appearing on the floor before the bed I lay in—as I dreamed I thought I'd awakened from my nap—and of a clown in a puffy bright-white jump suit and with orange hair and a red ball on his nose throwing back the lid and leaping from the box, and then another clown who looked just like him leaping out after him, and togeth-er they grabbed me and stuffed me into that box and put the lid back on. I recall the terror of that darkness, trying to scream but making no sound. Everybody's got a dream like that from childhood. I've come to believe such dreams have nothing to do with wishes. Rather, they're simply the cosmos signifying our doom.

That sock was my young and handsome, glib and profoundly stupid young father's conception of redemption.

I am a poet. I'm not very smart as smart people go. I think I have a higher than average IQ; I recall being told that as a kid. But it doesn't mat-ter. It's okay to be stupid if you're a poet. It's probably worse to have a higher than average IQ, but I don't care. I was the oldest of five, and when our father was in prison, I was the Boss of the Kids, compensating, poor-ly of course, for our mother's sweet incompetence. In that role, I assumed size to be the defining issue, and so it was.

Perhaps some poets are born, but not necessarily the great ones. Were he alive today, Milton might be the greatest sci-fi novelist. Donne might be a captain of industry. Dickinson might be in Congress. Whitman might get laid by pretty boys with sufficient frequency he'd settle for a simple, quiet life of bourgeois leisure and success in some gay urban Mecca; in other words, he might settle on being a great lover rather than a great poet. Shakespeare, who might be a theoretical nuclear physicist and practicing psychoanalyst, might also husband an addiction to cross-word puzzles. Perhaps people are born to greatness, but not necessarily to particular endeavors.

Nor was I born a poet, but rather was made one by a starry night on the cusp of puberty, as I took out the garbage in 1964. Since then, I have been doomed to perform the absurd activities associated with the role. Whether I am a good poet or a wretched one is, largely, irrelevant. I'll not talk about my own compulsive attempts to order the world in English-language verse. For at least nine to twelve hours of every day I hate poet-ry, especially my own, so, though I declare myself herein a poet, I shall offer no evidence, for none is necessary. It is the very nature of art in our time that the simple declaration that one is this or that kind of maker is sufficient to make one so.

My stubborn, mean-spirited, pathologically lying progenitor, as far as I can tell, has never wavered in his belief that he is superior to all other living creatures. A total of twenty years in federal and state prisons (this is a rough guess; the figure could be more or less) for the most ludicrously petty cons never came close to convincing him that he is stupid, and he is exceedingly stupid. The several occasions I have spent time with him as an adult have bubbled to the very brim of my patience with his rank stupidity. Yet always I have marveled at the tenacity of his ego. He has been bum rushed and, no doubt, butt plugged in Leavenworth, Attica, the federal joints in Georgia and in Harrisburg, Pennsylvania; he has suffered being oppressed by men who have settled for jobs actually working in prisons, which means they are not even smart enough to be criminals; for twenty-some odd years of his life he never took a shit or shower in pri-vate; for twenty years he lived with the unremitting smell of men's bodies, men most of whom probably thought him, as criminals go, a mere rabbit turd. I cannot imagine the humiliations he suffered, and have not asked about them, knowing him wholly incapable under most circumstances of speaking for more than ninety seconds without lying; yet I know he has suffered soul-wrenching humiliations, and for all he has suffered he is as certain in his early sixties as he was in his early twenties, before he'd done any time, that he is superior to all other living creatures.

I would like to kill my father. I realize that this is not an unusual desire. I am not overwhelmed by the desire to kill him; I usually don't give him much thought anymore. But if I were sitting across from him in a restaurant (an event, alas, which will never again occur), and he sudden-ly began to choke on a chunk of tenderloin, I would not rush to give him the Heimlich Maneuver.

I'd likely stare a long few seconds into the huge-eyed mask of terror his face would become, then rise and walk away. Or I'd take great pleasure hacking a hole in his throat with a table knife and poking a straw in it so he could breathe. Then I'd walk away.

It's not that he destroyed my mother, with the help of multiple sclerosis; or that he destroyed my childhood; or that he brutalized all of us when he was around; it's not that he was the king of failure. What fuels my loathing is that I have seen so many decent people brought down, twisted, their days littered with piles of psychic dog shit, for having suffered minute fractions of the humiliations my father has endured. Why has fate blessed such a stupid being with such a remarkable gift? Why is he allowed to be such a perfect American?

As I attempt to face my life as my father never faced, will never face his, I shall take as my patron shade Archilochos, that stumpy little soldier-for-hire who, legend has it, compelled with poetry an entire family to commit suicide. The daddy had failed, it seems, to deliver a promised daughter. Now that's aesthetic power! Those poems are lost, but imagine Mom, Dad, and the kids reading such verse, marveling at the quality of the prosody, the diction and wit, and sighing, hell, let's ride the Pale Pony, let's bite the Big One, because this guy's really good! Utter silliness of course. Auden proclaimed famously that "poetry makes nothing happen," though Sartre, admittedly in a quite different context, wrote (and this is the only thing from all of *Being and Nothingness* that I can recall, besides the days of tedium plowing through the damned thing) "Nothingness carries being in its heart." Between heartbeats there is nothing.

My father is heartless. He wept as a young man with a sock of pennies in his fist; he expressed infinite remorse innumerable times to my infinitely forgiving and naive mother; he suffered, surely, in all the prison cells he occupied; he suffered at the age of ten the death of a brother two years older than he; and certainly he suffered his father's stern silence and ill regard. But on that microscopic rack of the DNA gyre where the capacity for selfless compassion is determined, he has nothing. Most of us surely have somewhere on that swirl an antidote for selfless compassion, or survival——individual and indeed species—would be impossible. But few people are wholly incapable of brief moments of selfless compassion.

Years ago I got tossed in jail on the Fourth of July for an altercation I'd had with a slimy fellow waiter I'd caught stealing my tips. Before I was bailed out, I sat for hours in a holding tank packed with men, all black except for myself and a kid who seemed barely eighteen. One of my fellow travelers was a huge, muscular guy in cuffs and shackles. It seems he'd broken out of somewhere and killed a guard doing so; this I gleaned from snatches of conversation between him and a fellow he'd obviously known from childhood, and just happened to meet again in that hideous tank. He'd gotten all the way to LA., started a new life, and had returned to New Orleans, or so he said, to "pick up some things" from a sister. He was sitting on a bench feeding pigeons in Jackson Square when a cop recognized him. Surely he knew he'd soon be dead, and he certainly seemed at least mildly grave, yet he did something miraculous. Shackled and cuffed in a windowless stinking holding tank, awaiting return to a place where he would surely be killed, directly or indirectly, by guards for killing one of their own, he noticed from across the tank that the kid with long blond hair was weeping silently into his knees, and scraped and clinked over to him and asked what was wrong.

The kid choked out that he'd been busted with a pound of grass. He didn't say his father would be petulant with anger, but clearly that was what he feared. The big soon-to-be-dead guy in cuffs and shackles spent a minute matter-of-factly explaining to the kid what to do, whom to call and what to say. I remember it seeming to be good advice, and given with no ulterior motives. He'd heard another human in distress, and momentarily forgot his own. He wasn't trying to punk the kid, and there was nothing the kid could do for him. And given the guy's odd stature—a physically powerful man the cops had felt compelled to toss into the holding tank cuffed and shackled—no one of the dozen other guys in there commented on his making such a show of compassion in such a place, under such circumstances, to someone such as that kid. The big soon-to-be-dead guy wouldn't have thought to call his brief, off-handed response to that kid selfless compassion, but that's what it was.

My father is incapable of compassion except as a histrionic exhibition of Christian goodness. He has found Christ, and therefore is forgiven for every petty misdeed he has ever committed, and conspicuously fawns over the crucified Jesus. He lives just outside, or at least did until a couple of years ago, Tallahassee, Florida on several acres of land in a big ugly trailer. He's married to a decent, pathetic woman he wooed through the mail while in prison; she had a successful little business my father helped her with for a couple years after he got out of prison. He is the best she can do, and she is certainly the best he can do, and now he is secure and, as far as I can tell, legal, except that he walks around his property with a pistol strapped to his side. It is of course illegal for a convicted felon to own guns, and he owns numerous rifles and handguns, but as long as he shoots up only the vegetation and the small game scudding across his brief acres, no one will ever complain. He is master of his little white-trash fiefdom, and is an honored member of his church. Everyone in the community loves that he was a career criminal and that now, thanks to Jesus, he's one of them. He calls Catholicism a cult and believes the Jews got what was coming to them. He is definitely more dangerous, ideologically speaking, since letting Christ into his heart.

I shall never let Christ into my heart, or if I do it must occur somehow outside of language. Something nameless and unnamable and unutterably perfect must seek entry to a part of me I reveal to no one, and when I am profoundly changed I shall, I hope, have the decency not to talk about it. Even as poetry is the progeny of religion, it is its antithesis. Even addressing God, it is only prayer in linguistic drag; by its very nature it eschews piety and sets its declaimer above the saints (not to mention Plato's philosopher-rulers). No matter its subject, its subtext is always fucking, and getting fucked by, angels. Yeats's Byzantium was only that, a place where an old man might be fucked by angels. Stevens probably knew this better than all the Moderns, and God knows poor Crane was desperate to be fucked by angels, and that desperation was his glory and his destruction. Millay seems not to have made any bones about her own poetry's concern with angel fucking, and Dickinson's wicked synesthesias were protracted foreplay. Bless the tribe of angel fuckers. Bless my sister and brother poets.

I could have avoided my father unto either of our deaths had my youngest brother not insisted upon reentering my life. He showed up in a tired American luxury car; it was more than a decade old, and in the back seat was a huge Rottweiler he called Charley. My brother Chris was thirty, and I'd only seen him briefly three times since he was seven, most recently a few months earlier for a few hours when I visited our mother's grave for the first time. He was a stranger who gave off odd traces of familiarity. He'd just gotten through an ugly divorce (I'd love to know of a pretty one), and was, as he told it, clearing his head before returning to northern Virginia to start a new business. I let him in. My then-wife thought it charming that I was reuniting with my youngest sibling, the one I had helped raise until the family was split up. I felt waves of foreboding, but tried to connect with him. He was glib, even bright. He'd dropped out of high school and didn't read much, but he was relatively well-spoken, and expressed some fairly sophisticated sentiments about politics and religion. He was good-looking and had a sense of humor. I started to like him. I co-signed a loan for a new pick-up truck (he gave me the rebate). Of course, when he went back to Virginia he stopped making payments, and had stolen one of my credit card numbers which he used indiscriminately. Alas, he was our father.

So I flew out to Virginia and with the help of another brother, Arthur, whom I'd seen also but three times in twenty-three years, tracked him down. "Chris," I said, trying to remain calm, "why did you do it?" He did not or could not answer the question, but did invite me, calmly and seemingly in all seriousness, to kick his ass, which I wanted desperately to do, but didn't. Arthur suggested I call our father, whom he'd heard was doing quite well now. Perhaps he could help.

I had a ten-thousand dollar vehicle I couldn't afford to pay off and thousands of dollars of credit card debt Chris had further fattened, so, with the greatest of trepidation which would of course later be proved wholly justified, I phoned our father from Arthur's tattoo parlor. Dick told me to drive the thing down to Tallahassee and he'd "take care of everything."

My good brother Arthur was a very successful tattoo artist in Fairfax, Virginia. Bikers all along the East Coast sought him out, or so it seemed. His shop was attached to his home, which he shared with a woman seventeen years older than himself. She'd been his foster parent, became his lover (her own son is only three or four years younger than Art; I don't want to imagine that phase of Art's life; it must have been creepy), and by then they were married (I get faint messages, strangely enough through my ex-wife, that Art recently left her). She was, of course, still his mother, and their lives together gave off odd resonances. She was slightly crippled and walked with a cane, and he was therefore certainly daily reminded of our mother's infirmity. Art's wife/mother was a crack executive secretary and made pretty good money in D.C.; Art obviously did quite well with his business, and they lived in a big rickety house she had owned for years and where Arthur spent most of his time working. When he was not at home working, he was out bonking females younger and prettier than his wife, a fact he was quick to make known to me. He and his wife/mother had, it seems, "an understanding." She organized his daily life and showered him with positive regard and genuine affection and even allowed him to screw around; in exchange he remained with her and was not abusive.

He learned to do tattoos in a boys' detention facility, which Arthur claimed is worse than the adult facilities he subsequently occupied. I genuinely liked him, though I did not enjoy being around him. His pain was too large, and he seemed to think I could help him. He seemed to think that by talking with me about our mother, about our childhoods, he would heal. But nothing will heal my brother. And we are so different temperamentally and to some extent culturally that we really can't talk for long. He says things like "keep a tight asshole" for good-bye, and switches to a cartoon voice, Donald Duck's or Porky Pig's, for no apparent reason. He's had absolutely no formal training in art, and yet his tattoos (framed pictures of which lined his parlor walls) seemed to my untrained eye exquisite, and his odd and wonderful paintings have shown in New York. He's an artist from the gut, and I admire him greatly for that. He just makes me extremely uneasy. He, like Dick, owned lots of guns, and though he has a gentle nature, there is wildness in his eyes. He spoke with nostalgic glee of the time as a boy, a few years after Chuck and I were taken away, he'd derailed a freight train in North Carolina, and seemed a little hurt when I wasn't able to laugh along with him as he detailed the destruction. I fear his potential for being one of those weird white guys who goes nuts with weapons. Unlike our father who is a blustering coward, he has the courage to do much damage if the world is ever particularly uncooperative.

We were staying in a trailer when Arthur was born, a trailer outside of Sioux Falls, South Dakota. I was five, but I remember Sioux Falls, South Dakota, and that our father talked a lot about going to Puerto Rico. Dick went hunting one day with a man who lived in one of the other trailers, and brought home several squirrels which he cooked and I think tried to eat. There was a television in our furnished trailer which we could only watch if we draped a blanket over the cabinet and sat under the blanket as in a tunnel; the picture tube was going, and the screen was too dim to see in the daylight. I remember the day Joan brought him back to the trailer from the hospital, and then I recall nothing of Arthur until Chris was born. He bonded with our sister Theresa, who was almost a year older than he. I cannot recall him as a child except as her quieter companion. I didn't care much for either of them.

All of them, Chuck, Theresa, Arthur, and Chris were born on the road. I was born in Norfolk, Virginia, where our parents had grown up, met, and married. Chuck was born in Newport News which was not exactly on the road, but represented the first time Dick had had to get out of Norfolk, running from his first bounced checks. Theresa was born in Atlanta, Georgia, and my memory of her first day from the hospital is remarkably clear. She was red and ugly, and Joan was not thrilled to be leaving the hospital only a few hours after delivering her; the exhausted young woman seemed to nurse and generally tend to the wrinkled screamer with little enthusiasm. We were rolling again. We had stopped just long enough, a week maybe, for her to drop the kid. This was true for all three of the births I can recall. We were rarely anywhere for more than a couple of weeks right up until Dick was caught. We lived in cars and motels. Dick scammed banks and used-car dealers. I have no idea what those two young people thought they were doing.

The just man then has turned out to be
a kind of thief. You may well have
learned this from Homer, for he likes
Odysseus' maternal grandfather,
Autolycus, and at the same time he
says that he excelled all men in
thieving and perjury.

Book I 334 b

He circled the truck, sneering like an expert. He kicked the tires, popped the hood and looked around. It was a new white pickup truck with fewer than eight thousand miles on it; I couldn't tell what flaws he thought he was looking for. As a child I'd watched him innumerable times play the wary consumer with used-car dealers, when actually his major concern was getting off the lot with anything but what he'd driven onto it; the most recent APB would refer, of course, to the vehicle he was trading in, and so he had simply to get some trade-in credit and write a check and he was anonymous again in the Republic of Burma Shave, at least until the check bounced, but by then he'd probably have pulled the trick yet again. We kids learned not to develop sentimental attachments to automobiles. We knew we could count on living in a particular one usually for no more than a couple of weeks, and as briefly as half a day.

I wanted him to assume the loan, but of course he wouldn't do that. He insisted upon keeping the truck in my name and making the monthly payments. That way, he had me. If I angered him, he'd stiff the bank. I wanted nothing to do with him, but now I needed him. On a Fulbright, I'd impregnated a Czech while in Prague, Czechoslovakia during the Velvet Revolution, and so for several weeks, since the 2 a.m. phone call from my Czech darling announcing her predicament and soliciting suggestions as to what she should "do," I'd been living an immense lie with my wife. Awash in self-loathing for the lie I was living, and excited at the prospect of having a child in my life (for even in my fuzzy-headed shocked state I'd had no doubt that she should keep the child), I was in no condition to negotiate. I accepted his proposal, and thereby became connected to him, a situation I loathed and he relished.

I even tried to rewire my regard for him. He had mellowed, and seemed actually to try not to lie, and indeed for brief spells he lied with much less frequency than he had before. A lie would slip out every twenty minutes or so, and usually had to do with how much money he was now worth. At one point he said he was worth four and a half million. I just nodded and said "wow," but could not look him in the eye. Of course

I couldn't challenge him or ask for proof. He and the decent, slightly ridiculous woman he lived with were obviously comfortable; they'd eventually sell her business and probably had some other retirement funds. They had enough to live in modest, white-trash comfort for the rest of their lives, I was sure. I was actually happy for him, in a sardonic kind of way. He was definitely one for the Only In America annals.

That evening, he launched into his Jesus rap. I tried to be polite, and listened without comment. But his discourse became increasingly self-righteous and stupid, and my anger swelled. I stared at him. He was still a handsome man, and radiated still a modicum of charm when he wasn't holding forth. But the more he talked, the more I lamented having emerged from any gene pool to which he had contributed. I wanted to rise, go to him and, before he could grab the pistol he always kept within reach, pound him unconscious with my fists. He was talking about how Jesus loves everyone, even niggers and kikes, but only if they aren't Catholics.

He said nigger a lot. I hate the word. I balk at writing it. This repulsion is probably some liberal tick, but I've felt it since childhood. I become deeply sad hearing people, white and black, say the word. That sadness is my wretched sentimentality. And as I sat and listened to Dick's rant in which racism, homophobia, and sexism were focused through a simplistic and profoundly stupid reading of scriptures, I became more and more sentimental. I thought of my black students, my gay neighbors and colleagues, and my poor deceived wife and pregnant lover, and my sentimentality filled the trailer. I began to rant back at him, pointing out the inconsistencies in his argument. Of course he changed the subject from scriptural interpretation to my particular soul being doomed to hell. He was smug in his knowledge of my doom, even seemed to force back a smile. The only way I could avoid the most wretched of fates was to fall on my knees and pray with him. I told him I would rather eat Satan's shit than fall on my knees in his, my father's, presence. I screamed that he and his Fundamentalist cohorts are all fascists. He smiled and said that Satan was speaking through me. Satan, he informed me, is a liberal.

I burst out laughing. My anger melted. I asked him to explain.

His argument was simple: Satan encourages people to live according to a moral relativism; he didn't use the term, but that's what he meant. I suggested that what was moral relativism to some, was simply tolerance to others, and besides, does Satan encourage a redistribution of wealth through tax codes and social programs? Of course he does, Dick answered. So Satan had been responsible for my mother and the five of us kids living on welfare while Dick was in prison? Satan was responsible for feeding and sheltering us? Satan had us immunized and paid our medical costs? The Great Society was pure evil?

Yes, it was pure evil. Satan caused him, Dick, to do evil things and to go to prison, and then Satan put his, Dick's, family in his, Satan's, evil sanctuary.

I laughed in gleeful sadness. His sweet, pathetic wife entered the main room of the trailer where Dick and I sat across from one another; she smiled to see her dear, righteous husband—who had survived such degradation to find, finally, solace in the bosom of the Lord—getting on so well with his wayward, eldest son. She was a collector of things that had pigs on them, and one whole wall of the trailer was covered with plates on which various sorts of swine were dancing and smiling. My eyes teared with laugher. His life tethered to such a creature as she, and living in the midst of such profound kitsch, he sat before me, grinning like a smug, sainted idiot, and I recalled how much I had missed him as a boy in Elizabeth City, North Carolina where we lived after the first time he was caught, and in the projects of Norfolk, Virginia where we lived the second time he was caught and put away. Always, while he was away, life would be better when he returned. Always, when he returned, life darkened.

I had adored him. He had conned me into believing he was superior to all other living creatures. I was a lucky boy to have a father such as Dick, a man so fearless, so audacious, so, alas, misunderstood.

I was seven the first time he got caught. I remember the sirens, the flashing lights. It was, I think, midday, late winter or early spring, somewhere in central Florida. He screamed and punched the steering wheel. The three youngest began to cry. We'd been stopped before and he'd always gotten out of it. This time, clearly, was different. He ripped something from his pocket, paper I think, and gave it to Joan. He reached under his seat, grabbed the gun, and gave it to Joan. He snarled instructions to her. Holding the newest member of our troupe with one arm, she managed to hide the thing he'd given her in her clothes with the other. She stuffed the pistol in a white bag down by her feet. Dick got out of the car. He was out there a long time, fifteen minutes, maybe. Then he got back in and started up the car. I don't recall what kind of car we had, except that it was a pretty big one. I know the previous one had been a Chrysler.

Two police cars stayed behind us and two stayed in front of us. They kept their lights flashing, but their sirens were silent. They drove slowly, it seemed, and so therefore did we. Dick frantically gave Joan instructions. He told her what to say if asked this or that. We kids were terrified and silent, and for the duration of that slow drive did not exist in the regard of our parents.

Whatever it was they took us to—I suppose a highway patrol station —was quite lovely. I recall a steep, grassy hill that a policeman who watched us let us roll down and play on. The white-stone, three-story structure with two flag poles in front of it was not in a city; there were few other buildings around. They had taken Dick and Joan to the back of the building and a policeman watched us for quite a while before we were allowed to roll down that grassy hill.

I shat my pants. I was seven and mortified. I don't recall exactly how it happened, probably as I rolled repeatedly down that hill, too scared to go back into the building, but I will always associate my father's first being captured with the discomfort of shitty drawers. Stinking, mortified, confused, frightened, I was led eventually to the back of that building to a cell. As contrived and sentimental as it may sound, my father touched my face through the bars and promised he would see me again soon. He promised that everything would be okay. He told me to take care of everyone. He wept. I loved him unconditionally.

That evening Joan and the five of us were on a bus to Elizabeth City, North Carolina. Her mother and several aunts lived there, and Joan had phoned from the highway patrol station to have her mother wire bus fare and a little extra money for food. All the policemen or patrolmen had been very kind to us. Clearly, they'd felt sorry for us. While we'd waited for the money from our tight-assed vaguely Germanic grandmother, a chubby policeman or highway patrolman or whatever he was, they all were, had bought us stuff to eat and drink from a concession on the grounds of that bucolic bastion of law enforcement, and recommended that Joan get me cleaned up. He'd been very polite about it, indeed, seemed sensitive to my humiliation. Joan had then taken me to the bathroom, and I'd waited there naked while she'd gone out to the car to get fresh clothes for me. On the way out the door she'd dumped my drawers in a trash can.

The bus was packed and Joan slept deeply, her head propped against the window. The three younger kids, even Chris who was not yet a year old, slept as they always did in cars, lumped together like puppies. I don't remember where Chuck was, though he was probably right next to me, as always.

Ours is an unshockable age. No single life's trepidations have much resonance in a culture a significant portion of whose population will sit before cameras and calmly bear witness to an assortment of grotesque abuses. "Confessional poetry," an often maligned yet unquestionably predominate lyric mode that flourished through the '50s, '60s and '70s, and exerts strong influence even today, has been upstaged by talk TV. The point of a confessional poem is to posit the speaker, the poet masked (Plath often) or unmasked (Lowell, Snodgrass, even Sexton and most others), as a representative sufferer (this point has been espoused often), someone whose diseased consciousness is the direct consequence of a sick society. Lowell sang class, Plath and Sexton gender pathologies caused by, implicitly caused by a deluded, aggressively exploitive culture. Perhaps it is too easy to say that such poets have for our time become Shelley's unacknowledged legislators, if only because the culture obviously no longer needs such representation; almost everyone is willing to hold up bloody wounds to everyone else. We have transformed from a representative to an absolute democracy of the hurt heart, with Oprah and Jerry presiding over the spectacle of a nation waving pus-oozing wounds at the cameras while simultaneously thrilling at the sight on TV monitors. Lyric poetry, lyric art generally, dances on the margin between a culture's conception of appropriately public, and appropriately private discourses. When the distinction dies, or the margin gets blurred, the authentic work of lyric gets stifled. Angel fucking, of course, continues gloriously unencumbered. Perhaps this little vat of self-involved ejaculations, this little book you are reading, is merely part of such a national process, though I hope it is also about it, especially inasmuch as what I am remembering and misremembering herein has less to do with personal suffering than with my astonishment that I have been so blessed in a universe in which I may assume no transcendent agent, or agents, for blessings.

I am a forty-something American poet of the twentieth century's twilight. I have had an odd life. It has not been spectacular, and certainly not exemplary, just odd. Of the historical events that most determined me, Vietnam is probably chief. That is, missing Vietnam has made me what I am as much as anything else beyond the odd familial particulars. I missed Vietnam by less than two hours; that is, if I'd been born two hours later or earlier, I can't remember which, my lottery number would have been four rather than three-hundred and thirty nine, and I think I'd have been stupid enough to go, though by the time I'd have gotten there it would already have been 1973. How many nineteen or twenty year-old Americans even got sent over in '73? How many got killed? Maybe Vietnam's a moot point, chronologically speaking. I don't know. What's important is that my consciousness was not affected by direct experience of that horror. I've not been to war, so I'm not sure if I'm a coward. It is important to know whether one is a coward or not. I suspect that sometimes I am a coward, and sometimes not. I suspect that under some extreme conditions I would stand and face death, and under some I would run away, wretched and pathetic. I have faced relatively serious danger on several occasions and not embarrassed myself. But war is the Great Truth. We men and women who have not gone to war, or had it come to us, must remain humble before those who have, even those we find pernicious.

Dick used to tell me of his war days. It seems he'd had numerous adventures, and in one version of his life actually went to Korea. Pathological liars (I'm of course not credentialed to make this diagnosis, but nonetheless know it in my heart to be true), even bright ones, often cannot keep up with their lies; few, it would seem, maintain impeccable files on the times, dates, and narrative details of their lies. My father early in my life told me he'd been to war, but never repeated any version of that lie. I'm sure even he could not live with such a lie. So he pretty much stuck to the adventures of barracks life, and how he made sergeant in six months.

At the age of fourteen, a strapping lad, he'd run away, lied about his age with false documents he'd acquired God-knows-how, and joined the army, I discovered some years later. Of course, he'd called his mother after a few days and she'd fetched him, a pattern that would continue for many years. Dick was a mama's boy, and could always depend upon his sour little mater for bail-out money. She often wired us fifty dollars when we were on the road, sometimes as much as two-hundred, until Dick had gotten so hot she could not wire him money without facing legal problems herself. I rather liked her. She was raunchy and a little mean, but had a great sense of humor. Her father had been a sponge diver from near Athens (though I guess everything in Greece that isn't Athens is near it), and had founded and/or been the first mayor of Tarpon Springs, Florida (or so I was told by someone other than Dick, though I can't recall who). When I was old enough to figure out that Dick was a mama's boy, I realized Irene did not fit the profile of the doting, fawning matriarch. She seemed more the type who would have kicked a bad kid's ass early on and with sufficient vigor to keep him straightened out. But she'd spoiled her one surviving son, helped shape a disposition already predisposed to narcissism such that it could never wrench away from lurid self-regard. She was a tangy old broad who'd lost a twelve-year old son to pneumonia when Dick was only nine or ten; who'd married a forty-something year old man when she was twenty-three and had four kids with him; who drove a two-tone green Chevrolet my entire childhood and kept it nice; who loved to play poker and loved Perry Mason and who cursed, indeed, like a sailor, in Greek and in English. Irene was, I think, the kind of woman I'd like now as a friend.

But clearly she was a terrible mother, with no intuition as to when it is appropriate to embrace, and when to push away. She raised a classic coward, a man who could never face himself, even as he remained in a constant reverie of splendid self-regard.

Perhaps even in prison he remained thus afflicted, though I wonder how, with Lipless Louie's schlong pile-driving so many nights in his bung, he could have. I wonder if in some inexplicable sense a pretty man-boy such as he, an inmate marked to be punked early and often, doesn't become his own mother in the joint, and therefore come to regard his own body as only his own mother may. Poor man. Poor, poor man. When I was ten and saw him for the first time since that late afternoon he was behind bars in central Florida, I knew immediately that something was terribly wrong. He was fifty pounds heavier, all muscle. And he was clearly insane. I had no means of conceptualizing the change in him, but I felt it deeply. I could not affix "crazy" or "insane" or even "sick" to that change, but I knew that he was the embodiment of chaos, and yet he was the man, the concept my entire being had existed relative to for three years. "When Daddy gets home" was uttered innumerable times each day and night in our ugly little domiciles in Elizabeth City. Even Chris, just a big toddler, who could not possibly remember anything about Dick, awaited intensely his father's return.

And what returned was a monster, a big, muscled, crazy-eyed thirty-one year old man charged with a humiliation that whirred and crackled at the very core of his soul; whatever madness had propelled him into the

Republic of Burma Shave, to make a family there and drag it with him nowhere, had not been replaced so much as augmented by a greater madness, a fury he did not so much control as disperse judiciously. That is the father I hate, and the one I must learn to pity, reach back into my life and touch, console, comfort. He is not the one who would have given me a black sock filled with pennies; he was at that stage beyond the need to make such gestures to a child.

In Elizabeth City we stayed at first with Aunt Bertha, with whom Joan's mother was already living, and I recall some embarrassment on my mother's mother's part that she was having to stay there, but I don't know why she would have been embarrassed, except perhaps for the obvious reason: she'd married badly and now had little of her own, though her sons had bought her a quite nice house in Seattle, Washington which I remembered having visited once a couple of years ago, the last time I'd seen her. Perhaps she'd sold the house and was now simply in a state of transition. Bertha was one of several ancient great aunts we had in that small town who'd buried husbands and lived, it seemed, quite comfortably if modestly, alone in quaint houses on their dead men's retirement and insurance incomes. She had a prolific fig tree, and an old washing machine in whose rollers I immediately got my fingers caught. She was patient and funny, and I liked her much better than my grandmother, who was whiny and high-strung and who tried much too hard to make me like her, and who said devastatingly ugly things about my father when I was around; she said flat out that he was a liar and thief and should be shot. She was right, of course, but I didn't want to hear such things from her or anyone else at that point, in those first weeks, months since Dick had been caught and we'd come to Elizabeth City. She was wrong to have said those things, to have tried to turn me against him. If she'd not staked her relationship with me on an agenda of vilifying Dick in my seven-year old heart, she and I might have gotten on just fine. But we never did.

We arrived in April or May, and I attended the last four to six weeks of first grade. I remember, oddly, that particular teacher's face and body. She wasn't pretty, in fact, she was rather ugly, but she wore dark red lipstick that turned her fat lips into a stop sign, and I indulged in elaborate fantasies in which she stood before the classroom of kids naked, addressing us in that same stupid fake-happy voice she used with us when she was fully clothed. Mrs. Maple that woman's name was, I am just this moment recalling. I was seven and wanted to do something to ugly Mrs. Maple, a conjured image of whose dumpy naked body is lodged in memory. I think I was a little bit ahead of the curve in such matters, but maybe not. I certainly wasn't ahead of the other kids intellectually. I had somehow learned to read a little on my own and with Joan's help in cars and motels. I have no idea how. My bright and chatty oldest, Ema, attended first grade in Prague, second grade in New Orleans, and now is attending third grade in Prague. She's an excellent reader in both languages, but it's been lots of work. I've spent hundreds and hundreds of hours of her life reading to her and talking about what she's heard, and as she herself has begun to read, we talk endlessly about stories, about books. She sees her mother and me spending hours and hours absorbed in books, so all her life the idea of reading has been reinforced again and again and in numerous ways. Joan read to us a bit, but she herself did not become a voracious reader, nor did she begin to read to us in earnest, at least that I can recall, until Dick went to prison. Somehow, though, from the time I was learning to talk I liked the idea of books, and wanted desperately to know how to read. I remember when I was four holding a children's magazine with Humpty Dumpty on the cover, maybe that was the name of the magazine, even, but I remember sitting for hours staring at the print on page after page as though I could will myself to understand it, and then after much such effort weeping despairingly at the fact that my will had failed me in the endeavor. A couple of years later, in one of the several scattered grade schools I'd attend for no more than two weeks each—profiting therefore hardly at all by attending them—I was mortified that the other children could read and I couldn't. That first day, I took my reading book home, and showed Joan the page I was to read the next day. We went through that page again and again: "Up, up, up, oh Anne look! Can you see it, Anne? It is red. It is for us!" Those were the first sentences I ever read, and I was thrilled. The whole phonetics thing just kind of popped out of Joan's sounding the words with me, and I just got it. Of course, the next day I didn't read the words on the page because I didn't have to; I recited those sentences with gusto, and the teacher complemented me and asked me to read the next page. I was filled with terror at first, but looked at the words, and indeed tried. I didn't get through it—something about Anne's dog eating the red toy airplane, I think—but I sounded out a couple of words, and felt an odd triumph in my failure. I didn't mind the humiliation as much as a kid might who knew he would be hanging around. I knew that nameless school in that nameless city would soon be far behind me, and in a couple of days it was. After that, I bugged Joan constantly. Anything readable I'd try to sound out—I'm not sure how I even learned the alphabet, because I'd certainly not learned it in any of those three or four schools I attended all together for no more than three to five weeks; but however I learned it, probably from Joan, I was okay with the protean nature of vowels—and when I couldn't make out a word in a tattered magazine or on a billboard, I'd hassle her for help. Somehow, over time, I learned to read well enough that after only four weeks in Mrs. Maple's charge, I was passed on to the second grade. I was pretty much a little unsocialized animal, and I don't think I could write a lick; I'm not sure I could even count, much less do the simplest math when I arrived in Elizabeth City. But in that last month of first grade I somehow acquired enough of the skills necessary to move on.

My first day of school had been in Montreal. We'd spent three or four weeks in a nicely furnished apartment whose inherent bourgeois propriety we diminished by our presence. Dick had probably made a big score and was lying low. I'm sure he couldn't pull his scams in Quebec. I remember my excitement; I wanted so desperately to be normal. I didn't realize that that was what I wanted, but I knew other people didn't live the way we did. I lay in that dark room in that strange city where I'd already discovered that I couldn't understand people when they talked, the clogged breathing of my siblings all around me, and tried to imagine what school would be like. I feared a particular shadow because it reminded me of a witch puppet I'd seen and heard cackling in French that afternoon on Montreal TV, on a show hosted, I think, by a friendly bearded giant in a green jump suit and wearing a green Robin Hood hat that had a feather sticking out of it.

The next day I discovered that Dick had somehow arranged for an older boy who spoke broken English to accompany me to school. I liked that boy, but was shocked, entering the school from bitterly freezing weather, to discover that I couldn't understand anyone. I knew there were other languages because a few months earlier we'd spent some weeks in Mexico City. I'd watched Mexican television and marveled at the bull-fights and at what seemed the most ancient of cartoons.

But I'd never been on my own amidst strangers, much less strangers with whom I could not speak. I spent, I think, a week sitting in a room with boys who spoke a language I couldn't understand, listening to a stern male teacher who held me in utter contempt and yelled at me in French. He stuck me in a corner with nothing to do for the entire class period. The other kids eyed me as though I were a caged animal. It was hell, and I wept to Dick and Joan that school was terrible. That freezing evening Joan dressed me warmly and took me for a walk. She just held my hand and led me through the beautiful bright snow-crusted streets. She wore bright white boots, and we paused at a movie marquee, though I can't recall why. It felt wonderful being with her apart from the others. The next morning I ate her terrible oatmeal silently, and when the nice boy came for me, accompanied him with dreadful resignation.

After a couple of weeks, we left Aunt Bertha's house and moved into the top floor of a two-story house and got on welfare. We received a lot of fresh produce from relatives who had farms. Joan cooked beans, every kind—lima, black-eyed, navy, split-pea, white—collards with corn-meal dumplings, cabbage, and she loved to fry corn fritters. Everything got cooked with salt pork and/or hocks. The house was across from and par-allel to the elementary school and high school football field with its black wooden bleachers (the white high school football team, the Yellow Jackets, played there on some Friday nights, and the black one on others; I don't have to say who had the better band), and right on the edge of what was called Nigger Town by all the whites. Our house was literally the first one occupied by white people.

The white people downstairs kept a goat in the backyard. There was a large boy in that family who tormented me. His mother had seen the let-ters Joan received almost everyday were from a federal prison. Joan had managed to convince me that Dick had gotten out of that bucolic jail cell down in Florida, that it had all been a mistake, and that now Dick was "learning a trade" so we could all live well when he returned. The big, ugly snaggle-toothed boy downstairs every time I saw him chanted, "your daddy's a jailbird, your daddy's a jailbird," the meaning of which another kid had to explain to me. The same kid who explained this trope to me, I think it was Joe Brick, also told me there was no Santa Claus.

I confronted Joan with these propositions, that Dick was in prison and that there was no Santa Claus, and she confessed. What other lies was I believing in? I recall at the age of seven asking myself precisely that question. Could everything be a lie? Could I be dreaming? Could nothing be real? Why did my life seem so different from everyone else's? That summer I got cracked in the head by the back swing of a baseball bat; the black kid who did it was faultless; I'd stupidly walked into a pickup game on the football field, got smacked for a dozen stitches in a quarter-inch deep gash. And I had my tonsils out. I recall a fat woman kissing me all over my face, a nurse, Lord, I hope she was a nurse, as I came out of the ether sleep, and I recall recalling then the few seconds of horror I'd experienced as the doctor placed what had looked like a small sieve over my nose and mouth and dripped something on it, and that metallic, terrifying odor and weird echo-y feeling I got before blacking out. I hemorrhaged several times over the next couple of weeks, scaring the hell out of Joan and myself. One morning the bed Chuck and I slept in looked like a crime scene, and later that week I almost choked to death on my own blood on the side of the house where I played sword fighting with Jigger from across the street. The doctor told me to take it easy for a while.

But there is only one iterative event that defines that time in my life. Beginning that early autumn and continuing into the following spring, at least twice a week a boy younger than I by a year, maybe two, staggered at dawn through fog or rain and dimness naked, always naked, weeping wailing, "Richard, Richard Lee. . . Richard, Richard Lee," right up to Mirrimac Street, the brink of the white section of town, and always he turned there, still wailing that name, and returned, wailing, weeping.

Richard Lee, we learned that summer by which time the ghost had ceased his sojourns, was the pathetic creature's older brother who, at least according to Jigger's older brother, got stoned to death down by the tracks outside of town by some white men. The kid was a sleepwalker, and mornings rose still sleeping to search for his brother. He returned to bed, awoke, and carried on through his day more or less normally, or at least that's what was already the legend. He has haunted my entire life, and I know I shall never hear a more honest cry of love and loss. I have written wretched, sentimental verses about him, and yet, even though he is the essence of lyric poetry, I know I shall never myself write the poem he deserves. That first time I awoke to his cry was the most wondrous moment of my life. I heard my own first name being shouted in the raspy high-pitched voice of a child not a child. I thought he was imploring me to leave, "Richard, Richard Leave," and I was desperate to discover where he would have me go. I was so frightened of him I couldn't possibly run downstairs and out the back door to ask. It took considerable courage simply to look out the window, and when I saw that he was naked, and how contorted with pain his face was, a mask of such torturous remorse no real child could be wearing it, I knew I was witnessing the miraculous, and that the miraculous is tethered to the wheel of actual days and actual nights and all the blunt details of which they are comprised.

Most of which are decidedly unmiraculous. For example, I recently reread *Tropic of Cancer* and was impressed by what a reeking plug of pretentious woman-hating horseshit that book is. When I was seventeen, of course, I loved it. And I suppose the irony that how I just characterized it was influenced in part by Miller's boyish sensibility will be lost on few who read this. Boyish, yes, so much of American literature is boyish, but I'll not rant about that; others brighter, more erudite than I have already made and closed that case. There is a golden thread, or a yellow arc, a stream of piss, perhaps, between Twain and Miller.

Joe Brick was Tom Sawyer. When I read Twain in my mid-teens, I knew Tom because he was Joe Brick, whom I'd left in Elizabeth City several years earlier, except that Joe had bragged about fucking his older sister and had had a glass eye. When I was ten, just before Dick was to get out of prison the first time, Joe was my hero. He was tall, lanky, and honest because he was too stupid not to be. I often took his stupidity for profundity. I suppose Joe was not as glib as Tom, but psychically he struck a similar posture.

Though I have not been a particularly conscientious student of American literature as serious students go, I've been through the years fairly persistent, if scattered, in my regard for it. I realized in my late teens that my weird life resonated in ways which seemed to echo, at least faintly, the transcendent themes of American literature: The Missing Father. The Open Road. The Charming Rogue. Frenetic Movement. Boring, unkillable optimism. Tears filled my eyes when I came to that last paragraph of *The Great Gatsby*; I was eighteen, in my first semester of college in San Diego, and I believed that Dick, though much more stupid than Gatsby and not nearly as soulful, as humane, as capable of genuine emotion, had himself seen a green light, though a few years later I'd get a grip and just accept that if Dick had ever seen a light, it was probably just a red reflector on the back of a semi.

But back then when I read Twain, Irving, Hawthorne, even Poe, even, or especially, Whitman, and of course Melville, Dickinson, and then Hemingway, Faulkner, Frost, Williams, Salinger, I felt how American I was, and for the first time I could love what I was, what my father had suffered me to be out of ignorance and petty self-love and selfishness. My black sock filled with pennies became, as I absorbed the symbols of America through the predominately male aspect of American literature, itself a symbol, and as such something numinous, special. So it is with

31

youth: the soulful labor of understanding what things mean in their largest aspects becomes a sweet compulsion. Mid-life, as I cozy into it, is for recovering the particulars of life from the necessary yet always obfuscating and ultimately untrue symbols that define it individually and collectively. I need now for my sock of pennies to be only that, and for it to be, in my own mind, no less evocative of sadness and remorse for having been dragged from the American heaven of gaudy symbols.

Joe's glass eye didn't fit very well, and this was surely because he was still growing and his family couldn't afford to keep buying him new ones. He was always taking it out and fiddling with it, even using it to play marbles. He was quite a sport about letting us keep it for a day or two, but there was an unspoken rule that we'd give him ample opportunities to win it back. From a distance, when he wasn't wearing his glass eye, the left side of his face was darker, as though that darkness of his socket compelled the surrounding area by optical illusion to seem shaded, or as though Joe contained some of the night, and it sloshed out of him a bit.

The morning I heard him screaming out on the street, he wasn't wearing it. From my window I saw he held the only thing he loved, a lab mixed-breed, in his arms and wailed. The animal was limp and bloody, and when Joe screamed, sitting in the street clutching its head to his black jacket, his face was so contorted against the fact of his loss his sockets disappeared, but then he stared at the sky, and the darkness spilled from the hole in his face, and Joe was transformed that moment into something miraculous. His capacity for grief, and therefore for love, hulked enormous on the gray morning.

> Nor should a young man hear it said that in
> committing the worst crimes he is not doing
> anything out of the way, or that, if he inflicts
> every kind of punishment upon an erring
> father, he is only doing the same as the first
> and greatest of the gods.

Book II 378b

Dick had been out of prison the second time for maybe three months, and was in the bottle and lots of trouble. Joan was deteriorating fast, could barely move across a brief room without hanging onto furniture. She wept openly throughout the day, and we were all hungry. Some days I stole candy from stores nearby I was so hungry. I would walk through grocery stores and graze the produce, and sometimes even open boxes of things and stuff handfuls into my mouth before scurrying towards another aisle, my cheeks packed. Every afternoon I came home from school there was weeping and whining throughout the little house we'd moved into in Ocean View, a few miles from the projects where'd we'd been much better off. Dick was spending his days at Al's, drinking and reminiscing.

Al was in his late seventies. He lived in a stinking little apartment on Social Security and a bit of retirement he got from the shady insurance company he'd worked for. Al was Irene's best friend. He'd been a friend of the family when Charley, my father's father, was alive, and had even married Irene a little while after Charley died. The marriage had lasted a few months. They got divorced and remained great friends. I'm certain he'd been bonking Grandma Irene for most of Dick's life and right under Charley's nose, and when he'd gotten too old to bonk her, remained a friend.

I liked Al. One of my earliest memories—I was maybe two—is of Al showing me his teeth in a glass of water and laughing at my terror. He was pushing eighty and looked much older. He said he'd "sold insurance to the coons on Church Street for thirty years." His efficiency apartment was cramped and stinky with no real kitchen, just a crusty hot plate and an ancient toaster that was surely a conflagration waiting to happen, and a sink piled eternally with the same moldering, reeking domestic objects. He had a pretty good TV for watching the Friday Night Fights, and his bed, his fetid little cot, was something only a geezer resigned to death, and whose olfactory capacity had been demolished by over sixty years of daily whiskey and cheap cigars, may lie in. He drank whiskey all day but unlike Dick, didn't change as he drank. Al started drinking whiskey as soon as he woke up, so I suppose I never saw him sober. I was amazed, even at the age of thirteen, how he admonished Dick for drinking too much, for not knowing his capacity. Al was a religious drinker. He took it seriously, and did not like to see people doing it frivolously. He tried to teach Dick how to be a proper drunk, and I believe felt sorry that he had failed.

One day Dick came home from Al's in a truck he'd had for several days. He'd gotten a job with a small termite extermination company, had worked perhaps an hour or two, then spent the next few days simply driving the pickup over to Al's in the morning and staying there. I figured the owner of the little company was probably looking for him, but wouldn't know to come to our funky little place in Ocean View because of course Dick had not given our actual address on whatever employment form he'd filled out to get the job.

He brought some food, so was temporarily popular even with Joan, but inspected with obvious sinister intent the two shiny trumpets the junior high school had issued Chuck and me for playing in the band. I'd had more experience on the upright bass at our former school in the projects, and played the tuba quite well, really, but had wanted recently to switch to trumpet. Most evenings, though, I was too hungry to practice. I'd blow a few scales and get dizzy.

After we'd eaten, he told Joan he was leaving with Chuck and me. I was scheduled to get my ass kicked the next day by a very large fellow with a reputation for doing serious damage to people, so the idea of leaving that stinking house, the whining and weeping, Joan's palpable pain and despair, not to mention a serious ass whipping, sounded rather nice. I didn't know what Dick had in mind, except that he'd mentioned California, through which we'd traveled numerous times in cars during the years Dick had not been in prison.

Joan's face as Dick led Chuck and me out the door was expressionless, staring beyond me. I do not have a clear image of it in my memory, yet I know it was expressionless, resigned to her doom. I don't think I hugged and kissed her good-bye. I don't think I touched her or Theresa or Art or Chris, nor did Chuck. I wish I could recover the details of that moment. Surely I gathered stuff I wanted to take; surely Dick packed our clothes, such as we had. Surely there was conversation between Dick and Joan and me and Joan and surely Theresa, Art, and Chris wondered what was happening; surely there was noise. But when I recall the event it is packed in silence; it is stuffed into that wretched box my dream self got stuffed into after I'd been beaten viciously by my boy-father and given a sockful of pennies as compensation. Now, as further compensation perhaps, he was taking me away from the pain of my mother, removing me from it and therefore it from my sight.

I think Joan was using aluminum crutches at that point, and that they lay folded, crossed, in her lap. I think Chris wept that I was leaving because I was his big bubba who took care of him and he loved me and I loved him. I think Theresa and Art just huddled together, as they always did. I think the smell of piss-soaked bedding filled the air, and that the bags in which Dick had transported the food to us lay strewn about the living room. I think I couldn't wait to get out of there; I think I wanted that moment to embrace my mother and brothers and sister and promise that I would always take care of them. I think I was in despair to be leaving and elated to be leaving. I think there was a moment when I could have said, perhaps even came close to saying, fuck you, Dick, this is my family. I've been the main male around here for most of the past six years. I'm thirteen. I'm almost a man. And you're something broken and weird and sick. But I followed him out the door.

We left at dusk and Dick drove into the next morning. He had some cash, but hocked the school's horns in some Deep South city, Mobile, maybe. Roughly three years before, a few months after he'd gotten out of prison the first time, in Hawaii, after a big score of over a couple thousand dollars (I recall Dick, drunk, counting the cash in exaggerated gestures onto the motel bed, throwing down each bill into a pile as he bellowed the count; he thought he was being humorous), before Joan had begun to be sick, Dick had beaten her for something. *PT 109* had been playing at a theater near the kitchenette where we stayed. I'd been enchanted by the tropical island, and never wanted to leave it. But as she'd wept on the bed after Dick stormed out I'd crawled next to her and wept with her and promised I'd take care of her when I grew up. I'd promised her as she sobbed that I would take care of her even before I grew up.

In the truck, Dick chattered a lot about how we would start over in San Diego, just him and his "boys." Joan would be better off with just the three younger kids. She'd easily get back on welfare and, if he wasn't around, relatives would once again help her. Besides, after he got "situated" he'd start sending money back and eventually bring them all out to sunny San Diego. Well, that made me feel much better. After Dick got situated, we'd all be back together anyway, so I didn't have to feel guilty. Dick would take care of everything. He'd never in my life to that point taken care of anything except in the most immediate sense—getting food and passing it from a bag to the back seat, or pulling into a motel before dawn—but I was thirteen and could latch on to what in my heart I knew was folly and feel less remorse, at least for a while.

He quickly rented a small apartment in San Diego, bouncing checks to do so, of course. I soon discovered it was only a few blocks from his younger sister's house. I'd met her once or twice the first time we were on the road, but didn't recall anything about her or her husband and children. Their house was only the fifth or sixth proper middle-class house I'd ever been in, and they seemed rich to me. Barbara, thirty then, seemed to like me. She fed me constantly, and I ate everything. Raymond, her navel-officer husband, would shake his head and grin when I answered him honestly as to how many hamburgers I could eat. "Six," I answered the first time without hesitation, and when he produced them, I ate them.

Barbara saved our lives. Within weeks she decided that she'd adopt us. Raymond, one of the most decent people I've ever known, was probably more than a little frightened at the prospect, but pretty much went along with anything Barbara wanted. It was clear to everyone, even Chuck and me, that the family was doomed, that Joan was doomed, the younger kids were doomed, and certainly for the foreseeable future Dick was doomed. Barbara surveyed the situation, and observed that the brother she'd always loved and who'd always lied to her and cheated her, and his dying wife, whom Barbara had always had affection for, were unsalvageable. But the lives of a lanky thirteen year-old eating machine and his small and dour sibling perhaps seemed something she could immediately and positively affect in the midst of so much familial hopelessness. She adopted us such that our former lives were obliterated. We garnered perfectly legal new birth certificates which listed her and Raymond as our birth parents ("Katrovas" is not their name). Only a few weeks after we'd met her and Raymond, we were being encouraged to call them Mom and Dad. Dick disappeared, as he'd no doubt planned to do all along.

Barbara saved our lives. I would be dead or in prison had she not taken me into her life. Well, I would be dead or in prison, or a pipe fitter in a shipyard in Norfolk. All the sunshine seeped quickly from her demeanor, though. After the odd little courtship, after the paper work of the adoption, I don't know precisely at what point, but she became a dyspeptic, controlling person incapable of expressing affection openly. She soon regretted having taken us into her family, and not because we were bad boys; we simply didn't know how to act in her world. We didn't know the rules. And we were damaged. We probably needed, or at least would have benefited from, some kind of professional counseling for what we'd gone through, and to assist in the transition to a new life and lifestyle. But just as our pasts had been officially obliterated (to this day I don't know how one may legally generate a birth certificate that lists as birth parents individuals who in reality are not), we were strongly encouraged to obliterate our pasts in our own hearts. It remains a mystery to me that someone capable of such a life-affirming and self-sacrificing act as Barbara performed in adopting my brother and me, could turn out in her daily life to be one of the most mean-spirited and hurtful people I've ever known. Surely she'd been unprepared for the added burden, financial and emotional, two adolescent boys would represent to her daily life, two boys who'd lived most of their lives in cars and motels, and otherwise in domestic squalor. But when I look back now, I realize that the family allowance Barbara and Raymond received from the Navy increased to accommodate Chuck and me, so we probably weren't that much of a drain on their finances, and beyond that I don't know what Barbara should have reasonably expected. We tried to fit in, but were reminded daily and loudly that we didn't. Every failure, every misstep, was noted and admonished. Every attempt to garner a little self-esteem was slapped down and ridiculed. Within weeks of adopting us, even as the newly constituted family was preparing to relocate to Sasebo, Japan for three years, Barbara regretted having adopted Chuck and me, and continued to regret it for the next thirty years. Her regret was not born of our being particularly bad, because we weren't. . . oh, I pulled a couple of humdingers in Sasebo, but probably wouldn't have had I felt truly wanted, if I'd felt like anything other than a deeply regretted burden. Barbara saved our lives, and then proceeded to mess them up in tiny, persistent and pernicious ways. Good Fortune does exact costs, and how Chuck and I remunerated It for having afforded us middle-class opportunities was by enduring Barbara's meanness.

For all her meanness, she allowed me into adulthood to regard her home as my ancestral home, one in which I could never feel comfortable, but which by simply being there afforded some psychic comfort, especially when I was nowhere near it. A fundamentally decent, truth-telling person who, under different circumstances, could have been a corporate executive or business owner or high-ranking military officer or just about anything requiring diligence, common sense, intelligence and strength of character, Barbara, as strong as her maternal instinct may have been, probably should have marshaled it along with all her other strong and positive qualities to any life's work other than parenting, and I'm not saying she couldn't have had a successful career and been a mother; I'm simply saying she shouldn't have had kids, or any more than one or two. She has two daughters, one fortyish and the other almost, who have never married and have no children, but do have quite successful and fulfilling careers. They're very close to Barbara, and Raymond is the perfect man no man they've met or will ever meet will ever measure up to. The youngest son, now in his mid-thirties, is doing fine I'm told, but was incredibly fucked up as an adolescent and young adult, fifty times worse than Chuck and I—already out of the house by the time he hit puberty—ever were. He, wisely, moved as far away from Barbara as he could, to Maryland, got married and works in his father-in-law's business, has two kids, stays in touch with family, but remains, as far as I can tell, detached. His sisters still have rooms in the ancestral home, returning on weekends and holidays, and are otherwise living the lives Barbara should have been allowed to, but the culture wouldn't let her.

Barbara and her daughters remain close to my ex-wife, partly to piss me off, which the situation does but only a little because they truly are fond of her, relate to her. When Lois and I visited San Diego, she and "the girls," Barbara's daughters, would bond, form a three-headed pretty thing that shopped and generally enjoyed itself. They were three attractive young women—Lois is, in fact, a true and radiant beauty, and someone for whom beauty is sometimes an affliction—who would remain childless and therefore free to enjoy their youths in ways that mothers may not. The "girls" made noises to the effect that they wanted kids, but I doubt that they ever did or they simply would have had babies, and Lois, who also consigned child rearing to a misty future simply did not, in any sense, ever want to be pregnant, bear a child and help to raise it. She was and is a truthful, deeply moral person, yet there was one disgusting little lie she let fester in our marriage, that she wanted someday to have a child with me, that someday she indeed would give birth to our child.

A man can't compel a woman to want to have a baby. He can't compel her to turn away from her worldly passions and assist him in bringing a new person into the world if she is not so inclined. If there is a God, and surely there is not, may It bless all women who in a world such as ours choose to live childless lives. But marriage that doesn't include parenting may come not to mean a hell of a lot to someone who deeply desires children in his or her life, at least after a few years. And heterosexual sex performed in the context of fear of procreation may also cease to mean much, at least after a few years.

My first wife is one of the beauties of the world, and saying this I am considering her physical appearance as but one aspect of that condition. She is the most likable adult I've ever known. She is bright, intuitive and funny, and people always generally marveled that an angel such as she should ever have entangled her life with that of a self-consumed prick such as myself.

I met her in early June of 1976 by the time clock outside the employees' room of the Chart House Restaurant on St. Ann Street in the French Quarter of New Orleans. Bernie, who had first gone to Louisiana from California to be a dive tender at the beginning of the oil boom, had gotten me a job at the Chart House, where he was head waiter and Lois was a cocktail waitress. She'd recently returned from holiday, a rather bad one to California with a sick-headed boyfriend she'd just broken up with. I'd been working there for the two weeks she'd been gone, and had heard about the beautiful Lois, and there she was, stunning, literally, with the most gorgeous brown eyes that could melt all evil intentions in a man's soul. She was so far out of my league, so classy, so much the stuff of romantic myth, I literally got weak gazing at her that first time. I told Bernie I was in love with her. He laughed at me and said I was a slut, that Lois was way out of my league, everyone's league, and that I should just can it.

I was living at her apartment in the nine-hundred block of Dumaine within a couple of weeks. The one thing Bernie hadn't factored in was that I was a poet. Yes, I was a slut, too, but I wrote verse, and had read a lot of it, and Lois was an English major finishing up at the state university where I would someday teach, and loved poetry, read and wrote it herself, and she'd been waiting for someone like me, from Out of Town, with a weird and interesting past, who lived and breathed English-language poetry. Bernie, who'd known me for years in Coronado, who'd watched me get drunk at keg parties and smash my hand through rocks and bricks, who'd watched me be a shameless slut in the apartments we'd shared, wheeling in different women every night, and this after having been Louella's personal sex slave for over a year and then Colleen's complete idiot for another, Bernie was outraged. He was deeply fond of Lois and though he was my friend, sort of, he seemed to feel he was witnessing the coupling of the Holy Virgin with Frank Zappa. Bernie never got the poetry angle. He knew I read and wrote the stuff, but figured that because I played poker just well enough to lose lots of money to him, and because I was indeed a shameless slut, and because I'd let him use my '67 Mercury station wagon almost whenever he'd wanted to in Coronado, and because I'd let him sleep on my floor for several weeks once when I'd actually had an apartment and he hadn't, and because both our mothers were dead, and because in every other sense but the poetry stuff I seemed just a regular weird guy who'd shown up a few years ago at Coronado High School from somewhere in Japan acting and looking like a dork, he could ignore the fact that I actually called myself a poet, which to him was rather like a guy calling himself a certified cock sucker. Well, it was fairly obvious I wasn't a cock sucker, and didn't break into recitations of passages from *The Prelude* over at Dirty Dave's garage apartment when everybody was hitting Dave's nasty bong, so as far as Bernie was concerned I might as well be an Episcopalian as a poet; sans the vague poetry/cock-sucking association, they meant about the same to him, and his faith in some fundamental order in the universe seemed shaken by Lois's and my cohabitation.

Those two months with that beautiful, dreamy twenty-one year old woman transformed me. She was my first real love, the only real love of my youth, and New Orleans and its weather were conspiring to intensify our romance over those charmed weeks. It rained like clockwork every day just long enough to cool everything down, and George Benson's "Masquerade," with its sweet little scat riffs, wafted out of every window, every bar, every moment in the Quarter. Each day red beans and rice and sausage and French bread and Barque's Root Beer at Buster Holmes' on Burgundy. Each night hard work and tips at the restaurant, then drinks and dreamy talk and sex. The famous humidity of summer in New Orleans rendered the occasional breezes that slinked off of Dumaine over the tiny balcony and through the open storm doors and across our naked bodies that much more friendly-seeming, and I was in love with a mysterious and ravishingly gorgeous woman who was surely but the corporeal essence of that sultry city, the human form it manifested for whatever otherworldly reasons.

I was at an age when romance was not only possible but necessary. And no young man, or woman for that matter, with a poet's heart could have failed to love that young woman intensely and exclusively. Petrarch would have choked on his own words trying to describe her, her brown thick hair that, fanned out over a pillow, seemed afloat; her huge liquid brown eyes which at all times were a bastion of sadness and yet when she laughed invited one's soul to languish beyond the knowledge of human degradation. Her small and perfect mouth from which no lies issued.

I was to go to the Breadloaf Writers' Conference in mid-August, having been awarded some goofy "work-scholarship" to the program, no doubt less for having demonstrated merit than financial need. The fact that our affair had a time limit, that the whistle would blow on our love making, the bell would ring and the game would be over, of course served to intensify our feelings. Though as mid-August approached, and Lois's final year of college loomed, and I too had to return after the eleven days in Vermont to San Diego State to continue the activities that passed for my studies there, intensity gave way to sadness that gave way, in Lois's heart, to impatience; she clearly wanted me out of there so she could get on with her life. Our little summer thing had been fine, but now she had to get serious. She'd done the I-fucked-a-crazy-poet thing, and now had to get ready for the grind of taking twelve to fifteen hours at the university, working forty hours a week at least, and keeping a maternal eye on her beautiful and wise-but-ditsy mother and three siblings who lived scattered about town.

She packed my things and even bought me stuff for the bus ride to Vermont. She may have even slipped me a little extra cash; she made much more at the restaurant than I did and was, is, famously generous. If she were given back all the money she's over-tipped over the years, she could pay off her mortgage.

At Breadloaf, the work I would do entailed, according to the official letter, my being a waiter for all three meals each day. I found this intriguing if only because for my three months at the Chart House I'd wanted to be a waiter, but they wouldn't let me. They let me bus, but otherwise I worked the broiler, mostly as a broiler assistant, but sometimes as the actual "broilerman." And I was, in fact, the absolute worst broilerman in the history of that storied franchise. My incompetence I'm sure is legendary. I imagine present-day broiler assistants being mentored by broilermen, shown the ropes, all the little things that add up to success at an exhibition broiler, and of course an integral part of any serious mentoring process is the passing on of a sense of history, and most of such institutional history is comprised of heroic tales and cautionary tales. My example would certainly fall into the latter category. After telling his B.A. (Broiler Assistant) the story of how, in 1974, in La Jolla, a broilerman turned out seven hundred and twenty-three dinners with the assistance of only one B.A., and him a rookie, a seasoned broilerman breaking in his own starry-eyed B.A., who of course dreams of someday himself being a broilerman, after relating the heroic tale might pause, shake his head sadly, and recount how, on a Sunday night in the summer of 1976 in New Orleans, a broilerman, working alone on a light night, had a dozen teriyaki steaks "comped" (restaurant lingo for giving something free) because they'd been ordered medium-well, and the monster had managed to overcook them. Vesuvius. Nero. Me. Forget the fact that every night I threatened to kill at least one waiter, and needed a couple of minutes every hour I worked behind the broiler to go back to the kitchen and punch and kick the freezer door before returning to the carnage charring hideously before the horrified eyes of the entire restaurant.

At Breadloaf, the "work" was a joke. We donned silly white work coats and, as I recall, set up trays and delivered them not to people but to the places where they sat. There was no real service involved, just a few minutes of hustling about before sitting down with everyone else and eating.

I was fairly star-struck. Poets and fiction writers whose books I'd read earnestly, moseyed about; some were strutting, condescending assholes, some just regular folks, some condescending assholes at least attempting to be regular folks. The caste system at Breadloaf was infamous (I hear the whole show has changed for the better in recent years), and enough's been written goofing on it; I'll not pile on. But, Christ, it was all quite silly, the segregation according to career status, the vaunted Pecking Order, which I was so far down on I could actually relax a little. Richard Ford, not famous then but highly respected by other writers, was there; pre-Garp John Irving, into whose face I spiked a volleyball and who acted as though he was going to wrestle me to the ground and give me noogies for having done so, was there. Galway Kinnell, whom I worshipped, stupidly, visited for a couple of days. Daniel Halpern, a poet who over the past twenty-five years has been also one of the great entrepreneurs of American literature, someone to whom many people in large measure owe their careers, was there. Mona Van Dyne, a quite wonderful poet who bummed cigarettes from everyone, was there. Marvin Bell, a smart man and cunning poet of whom I've grown more fond in recent years, was there. Stanley Elkin, brittle, eloquent, darkly funny, was there. David St. John, Gregory Orr and Ca were there. There were of course other luminaries I'm simply not recalling. And then there was Mark Strand, at the time the most imitated poet in America, whose resonant minimalism, in which simple declarative sentences are lightly charged with surreal dissonance, was a most attractive model for bright young hopefuls who hadn't read much else. Strand was my mentor, and conducted a manuscript conference with me. He didn't say much as he gazed upon my several pages of the rankest imitations of his work. He pushed around a few commas, occupying a chair in the middle of the barn where the conferences, as I recall, were conducted, though we may have been sitting out under a tree, but wherever we were he mumbled a few words over my horrible poems, obviously not having bothered to read them before sitting down with me (and there was no reason he should have after just glancing at them; what they were was so immediately apparent). He obviously would have preferred being anywhere else talking about anything else and, Lord, do I understand that feeling! As he spoke he would halt from time to time, not seeking words but rather simply allowing himself to drift off in brief reveries, sighing and staring off in a way that had absolutely nothing to do with me or my little poems in which he saw his own genius reflected back to him in grotesquely sophomoric distortions (I was imitating just about every published poet in America; I'd just thought it good form to show Strand the poems of mine that imitated his).

As I got up to go, Strand paused, as though finally he was going to say something that would change my life, and stared off a second; then, as though just noticing that I was still beside him (half-turned to leave but pausing to hear one last word from his mouth), he asked without taking his eyes off whatever in the distance had invited their regard, "Are you having a good time?" Solemnly I answered in the affirmative, though only because not to would have seemed rather silly, and he nodded slowly, gaze still fixed on the Distance, and finished our session with the wisdom I'd so much hoped he'd impart: "Good. That's what's important."

Well, shit, there you go! Finally, someone was telling me what was important, and it seemed at the moment considerably doable. That night I had sex with a blond conferencee, and the next night with another whose hair color I can't recall, and finally, after an intense and confusing, starry-eyed week at the famous Breadloaf Writers' Conference, I was doing what the sage Mark Strand said was important, and I thanked that patrician poet, that self-consuming star, that quintessential Handsome Man silently every night, as though in prayer, for the duration of the conference.

A year or so later he learned I was running the readings at San Diego State, and contacted me for a gig, for which I came through. As often happens with such impromptu affairs, the money lagged behind the performance, which I'd informed Strand would occur, though he proceeded to phone me every other day for a fortnight for his three or four or five hundred bucks, as though I, a student, had any control over the bureaucratic machinery of an organization servicing over thirty thousand customers. He finally got his money, and I relief from his patrician, hectoring voice.

I proceeded in San Diego to read, write, and participate in the making of numerous two-backed beasts. A lot. And I'm too old to be proud of having lived the way I did then; I am indeed embarrassed by how much I read, wrote, and bonked, if only because the three activities became so oddly connected, so oddly dependent upon one another. I shall of course never again read nor bonk with such vigor, though I may indeed by virtue of diminished capacities in those first and third activities actually accelerate my accomplishments in the second. But that's probably just wishful thinking.

At this point I was a sixth-year senior with several thousand credit hours, or so it seemed, mostly in English and Creative Writing, though also scattered throughout the liberal arts and social sciences. I'd taken and passed courses in Spanish, Italian, French and Latin and could neither speak, understand, nor read any of them. I'd taken quite a few philosophy courses, though had ended up reading the texts, numerous additional works by whatever major figures were being covered and often works and commentaries on and by tangential figures, and otherwise had shown up in class only for the mid-terms and finals. I even read *Critique of Pure*

Reason, comprehending not a single sentence. And I did a lot of reading like that. I would joyfully give hours, days, weeks over to Great Books of philosophy and social and critical theory, understanding almost nothing of what I was reading and yet plowing on, puzzling over everything, certain that Truth lay somewhere behind the thick brambles of syntactical complexities and the forbidding walls of Grand Abstractions.

Yet I have to say that the most important courses I took at San Diego State, besides the poetry-writing workshops with Glover Davis and later with Ca, were in Women's Studies, a discipline that was still quite young. I took my first Women's Studies course for all the predictably wrong reasons, chief among them being that I thought doing so would be a swell way to meet even more women. So I was quite happy to observe that in Sandy D's Women In Literature course I was the only male (that I can recall), besides a very quiet and sincere gay guy who sat near the back, among perhaps forty females. Closer inspection, however, revealed that those women did not collectively reflect the shiny San Diego State ideal: tanned, pretty, pert, scantily clad, quick to smile, not quite smart enough to have gotten into UC but worldly, that is, superficially sophisticated, solidly middle-class. On the faces of those women, some of whom approximated the Ideal, seemed a seriousness that ranged from morbidity to youthful earnestness. I felt as though I were not in a university classroom, but a church choir.

But I remember that D was quite good—engaging, energetic, very well read and articulate. And I enjoyed the reading and participated in class discussions with gusto. . . too much gusto. A couple of times, D, as has so often happened to me while teaching off the cuff—and off the cuff is the only time one is ever really teaching—paused to recall a name, and glanced over to me—I'd established in her eyes that I was an English major with several thousand credit hours under my belt, and I'm not certain if there was another single English major among the forty or so other students—and I'd promptly supplied the name for her. Well, as it turned out, her looking to the only butch male in the room for assistance did not sit well with some of the women in the class, and there were grumblings, but the extent to which I was not just an anomaly but a representative of the Enemy became apparent to me only after several weeks when one day D had us break into groups of five and discuss Chopin's *The Awakening*. I'd read the hell out of the book. I was ready. I was firing on all eight. My head hummed and rumbled with ideas. I was ready to burn rubber, leave beautiful black tread marks all over Chopin's sumptuous prose. I was going to bring in all the obvious D. H. Lawrence stuff. Lord, was I going to roll! And when my group got its chairs angled towards one another, I popped the clutch. I was dazzling. Brilliant. Insightful. Completely full of shit but so brazenly so I achieved that sporting luster of the glib half-educated. Contrary to Pope's directive, I had not drunk deeply but taken a thousand little swigs; however, that was not my problem at that particular moment. My brilliance or foolishness was not the issue; the issue was my presence, and the nature of my presence, what I assumed about my own social being.

Two women whose names I did not know and would never know, taught me more in ten seconds than I had learned in six years. As I babbled, they sat quietly, which of course to me seemed perfectly appropriate, then perhaps five or seven minutes into my diatribe they looked at each other a long second even as I continued to hold forth, and then, simultaneously, absolutely simultaneously it seemed, they rose with somber deliberateness and carried their books and chairs away from me, sat facing one another, and began chatting cheerily, even as I continued with my dazzling discourse.

The two who remained took their cues from the ones who had moved away, but instead of even bothering to move their chairs, simply looked at one another and started talking. I sat and listened because I didn't have much of a choice. At first they didn't seem even to be talking about the book, only their own lives, but then what they said about their own lives began, or at least seemed, to have a bearing on the life of the woman Chopin had so tenderly drawn.

My life was not profoundly changed. I did not at that moment want to be a woman, nor did I suddenly feel myself a lesbian trapped in man's body nor even in any real sense enlightened. I was still a swine and a slut. But I became a slightly better listener, and wanted, truly, after reflecting upon what had happened, to earn the respect of those women, who happened to be lesbians, but whom I correctly came to see simply as politicized, enlightened women.

Lesbians—especially if we allow the broad definition which includes all politicized, enlightened women regardless of their sexual predilections—are the vanguard of consciousness. They will be the mothers of the new world, or we're (and not just in the cosmic sense) doomed. We, all of us, are therefore likely doomed. No one stands in and out of nature more profoundly than a smart lesbian; no one is better equipped than a smart lesbian physiologically and culturally to understand that it is the human condition to stand at once in and out of nature, and to understand that all of civilization is a necessary lie. Smart lesbians, whether they write poetry or not, are supreme angel fuckers. Stupid lesbians (and these we must define only in terms of sexual predilections) wallow with the rest of us—non-angel fuckers generally, and straight-male angel fuckers—though I don't think there are too many: four or five in the contiguous United States, and three of those in New Orleans, Louisiana.

My ex-wife has grown into a good thinker trying to come to terms with the historical oppression of women through an exhaustive study of the history of dance and its relation to literature. She herself began dancing seriously at an age most serious dancers begin winding down their careers, and got very good quickly, primarily due to the luck of being mentored by an odd, brilliant and slightly mean little Serbian who had trained at the Kirov and who supplemented his meager teaching income by selling Christian Orthodox icons he fashioned himself out of scraps of wood, copper, and pictures he cut out of books and magazines.

I was and still am quite proud of my ex-wife. She has a terrific work ethic, and truly loves the rigorous craft of dance, and it is gratifying to witness that in her late thirties and now mid forties, after a decade of hard physical work that seemed to be heading nowhere, she has managed to derive from her passion for dance a project worthy of her passion and appropriate to her age. I think she is becoming a fine scholar, and will produce work of genuine value. Until a couple of years ago, that is, until a messy little spat that included lawyers, I'd wished she weren't doing it, at least partially, on my nickel, but I'd figured it was only right, only fair, that I financially supplemented her life as she changed it in an honorable, appropriate way.

But divorce has definitely strengthened my feminist world view. Every woman who can work should, and society should be organized such that no woman is denied on the basis of gender the opportunity to achieve economic independence, especially my ex-wife.

I'd married her, both times, ridiculously. The first time, I married her as a way of getting away from Ca, with whom I was cohabiting in a gorgeous log house, outside of Charlottesville, we could not afford. Ca and I had gotten past the stage where we were lying to ourselves and each other about marriage; that is, we were no longer announcing to the world that we would get married, which was wise if only because by that time I was sleeping around in Charlottesville, and she was going steady, so to speak, with a sweet-seeming, superficially brilliant British Terry-Eagleton Marxist Lit-Crit fellow whom she later stupidly married, and subsequently dumped (actually, I'm not sure who dumped whom, but whether the dumper or dumpee, he had to go; Ca was clearly too much woman for him).

I had stayed in contact with Lois over the three years since I'd seen her last; I called every few weeks to tell her I loved and missed her, information she seemed to process with casual good humor. One day on a whim I phoned Lois and invited her to visit me and Ca in Charlottesville, and to my astonishment she accepted the invitation, and arrived on the weekend preceding Mardi Gras, which of course meant little to Ca and me but a lot to Lois; she'd used my invitation as an excuse to get out of the French Quarter and away from the maddening frivolity of Carnival.

Actually, I'd earlier invited Lois to Ca's and my wedding, and though I'd not spoken with her at that point for several months, she'd said immediately that I shouldn't get married, that she, Lois, didn't want me to marry Ca. This had thrilled me a little, so when Ca and I had settled into our separate intimacies, I invited Lois to Charlottesville fully hoping to reengage with her. And so it happened, and I announced a few weeks later that I would go down to New Orleans to visit Lois while Ca herself was out of town. Just how incredibly goofy Ca's and my relationship had become is indicated by the fact that I only felt free to roam because Ca, too, would be on the road.

I can't recall if Lois picked me up at the train station where the Southern Crescent had deposited me. I knew the city, though, and made it to the Quarter, the apartment on Dumaine. Lois was in the death throes of a relationship with a pretty guy who was pursuing a degree in Truth and Beauty. I muscled him the rest of the way out of the picture, and set up shop. Lois and I drank a lot and I think dropped acid and decided, after a ridiculous poetry reading I gave in the courtyard of one of her best friends, to get married. Just like that. Fucked up on I can't recall what, on the cusp of RR's lovely courtyard, in the shadow of the door leading to the courtyard, Lois or I got the idea that we should get married. I may have even raised the issue during those summer months in '76; perhaps I'd blurted out that I'd someday marry her, despite the fact that she was at that point very sweetly kicking my ass out of town.

Of course all the details of this time Lois would know; she'd know how many days I was in town, when her odd boyfriend hit the street, what time of the day and on which day the idea of our getting married came up, which of us raised the idea, what drugs we were taking, and what madness happened next.

All I can now recall from that blur is that we got physicals for a marriage license from an ancient physician who serviced the drag-queen community in the Quarter. He felt our elbows, grumbling something, and signed the papers. Why did he feel our elbows? Will someone tell me why that doctor felt our elbows? Anyway, I also remember that we then got drunk and fucked up on something else or maybe just whatever it was we'd been getting fucked up on, and Lois informed me that she would stay with RR on that night before our marriage, and I would remain alone in her apartment. The next day we staggered down to the courthouse and were married by a woman who seemed mildly distracted in her black robe (Judge Connick, wife of the D.A. and mother of Harry Connick Jr.; she died soon after of cancer). I recall standing there as the judge droned, saying to myself, "What the fuck am I doing?" When the judge asked wild-eyed Lois, who'd no doubt pulled an all-nighter with RR, if she'd take me as her husband, Lois gave a little shrug and said, "sure."

Then I returned to Charlottesville and Ca immediately told me she wanted us to try to have a more conventional relationship. I don't know if the Brit had angered or temporarily dumped her, but she was making noises I didn't want to hear. My fellowship would be up in a few weeks and I'd be released to return to New Orleans. The Stanley Kunitz Festival was firing up, and a lot of famous poets (not to be confused with famous airline pilots or famous proctologists, though to be a famous poet means about the same thing) were converging on Charlottesville to honor a truly honorable and wonderful man and terrific poet. James Wright died that week, and the news saddened everyone at the "festival" (an unfortunate designation; it conjures images of noble Kunitz dashing among crowds dressed as a harliquin); I recall Jane Miller, a gifted and original poet, being particularly stunned, though I think she and everyone else knew that Wright was fading. Jane and Olga Brummas and Tess Gallagher, as I recall, hung out with Ca. Jane and Olga had visited Ca and me in Provincetown months earlier, so I knew and quite liked them. Dan Halpern, Robert Hass and Peter Davison were prominently about. I think I said something really stupid to Hass which I hope he can't recall; I certainly can't. All and all, except that Ca one night tried to shoot me with a high-powered pellet gun, the kind that brings down small game, everything was swell.

I'd simply made it clear I was going back to New Orleans; I hadn't even told her I was married, and would not have the courage, would not have the balls to tell her for at least another couple of months, and then only in a letter and only because Lois told me that if I didn't she'd kick my ass out, or something to that effect. I was a wretched coward in the matter. Even though she and I were not sexually exclusive we did have a genuine emotional bond. I'd bought into, implicitly accepted the terms of our relationship, and breaking those terms was no less an act of deception and betrayal than if our relationship had been more, shall we say, traditional. Ca had been a good friend and mentor; our time together had been one hell of a ride. We'd have stretches of time when we officially hated one another, but always, always we reconnect.

One of the oddest and sweetest small moments of my recent life was walking through the streets of Prague's Old Town with Ca, my oldest daughter Ema, then six, and Ca's beautiful son, a few years older than Ema. Ca and I looked at our gorgeous, smart kids, and at each other, and grinned like idiots at the time and distances we'd come to be on those streets, walking with those children. We laughed and goofed like siblings, and I suppose that is what she has always been, my bossy older sister, my stubborn, sometimes mean, sometimes deeply caring and giving sister. I was sexually attracted to her in the beginning, and perhaps she was to me though it's entirely possible she wasn't, but all that played out, withered for her probably even sooner than for me, in the first months of our being together away from San Diego, and our intimacy became that of orphaned siblings, two people who knew one another's minds and hearts as siblings may, and became emotionally dependent upon one another not as lovers but as intimate blood relatives. Of course that is why we could endure, even thrive, as non-sexual partners in Charlottesville, and why when I left her for New Orleans, for Lois, she could feel betrayed, for a doting younger brother who tended to her emotional life, whose proximity meant she could not be lonely, was in fact leaving her to be with a woman not as a sibling but a lover.

As Ema and I walked with Ca and her son, I recalled, shared with Ca as we shuffled over "cat-head" sidewalk stones, how I'd walked Dominika briskly through the Prague Zoo on August 28, 1990, and later through the Old Town Square where the four of us were now strolling. I'd had to be back to teach in a couple of days, and Ema was late arriving. The last doctor to do ultrasound had hinted (it was then official policy not to reveal gender) that it was a male, so when the nurse told me it was a female ("holka" or "holčička," I can't recall which form of the word she used), my joy was doubled, trippled. I'd been flooded, I told Ca, with the realization that I needed to father a female and give her the life Joan had been denied. Ca understood this sentiment, and spoke about the birth of her son in Paris.

At four-something in the morning of August 29, 1990, I was awakened by Dominika's gasp. Her water had broken. We gathered her prepacked stuff in that little apartment on Rybna (literally "fish"), and taxied to the drab maternity hospital she'd been assigned to. A week earlier, hormones cooking, Dom had wept at how drab and depressing the place seemed as we visited it on a dry run.

Once Dom entered the long hall of women, all of whom had gotten gloriously knocked up in the midst of that giddiness which was the Velvet Revolution, we were separated. Except for one doctor, men were forbidden beyond the Door. I yelled at a surly nurse who wouldn't check Dom's progress; she didn't speak a word of English, and my bad Czech only confused her. But I doubt she'd ever seen a man more crazed than I, more seemingly capable of dangerous behavior. I was soon informed that Dom was okay, and that the baby had not yet been born. After a couple of hours, a little after dawn, I slunk back to the apartment. I returned in the early afternoon to discover that indeed the child had emerged, and was female and healthy.

The next day a nurse whom Dom had befriended sneaked me beyond the Door so I could hold Ema before returning to New Orleans the following morning. I passed rooms where women were waiting to deliver or had already delivered. Pained or exhausted, none seemed at all concerned by her quarantine, though of course such concern would not reveal itself to one passing by, merely brushing against their lives. I had expressed incredulity that I would not be allowed to witness the birth. Dom later informed me that she was quite glad I had not, and to have been folded into an enclave of women for the event of birthing seemed wholly appropriate to her, especially at those moments of greatest physical suffering. That drab, Dickensian structure which seemed to siphon the natural light of day, that dark building which had made her weep a week earlier, had become a house of relative comfort as, pale and drained, her body repaired itself from the savage event.

I held my daughter for ten minutes or so and, thirty-seven years old, began, finally, to finish the process of becoming an adult. It would take a few more years, but finally the transformation from a protracted adolescence into the sweet sadness of adulthood had begun. Finally, the desire to live for something other than myself glowed within me. My fear of death became the fear of leaving another human being less secure in the world. Nothing would keep me from parenting that child, even the woman I'd divorced and with whom I was still living back in New Orleans, that weird city to which I would return the following day, that shattered province of the Republic of Burma Shave.

Are these not the reasons, Glaucon, I said, why nurture
in the arts is most important, because their rhythm
and harmony permeate the inner part of the soul,
bring graciousness to it, and make the strongest
impression, making a man gracious if he has the right
kind of upbringing; if he has not, the opposite is true.

Book III 401e

I f it were something one could actually see, I'd have seen most of it
before the age of seven. It isn't; I didn't. The very word is as something
made almost entirely of sugar that dissolves, leaving a faint aftertaste
in the acids of the mouth. This figure is equally applicable to "memory,"
and the nexus of "America" and "memory," at this moment in history
when Self is the supreme commodity, is childhood. In a rare fit of lucid
resolve, I decided recently I would cure myself of that peculiarly
American sickness the critical stage of which is morose attachment to
memories of childhood; however, I still watch enough television to know
just how unrelenting that medium can be at keeping us childlike, that is,
uncritically receptive.

I also know that to break a fever one must usually ride it out.

As a child, I was as uncritically receptive as the next, and though I
was born smack dab in the middle of the Golden Age of Television, I did
not spend as many hours in front of the screen as others of my generation.
I loved television, but the circumstances of my life not only made it
impossible for me to watch as much as I desired, but also created an
inverse relation between myself and television relative to what I now real-
ize was, and is, the norm: I experienced it not as a means of transport
from a static environment but rather as a fixed point, a touchstone.

By 1960, a few months before Dick would be caught in Florida, there
were seven of us, the youngest, Chris, still inside Joan. We'd been on the
road since before I could remember, changing cars every few weeks,
sometimes days, and staying in motels at roughly forty-eight hour inter-
vals. I therefore viewed America through the window of the backseat of a
car, and also through that other window when we stayed in motels. My
relation to what I viewed through both windows was one of uncritical
receptivity, yet whereas what passed the car seemed distant, redundant,
and uncaring, the world I viewed through the TV screen was close, var-
ied, and constantly concerned with me. No matter what seedy little motel
in what ugly little town in what boring state we lost ourselves, Captain
Kangaroo and Little Miss Sunbeam would be there, waiting, along with
Bart and Bret and Paladin, the Cisco Kid, the Lone Ranger and Tonto,
Mickey Mouse and the Mouseketeers.

I recall leaning onto the passenger-side seat which my mother will always occupy in my memory, and asking, "What's a merica?" I was roughly eight months from my seventh birthday. The sky was dark. Two younger brothers and a younger sister were sprawled around me, breathing through crusted nostrils, and a third younger brother lolled in the most comfortable space in the car: swelling Joan's stomach. Dick was in his long-distance coma behind the wheel. The gray rabbits bounding across the road at the vague limits of our high-beams, and the furry blood-splotched carcasses of the ones that hadn't made it were no more nor less real to me than Captain Kangaroo's Bunny Rabbit—that mute, bifocalled little prick of a puppet who made a lucrative career of tricking carrots from the gullable Captain—but were certainly less engaging.

"What?" my mother whispered.

"What's a merica?" I asked again.

This may seem a naive question even for a six-year old to ask, but I'd not attended any school yet. I'd picked up how to sound words out a little, though I'm not sure I could recite the alphabet, and couldn't do much with numbers. I'd probably heard of mericas in a song sung on TV late at night in a Holiday Inn just before the shows stopped and bugs swarmed all over the inside of the screen:

A merica, a merica
God shade his gray sun tree. . .

"Just a word," Joan mumbled, half asleep. Of course, this wasn't enough.

"But what does it *mean*?" I whisper-whined. Her eyes opened slowly. Her fingers, laced over her ninth month, began to drum lightly.

Joan was a beautiful woman. She was beautiful enough to be on television. As I stared at her shadow-softened profile, I saw that peculiar smile take shape which meant she was about to say something to me without really talking to me. It was a thin, crooked smile which meant her voice would be more breath than words.

"The Republic of Burma Shave," she breathed, letting her tired, dark, beautiful head roll toward the window glass where she would keep her forehead pressed against the coolness until dawn.

I turned my cheek and rested it on my forearm which lay across the top of the seat. A rasping body curled just behind me so I couldn't sit back, but I didn't much care because the one talent all of us had developed was to achieve relative comfort in what cramped space was finally allotted when the chips, as it were, had fallen for the night. I realize now that everything I am, for better and for worse, depends on that moment, which was many, many such moments: Joan pregnant and sleeping upright; Dick achieving Zen-like oneness with the road; my siblings breathing as from the clogged center of the earth; the hum of rubber over asphalt vibrating up through a ton of steel, plastic, glass and flesh. My dreams were reruns.

I had only the vaguest sense of how others lived. The Nelsons, Ricardos, and George and Gracie all lived in their own places like the people whose houses we passed in our cars, and like the odd relative here and there we'd vex from time to time. Even Fred and Alice ("Mom, what's a honeymooner?") had a little place, though it looked pretty drab, a bit like motel rooms in the desert, places I hated because some of them didn't have televisions, or if they did, only got one fuzzy station.

Two days through desert with a burlap bag strapped to the grill (we'd filled it once with orange pop and the water everafter was tainted with a sugary mildew), another day through mountains and into snow.

Just out of mountains ("don't worry," Joan had said, "our angel has a secret button that'll let us float down if we skid off the road"), we stopped in a little town that was glazed with frost. We waited in the car while Dick was "doing business." He came out of an old brick building holding new license plates wrapped in wax paper, then took us to a motel on the outskirts of town. I no sooner got the TV on than he made me wash up and change into fresh clothes. Back in the car he told me that when we got inside my name would be Mike.

I liked that bank as soon as I saw it because it had revolving doors. Dick introduced me to a man in a brown suit and made me shake his hand. The man's smile reminded me of a game show. Dick sat in a chair across from him and they chatted like they knew each other, though I knew they didn't. Dick put me on his knee, which I hated, but I knew instinctively that my job was to keep my mouth shut and be a synecdoche for a good man's good family life. So I sat there balanced on his hard knee, seeing the man as Dick saw him, admiring how, though he was leaning back away from his cluttered desk with his elbows propped on his chair arm and cigarette smoke swirling from his fingers around his head, he seemed to wear that desk. I wanted a desk like that, with a black telephone and lots of papers and pens. At one point Dick made me stand so he could reach into his back pocket for his wallet. He plucked several cards from the good-smelling leather, and then a neatly folded piece of paper that, opened, had numbers printed on it here and there. The man smiled and nodded, then pushed something in front of Dick. Dick wrote briefly on both what he'd pulled out of his wallet and on what the man had put in front of him. Then he shook hands with the man who gave him something that looked itself like a wallet. I knew as we passed through the revolving glass door I could stop being Mike, though it didn't really matter. There wasn't much to it.

Snow fell hard that evening. Joan went into labor. Her weeping and writhing scared the younger children. I was scared, too, but didn't cry. Dick told me to watch the kids while he went out to see if there was a hospital close (there was no phone, only some kind of buzzer that the office could use if a call had come in for the occupant). When he opened the door I glimpsed, in yellow-bulb light through wind-whipped swarms of snow dust, white mounds where cars had been. I told the kids to lie on the floor. I spread a blanket over them to muffle their whimpering. Joan seemed foreign and terrible. I didn't dare approach the bed. I turned on the TV. She screamed louder, making noises I'd never heard. I turned the volume as loud as it would go, draped a sheet over the cabinet the way we had had to when Art was born, and squatted under the glowing tent. The noises Joan made were drowned out by a roaring laugh track, but the screams weren't. I ran into the bathroom, locked the door, turned out the light, put the seat down on the toilet and pressed my cheek to it mumbling, please, please.

I wasn't praying. I didn't know what that was. My pleading was raw and random. I was awakened by a pounding on the door and Dick's furious voice. I opened the door. He pushed me aside, lifted the seat and pissed. The kids were still under the blanket. Joan writhed slowly and moaned gently, flushed and sweating. Dick had turned down the sound on the TV. I heard a quick, sharp honk. Dick lifted Joan, ordered me to open the door, and carried her to the cab. The cab's chains crunched them away and I watched the red taillights dissolve into the snow-swirled traffic at the outskirts of wherever we were.

I turned to the sleeping, blanketed lump left in my charge, and, as I closed the door on a cold wind, began to weep silently. I switched off the overhead light, stepped over my brothers and sister, and curled up in front of the television's gray glow. It flickered through my eyelids and in a moment I was empty and peaceful, drifting to sleep on the violin-thickened strains of an old movie.

The next afternoon, Joan listened to *Queen For a Day* from the bed, pale and quiet, staring at the ceiling. The human being who would one day rip me off for a pickup truck was asleep in a bed we'd made from a bureau drawer. *Queen For a Day* was one of my favorite shows, though I found it puzzling. Women took turns telling how messed up their lives were, and the studio audience voted, by clapping, for the one who seemed the most messed up. Though it was a kind of game show, clearly it was a precursor of the day-time audience-participation interview/talk show of today as well. I liked the part where they clapped. The winner got prizes and wept for joy. "Democracy in action!" Joan had exclaimed more than once, never explaining what democracy was; this time she just lay there staring off. Several years later, when Dick would be in prison and she'd be crumbling from a then-undiagnosed muscle disease, I'd see her like that often, though I'd be spared by dubious good luck the pain of her final pain and wretched dying.

The queen for that day was "a housewife from Miami" whose husband was in an iron lung. That one gave me fits, but I didn't dare ask Joan about iron lungs. She was clearly in no mood for questions. I briefly tried to imagine it, but I couldn't really come up with anything. It certainly sounded like a winner! The audience went crazy, the little needle on the speedometer that appeared under her chin jerked to its limit, and the man with the nasty little moustache who ran the show gave her kitchen appliances, Maytag of course, and a vacation to California and she wept for joy.

My main task was to keep the kids from messing with the future criminal while Joan was incapacitated and Dick was out doing business. The kids accepted my authority with passive sadness because I was larger than they and quick to exhibit the inherent advantages of that fact. The burden and privilege of authority were mine, and I carried both aspects with less than regal grace. I was a brutal older brother. This new one, though, I would not brutalize until we were adults and he would challenge me to a fight. For the next seven years he was mine. I would, sometimes, almost as much as Joan, tend to him, right up to the time Chuck and I would leave with Dick for California. From that time of our parting, I'd see him only twice, briefly, before he'd rip me off, once for two or three hours when I was passing through Virginia Beach the summer he was fifteen and I was twenty-two and on my way back from Breadloaf; he and Art were spending the summer with our Aunt Joyce, whom Dick could infuriate inexplicably simply by calling her Murdle, and yet whose only criticism of Dick was not that he was a petty criminal, but that he "did it all wrong." The second time was when he was a twenty-three year old Cadillac salesman whose every utterance seemed obsequious and loud. He'd ask me, in his North Carolina twang, "So what's the bottom line on this poetry business, bub?"

But now I was a noble hero fending off the alien hoards. Joan kept asking me to refill her glass with water from the bathroom tap. The baby was sleeping, and she'd lift her head with much effort to cast a weary glance at the pink, swaddled product of her previous night's pain. I would never know how Dick got the two of them out of the hospital so quickly, nor, of course, at the time was it within the realm of my natural considerations. I possessed fairly vivid recollections of the two previous births, and in neither case had Joan languished in professional care.

My vigil over the new citizen was interrupted only by the theme music of *The Three Stooges*, the zippy strains of which made my heart race and washed away even this solemn new sense of responsibility. I shoved the three-headed bundle from in front of the screen, and stationed myself six feet from the action, half-lotus. This was my seminar on violence, and my siblings were the nervous rabbits on which I'd perform assigned experiments. Chuck would, as a result, become a career naval officer and staunch supporter of a strong defense.

After the last pie had struck the last stoogy face and the credits began to roll across the screen to that adrenalin-pumping theme song—"Three Blind Mice" done double-time— I faced my second-in-command with my fist extended perpendicular to his chest, and ordered him to strike down on it. "Come on, hit it!" I commanded, and with side-glancing trepidation he did so, and braced for the stiff-armed three hundred and sixty-degree arcing hammer fist that would find its mark on the bull's-eye cowlick in the middle of his crew cut. I supplied my own stoogy sound effects and laughed hysterically. He whimpered off to a corner of the motel room, the seeds of a military temperament taking root in his four-year old soul. The next-to-last time I saw him, at least twenty years ago, his ship, a nuclear-powered aircraft carrier, had docked in San Diego where I was then living, and he took me on a tour of the thing. He conducted the tour amicably and with pride, but seemed under all the spit shine like a man itching to kill something, something big.

I was not very patient. After *The Three Stooges,* programming entered the wasteland of news and talk shows (*Girl Talk* hosted by Virginia Graham), and that always made me irritable. I'd turn the sound all the way down and twitch about the room for the couple of hours until (what a few years later would be known as) prime time. Now, though, I resumed my station by the drawer, reaching in once in a while to touch the small sleeper.

The weather had calmed outside. Joan lifted herself with much effort, and took the future con man from the drawer and nursed him sitting upright in bed with her eyes closed. Dick came in stomping snow from his soaked black shoes. Joan's and Dick's eyes met and Dick smiled broadly and arched his eyebrows, a facial gesture I would come to hate, but now it signaled good news so it made me excited. I knew it meant we had a new car and probably a bigger one than the last. He was holding two white bags which made me very excited. I could smell the fries and see the grease stains at the bottom of the bags. My heart began to pound. We'd not eaten since the night before. He doled out the burgers and fries, and my siblings took their rations and moved as far from me as they could. They didn't want to be close when I was in a feeding frenzy. From the moment I ripped the wrapper off my burger my mouth was filled beyond its natural capacity, and I finished just as the others were settling into their nests. My second-in-command was savvy enough to lock himself in the bathroom. Theresa and Arthur, three and two, respectively, chewed their burgers and nibbled their fries by the bedpost together, never taking their eyes off me. But I left them and their booty alone this time. From the tone of Dick's voice as he spoke to Joan, we were in for a period of prosperity. There would be burgers and more burgers.

Television can be torture to a hungry child. Though I'd never seen a television chocolate cake in real life— the black frosting swirled in hundreds of little waves from top to base— I knew that a good mother was one who made them that way. The few times we'd stayed in apartments or kitchenettes, Joan had cooked very little, and then almost strictly from cans. Only a couple of times did she try to make cakes, and the frosting was flat, thick, and boring.

When we were really hungry, desperately so, and Dick was out doing business, we'd wait in a motel room, lethargic, watching television. Once I started crying while watching a commercial for Duncan Hines, and Chuck, Theresa, and Arthur started crying with me, and Joan began to weep with us, and all our eyes were fixed on that frosting-swirled monument.

A couple of years later, while Dick was in prison for his first three-year stretch (five to ten, out in three; the only advantage to being wanted for little crimes in so many states, I suppose, is that most don't bother to prosecute beyond the federal charges, but I really know nothing about this aspect of Dick's legacy), and the five of us kids and Joan lived in relative comfort on a hundred and sixty-nine dollars a month from welfare, I proudly explained to my friends, before the goat-fucking punk downstairs told me otherwise, that my father was out of town learning a trade.

But Dick's only skills were bouncing checks and ripping off car dealers. His dream, however, was to be a legitimate businessman. "Legitimate" was an adjective he used often back then, and his dream of legitimacy soured years later, before his Jesus scam, into schizophrenic fantasy. I saw him one more time in my early twenties, and he related to me the shrewd manner in which he'd recently acquired offshore drilling leases in the Gulf of Mexico. Before I left his sleazy motel room, he, of course drunk, pressed a personal check for thirty thousand dollars into my palm, and as he did so arched his eyebrows and smiled, and I wanted at that moment to kick him in the nuts and beat him bloody.

The Millionaire was coming on just as Dick started packing us up. It took the *Queen For a Day* theme of remuneration for suffering much farther, and was also a more romantic, more civilized fiction. The formula was simple: A multimillionaire covertly searched out a person down on his or her luck and sent a butler to give that person a check for a million dollars. Tweaking Horatio Alger, it seems now an oddly more accurate model for what a few years later would be called the Welfare State. Much humbler, *Queen For a Day* seemed downright neighborly; its intimate yet raucously democratic game-show format, within which a kind of Fundamentalist witnessing took place, celebrated the largess of a local church sending Christmas groceries to the Widow Jones. *The Millionaire*, with its pontiff-like source of centralized, quiet power, had an Old-World, and of course old-money, grandness to its giving, rather like the federal government, though of course a bit more generous. Regarding money, Dick is a creature of the former who dreams himself an occupant of the latter fiction. He slithered across the continent subsisting on the small, countless payoffs a sturdy lie mouthed many times may garner, dreaming all the while a heavenly legitimacy in which some nameless Force would reward him with incalculable riches. It was as though he truly thought that if he just kept moving something outrageously wonderful would happen. That was the grand lie he told himself, though the lie that was his currency and passport through the innumerable precincts of the Republic of Burma Shave was small, embarrassingly small. As liars go, he was a one-trick pony: a television actor who can play only one narrow role, the henpecked husband or the laconic, stogie-chomping gangster from

Nowhere, or only the voice of commercials for toothpaste and shaving cream.

The new car was large and awesome, the best we'd ever had. The *cry* in Chrysler seemed inappropriate to such a chrome-bespangled, fetching thing, though the bright vowel at the heart of the word suggested the thing's waxed newness. Dick packed up what little we carried with us, and after several hours of the kids bouncing on the slick vinyl and all of us inhaling the heady scent of a new car's interior, night came on, clear, cold and precise with stars that seemed to follow us. Chuck, Theresa and Arthur slept in a bunch on the seat under army surplus blankets that smelled of mothballs and the loneliness of closets, and I curled up in the space at the top of the backseat, in the rear window, covered with Dick's jacket that smelled of his sweat and aftershave. The curved window was an observatory when I lay on my back, and when I turned on my side to observe the faint glow of our taillights on the snowbanks at the sides of the road, to see as well the pearls of traffic lights, far away, from where we had traveled, my position was one that felt like destiny. Though, of course, I had no such concept in my life, the memory of the feeling that filled me as I lay shifting my vision between the broad field of stars that followed us and the faint lights of distant traffic, is the measure by which I now understand the word. It has little to do with where one is going, and nothing to do with where one has been. It's the supersentient moment of trust in blind movement toward anything and nothing, the dry whir of artificial heat and the steady whine of new tires through slosh.

I lay counting the stars of a moonless sky, fixing on one a long time and promising myself that tomorrow night I'd find the exact same one again. As I stared at my star, which was neither a faint nor a particularly bright one, an ordinary star I knew I'd lose forever after that night no matter how hard and long I now stared, I visualized the letters of the first words I'd ever recognized as words: Joan would read aloud the little signs, one by one, until the last, when all of us, from Dick to whomever was youngest on that highway on that day in that week of that month of that year, would yell in unison those words printed in bold caps: **BURMA SHAVE**. The wisdom of the land thus appeared to us on the highways of America.

And we were off again. Their stomachs full, my siblings slept as one. In the darkness of the car, I closed my eyes and dreamed a waking dream of television cakes and burgers as my American mother held a future salesman, and crook, to her breast. In the Republic of Burma Shave the sins of the father can be taken to the bank, and every mother's son gets an even break.

> They are like the faces of those who
> were young but not beautiful after
> the bloom of youth has left them.

Book X 601 b

And I have gotten a better than even break. I have been incredibly lucky. I have also been single-minded. The first time I saw Dominika, I was definitely swimming upstream; I was a big-buck salmon with SPAWN AND DIE tattooed on my fin. I was the eldest moose whose huge rack rattles in the wind when he blasts forth his affections in deep-bass mating calls. I was a dog, a stallion, a hare, and, ostensibly, no longer a slut. I was thirty-six, childless, and beginning to fear death with a mid-life soulfulness. She was beautiful, incomparably, in a northern-European sort of way. I'd never been particularly attracted to blond-haired, blue-eyed women; that is, I'd certainly never found the type any more attractive than the others. But she addled me. She had voluptuous hips, and the first thing I thought upon seeing her across a room at a cheesy wine and cheese reception was that she was definitely a breeder. Her voice, mildly and mysteriously accented, was the sexiest I'd ever heard. That I was quite married to a fine person who hadn't a clue I was constitutionally capable of even being attracted to another woman (sweet, foolish woman), at that stage of our relationship, was a detail I'd address in due time.

What ensued, of course, was because I transformed into a meta-coward. It's a story so old, played out so often, that any man attempting to recount and thereby atone for his deceptions, his hulking mendacities, either breaks under the pressure of self-critique, or feels compelled to launch into so sorry a tale of self-justification his wretched soul only plunges deeper into pettiness. What I'm talking about is the essence of comedy. A guy is funny as hell when he's lying from the loins.

I told my blond beauty, my sexy Slav that yes, I was married, but that I and my partner had drifted apart. We remained good friends, but our lives were, at best, contiguous, hardly intermingled. She lived her life, I mine, and though we were superficially kind to one another, we were little involved emotionally. Lois was obsessed with dance, ridiculously, considering her age, and I felt exploited; surely if she were not married to someone who did not complain (very often) that though she was deathly frightened of becoming pregnant (hardly an issue, given that our sex lives had so much diminished of late), and therefore was burdened neither by having to parent a child nor even by having to fret over conceiving one, she felt no obligation to earn more money than she scraped together slinging cocktails two or three nights a week in the French Quarter. I was, in fact, subsidizing a lifestyle I did not particularly approve of, and whenever I broached the subject, suggested mildly that perhaps she was spending too much time in the studio which might be better spent finishing graduate school or developing a meaningful career, she became something out of a Japanese horror flick, Ballerinza, towering on pointe, her tutu ablaze about her waist, and roared her displeasure as I cowered in the rubble of Tokyo, Louisiana.

This was true, and it was utter horseshit. Truth in the service of deception becomes what it serves, and any ulterior motive is a lie of omission. I didn't confess these circumstances because I desired greater emotional intimacy, but rather, and oh so simply, because I wanted to bonk that exotically gorgeous young woman; actually I wanted to impregnate her, but I didn't understand that yet. We proceeded to bonk ourselves silly for the six weeks of the Eastern European Language Institute on the Chatham College campus in the Squirrel Hill section of Pittsburgh. She'd been brought over from Czechoslovakia to teach Czech, and I was a student of Serbo-Croatian. She did fine; I was the class dunce. The course required hours of out-of-class work, and I was much too busy bonking the Czech teacher to apply myself appropriately. The Fulbright organization, in its infinite bureaucratic wisdom, had decided that since I was going to be the Writer-in-Residence at the University of Ljubljana in Slovenia— where fewer than two million people speak their own beautiful Slavic language—it would be a swell idea for me to learn a little of that language the Slovenes themselves were forced to learn in school, and which they looked upon as the language of their oppressors. In unintentional solidarity with the Slovenes, I screwed Czech and spoke no Serbian. The entire six weeks, five hours a day Monday through Friday, I sat in a cramped seminar room with six other folks, all much more eager than I to absorb the paradigms of sound and grammar, and was tormented by a well-meaning, quite bright fellow who loved teaching the language much more than seemed appropriate. I sat next to a young woman whose biggest complaint was that her six years of formal training in Russian were interfering with her acquisition of Serbo-Croatian because the two languages are so similar. By the second week she was cheerily conversing with the instructor as I listened on as though to the clicks and whistles of precocious sea mammals. The instructor gave me a C+ for the course, in much the same spirit as I have given Cs to clueless business majors suffering through required literature courses.

Three weeks into the language program and two weeks into my affair, Lois phoned my room as Dom and I were bonking, and informed me that her beloved mother had been diagnosed with breast cancer. My first thought was that this information was coming at a most inconvenient time, not in terms of the present moment's halted passion but rather in the larger sense of how and when I would confess that passion in the midst of the protracted turmoil her mother's illness would likely produce. The fact that her mother was someone I admired and loved, at least a little, struck me only later, and when it did I felt, properly and deeply, ashamed for having initially felt inconvenienced by her horror.

When the program was over, I couldn't let my Slavic beauty simply disappear into the red maw of Stalinist communism. I would save her! I would drive up to New York from New Orleans before her plane left and spirit her back, showing her much of America in the process. In New Orleans, I would convince Lois that my motives were pure, that all I wanted was to save this waif from the vagaries of a corrupt political system. Dominika would seek asylum, and I, we! would be her sponsor.

Dominika, who had visited friends in Chicago the week following the program, realized immediately that I was at least a little insane to think she needed or even wanted to seek any kind of asylum, but did rather fancy the idea of a road trip to mythical New Orleans. Lois, distracted by her mother's travails, thought it sweet of me to take such an interest in someone so unfortunate as a poor commie language teacher, and sanctioned my drive to New York. I would be leaving for Yugoslavia in a couple of weeks, anyway, and what we would probably do is officially invite Dominika back in the spring, and then begin the process. . .

Intimate proximity so often engenders emotional numbness, such that one may know least well the individual who haunts the very core of one's privacy. How could such a bright and intuitive person as Lois be so profoundly stupid about what I felt? How could she assume me emotionally two-dimensional? Because I lied, yes, but when I didn't lie, she did not register what I said or exhibited. I raged against the world for all the years we were together, achieving a small professional success, of sorts, despite the vigor of that rage. When we lived in the French Quarter, I would go out into the street after midnight to conduct fist fights with, pound the crap out of, big, drunk, loud boys who, by smashing hurricane glasses and beer bottles against the wall of our balcony, were doing nothing more than what was expected of them by the local chapter of the Better Business Bureau. I conducted myself in such a way professionally that a band of tender souls, who'd thought themselves emotionally harmed by my frank disdain for them, attempted to derail what should have been my *pro forma* tenure acquisition by declaring me egregiously "uncollegial." And they were right to charge that my using the truth like a blunt instrument was hardly a friendly act. Indeed, figuratively flipping off senior colleagues, just because you think that your little bit of good luck in publishing makes you impervious to their negative regard, is the stupidest professional hubris. Professionally as well as personally, I have always been celebrated and damned with equal vigor and pretty much by equal numbers.

But for all my rage against the world, I hardly ever raised my voice to Lois, and any physical response to her other than tenderness was unthinkable. And we created for ourselves a fiction of intimacy, a kind of heart's golem, which bore on each of its foggy shoulders each of our emotionally partitioned lives.

She lived a full social life, dancing, working a bit, being with a wide range of friends and family from whom I largely felt not so much alienated as abstracted. New Orleans was her city. We'd returned there after I finished graduate school only because she'd calmly, even cheerfully, informed me that she was returning, with or without me. I took the only teaching job available, slogging through, in the beginning, four composition classes a semester. I was, of course, lucky to have a teaching job anywhere, much less in the one and only city on the planet my mate would occupy. And for all the uncertainty of the job, the grind of it, my ambition to advance solely on the basis of my publications and often-inspired if edgy teaching; for all the hours I spent alone working, but also waiting for Lois to return from this or that social event or from a late night at the bar where she served cocktails, I could not speak the truth to myself, that I was unhappy not just in the existential sense that any sane adult must be, but at the very root of the specific life I was leading. How could I not be happy with such a beautiful, sensitive, bright and supportive woman? She never criticized me. We laughed together often. She liked to socialize and I didn't, or thought I didn't, but we seemed to work that out fine, simply living separate lives and coming together once in a while to give reports.

I was never so lonely as sometimes when I was with her, and such times were often the most civil, even fun. That old paradox of intimacy was a dull film between us: to be truly intimate one must be absolutely honest about one's passions, though to be absolutely honest about one's passions is often to confess a desire to break that intimacy, if only for awhile. Lois thrived on the myth of our marriage. She believed, truly believed, that she was my compensation for a lost mother, and believed, as only a Catholic, or a victim of some other form of psychosis may, that she was "spiritually" connected to my dead mother.

And under such emotional circumstances, how could I not, even brimming with resentment, carry the envelope in my luggage to Prague? Having gotten it that far, how could I not pluck it from my suitcase and fold it into my jacket pocket, and trek from Dominika's apartment on Rybna across the gray and saint-flanked Charles Bridge, through the first excited and primitive street commerce and bad-if-soulful musicians and painters, into Lesser Town, up the steep hill past minor embassies, through the Castle's gate (absurdly guarded by pimpled and pomp-puffed, over-dressed boys shouldering absolutely useless rifles), past the presidential suites and supporting stuff of the spanking new Republic, into the blackened and bedeviled Gothic hush and quirky majesty of St. Vitus Cathedral; and once inside how could I not seek out the stone lion she recalled from when together, in the midst of the Velvet Revolution, we'd gazed upon it—"somewhere on the right facing the rear altar" my Catholic ex-wife with whom I was still cohabiting reminded me at the New Orleans International Airport—and once there how could I not do as ordered— yes, she had ordered me, yet with such sadness and discrete charm I at first thought it a truly collaborative enterprise—toss that envelope into the space behind the eternal lion, where surely it would not be detected (by mortals) for a thousand years? Months earlier, visiting Joan's grave in Elizabeth City for the first time, at Lois's insistence, I had worked a crucifix, as she'd ordered me, into a wedge between the moist dirt and the marble headstone, and the delicate silver— chain and all— had actually seemed to be drawn down.

Nine months before I tossed that mysterious epistle behind the stone lion (I didn't dare break the seal of the envelope), Lois had insisted upon coming first to Ljubljana, then Prague. She had never been to Europe, and I'd felt that I owed her Slovenia and northern Italy, yet the jaunt to Prague, my allowing her to come, was the dregs of my insanity, even though the Velvet Revolution, or whatever CIA-orchestrated affair it actually was, I'd not foreseen, but nor had anyone else I knew, Czech or not.

But how could I not "allow" her to come? As delicate, as authentically fragile as she was and is still in certain respects, she had dictated every aspect of my life since we'd stood before that distracted judge at City Hall and Lois had shrugged and said, "sure." In the years that followed, I'd bluster, usually only a little; she'd win. I'd relinquished my life to her, and even in the midst of my mendacity, my passionate lie, I could not overcome her will. I realize now hers is among the stronger wills I have ever encountered. I also now know, as a consequence, that human will certainly has nothing to do with gender, but is simply a force of nature among other forces. Chaos theory says a butterfly's wings may vex the currents which ultimately may vex the currents which play upon the forehead of a child who blows a bubble that climbs the slightest wind and, popping, sets in motion the motion of air across ascending heat that bubbles up into what will, indeed, determine the particular gust of air that congregates with others in such a pattern that a butterfly is swirled to its death; and another child, on the other side of the planet, happening upon it, may shed a tear or giggle in such a way the air is disturbed in such a way a surging front is vexed and dies, and dying does not vex a countervailing front which gathers into what will therefore not be the killer storm an old man, whose house has been flooded fourteen times, fears every waking moment of his waning life. What is human will, gender-determined or not, in the midst of such processes? Yet the one set against your own, such as to seem your own, becomes the vortex of your life, the agent by which you are slowly diminished and finally sucked away.

I stood there before that ancient lion, dripping absurdity, yet for the moment heartened by having kept an insane promise to toss a letter to my dead mother behind something ancient and immovable in a city where, alas, if Joan's soul wanders, I doubt it will visit in a thousand years. I stood there realizing that the ridiculous act I'd just committed was yet another indication of Lois's power over my actions, my life. Was she aware of that power? I think she took it so for granted even in the midst of my mendacities, lies she slurped down without first inspecting, that it was not even an issue to her. Nine months earlier, as what would be called the

Velvet Revolution was occurring, she arrived by train in Prague from Vienna, and Dominika and I fetched her from the station together. Dominika, drunk on current events, was willing even to put up with the presence of my deceived wife, whom she neither liked nor loathed, though she fully expected to supplant her.

They had met in New Orleans and gotten on very well. Dominika, correctly, saw my relationship with Lois as a mess I would have to clean up, and though she certainly desired that I should get on with the mopping, she could afford to be patient. Sure, it was odd that Lois was in Prague, and doubly so considering what was happening around us. But I was there primarily to "be" with Dominika, though ostensibly to work with her as well translating and interviewing Prague poets, a project for which the Fulbright folks had relinquished a little extra money.

It was fairly easy for Lois, though I have to believe it would not have been for most other bright and worldly women, not to assume I was physically intimate with the beautiful young woman with whom I was obviously sharing a one-room flat and with whom I was daily "working." After Lois's first night in Prague, during which she and I slept together on the floor of Dominika's flat, Dominika arranged for Lois and me to use Dominika's brother's pathetic little flat on the other side of town for the days Lois would be in Prague. During that time, Lois managed to hook up with the Czech National Ballet, and so was able almost every day to work out with the best dancers in the country. As the petty regime crumbled, as the Czech people marched in the streets, she did her deep balletic squats at bar, and joyfully sweated in her black leotard. Once, she and I joined Dominika and E, Dom's gay friend, on a huge march with tens of thousands to Charles Bridge, which when we arrived from Wenceslas Square was blocked off by the police/army, and I recall Lois's discomfort, just a little greater than my own, though what I felt was closer to embarrassment at the privilege of being where I was, a privilege I knew I didn't in any sense deserve.

It was that night, I think, or perhaps the one following, while Lois and I were waiting in Dom's flat for Dom and E to return from something, that Lois asked me, offhandedly, almost jokingly, if Dom and I were more than we seemed. Yes, I said, though if I'd thought about it I'd have answered no, that Dominika and I were precisely what we seemed. But had I slept with her, Lois wanted to know.

I had hoped that all the obvious evidence would simply speak for itself. I had even back in New Orleans confessed deep feelings for Dominika. Surely such a question was unnecessary. Surely as civilized, worldly adults we may simply observe the obvious and proceed with quiet dignity from that knowledge. But she was asking me point-blank if I was physically intimate with a beautiful woman with whom I'd obviously shared relatively cramped quarters for weeks before Lois's arrival. I said, evenly, matter-of-factly, "yes," and the Velvet Revolution became that moment a minor, barely discernible disturbance against which a truly cataclysmic event raged. A vital people's shucking off of fifty years of totalitarian oppression, first Nazi and then Stalinist-communist, became merely the peel of sardonic laughter in the midst of an unrelenting artillery bombardment. Until that moment, my lying had been simply, at least largely, a matter of silence. I would from that moment join the motley ranks of the pernicious double-minded, which is of course a condition of insanity. What a bumbling, two-minded fool I became! Yet whatever real, undiluted compassion I have in my heart, until then largely untapped, I discovered thus afflicted, and thus afflicted I became therefore more fully human, which perhaps doesn't mean a hell of a lot, though it may be the only justification for talking about my odd, small life.

When children play the right games from
the first, they absorb obedience to the
law through their training in the arts,
quite the opposite of what happens
to those who play lawless games.

Book IV 425

I and my new family arrived in Sasebo, Japan in the autumn of '67. It was in Sasebo I'd first get drunk, first take drugs, and first get laid, and where I'd study karate and first witness people gather in large numbers to affect changes.

Whenever a nuclear-powered aircraft carrier came into Sasebo Harbor, thousands of students from the north, I guess mostly from around Tokyo, would pile into trains and flock to Sasebo, the southern-most major port city on the west coast of Kyushu, to protest. The day before their arrival, bilingual fliers (perhaps they were only composed in Japanese and I simply recall anecdotal descriptions of what was written on them) would appear all over town, even on the U.S. naval base, accusing the carrier of contaminating the waters of the bay with radiation. The accusation was in every sense untrue, but had particular resonance considering how close Sasebo is to Nagasaki. I'd heard the students were communists and, therefore, if not evil, certainly dangerous. But they were just kids, only a little older than I, born during or just after the war, and who therefore shared early memories of the adults in their lives putting all their lives back together in the wake of great horrors. Even then, for all my ignorance and for all the propaganda my regard for them was soaked in, I admired and sympathized with those students.

We'd leave Sasebo at the tag end of '69, between Christmas and New Year's, so I didn't receive the same media drenching of anti-war protests as my contemporaries stateside. *The Stars and Stripes*, when I bothered to read it, and Armed Forces Radio, which I did listen to almost nightly (for almost three years I listened to a half hour of Johnny Carson most week-nights, and to many of the old pre-TV radio shows. It was really quite wonderful, and put me experientially in touch with the preceding pop-culture generation) reported domestic turbulence in less dramatic detail, perhaps in some respects even more responsibly, than did media in the States. For more than two and a half years, *the* two and a half years of "counter-culture" turmoil, I did not view the Vietnam war on television, nor did I observe footage of college protests. I had a vague sense that things were cooking stateside, but this was culled mostly from marines and sailors only three or four years older than I and more recently over from America. My main venue for meeting and being briefed by such folks was the karate dojo on the base, where I spent some of the best hours of my teens.

So when I sat, I think with George and Chris and Leo, the first time on the C.P. Building (I've no idea what the letters stood for) which housed the American bank as well as the D.O.D. school we attended, and which shadowed a tiny river (or protracted ditch) that separated the American sector from the rest of Sasebo proper, and watched the thousands of black-uniformed students, all male, march double time in mechanical syncopation and seemingly perfect order, in waves of—I think—a hundred at a crack to traverse the stone bridge and smack into hundreds of white-helmeted, dark-blue uniformed, huge-shield wielding riot police, that became my image of "student protests." Dozens, it seemed, were knocked over the railing of the bridge into that ditch which lay at least ten meters below. But they kept coming, in wave upon wave. Each box of a hundred was directed by a guy with a whistle and a white rag tied around his head. He, and I think everyone else, wore white gloves. He shrieked and yelled a double time, then as they reached the bridge, a triple time cadence, and that hundred-boy box would pile into the thick clump of baton-swinging cops, get seriously beaten, fall back or get dragged away by medical personnel on the sidelines as another box got revved up. It went on for hours. My friends and I watched from several stories up, chuckling and shaking our heads. I learned one big thing in karate dojos and watching student protests in Japan: Don't fuck with the Japanese. Dangerous as my liberal heart knows it is to generalize about "a people," I can't help but believe that, generally, the Japanese harbor a seriousness about life which must have been (generally) true of ancient peoples. This may be partly due to an intense and unique island culture's evolution out of a feudalism more oblique and enduring than the West's, and partly due to their being the only member of the We've Been Nuked Club. Even as I feel a strong sentimental bond with whatever the counter culture was, indeed feel shaped by its ideology, and therefore even though I didn't participate in campus protests, feel affection and respect for those, three or four years older than I who did, I can't help but view those events in retrospect, even Kent State, as having been at least partly false. Revisionist popular-culture history which vilifies the participants in late-'60s activism and apotheosizes the poor misunderstood vets sickens me. And yet I can't help but observe that none of those Japanese students who stupidly, insanely piled into those shielded riot police was expressing himself through a lifestyle. None was haunting the periphery of a youth culture which lived off the prodigious fat of an unprecedentedly prosperous society it defined itself against. They may have been nuts. They may have been wrong. But they were to a person goddamned serious about their lives, as only the best and worst in America, a small percentage in either direction, were, and are.

It's difficult to tell how serious the Czechs are about their lives. For the Czechs irony is religion, and that is why I love their culture, or that minute fraction of it I may ascertain in translation, and from what little I understand, will ever understand, of their language. The Japanese, despite or perhaps because of the fact they were so utterly defeated, still harbor a heroic ideal, a black pearl, in their culture's heart. I mean, they're a little Greek: implicit in heroism is tragedy, and surely most of the Big Boys in the Japanese armed forces knew fairly early on, probably at the very beginning, that their grand enterprise of conflagration and domination was doomed. It is the essence of heroism to proceed, after *anaknorisis*, into the maw of doom. Only by so doing does one maintain dignity, the only thing worth sustaining unto death. The Czechs, historically, have said to hell with it. We're tiny; Germany/Austro-Hungary/Russia are huge; from time to time we'll puff up and sing operatic nationalism, but when the patriotic chips are down, we'll display the better part of valor. Two beautiful facts define, for me, the Czech national character: first, a Nazi governor called them "laughing beasts," and second, during the Soviet invasion of '68 (according to Kundera, among others) young women posed provocatively before tanks occupied by scared, weary and horny Russian boys, igniting them (as it were); the damage done, the women fled.

Heroism is a function of biology; its apprehension and interpretation, though, are always ideological, even as its essence lies in the indeterminate zone where the creature embraces the angel.

Physical fights are ugly. Some boxing matches are beautiful, truly beautiful. Several of the most aesthetically transcendent events I have observed have been boxing matches. But fights, the kind males are encouraged by history to define themselves by, are wretchedly ugly, obscenely grotesque. In the karate dances I learned as a kid, the idealized battles between men who did not hold weapons was beautiful. The economy of movement, the seamless merging of form and function, the stylized dignity of those dances, those *kata*, overwhelmed me. I learned them voraciously, and practiced incessantly. They represented the same spirit that compelled thousands of kids to heave themselves systematically, precisely and even beautifully, as well as stupidly and absurdly, against men who would beat and maybe kill them.

That there must be an aesthetic dimension to violence is a tragically beautiful idea. The image of neatly attired Red Coats in their neat little rows-upon-rows getting picked off by coon-skinned colonists sniping from behind rocks and trees sums up America's response to that most civilized medieval ideal. Of course, Pearl Harbor and much of the rest of the Pacific War hardly seemed the spirit of the noble samurai confronting that of the mercurial Yankee, though that may simply be because the samurai in that case knew they were not engaging other samurai, and therefore dispensed with the code of honor, a code which like all martial codes only operates when both combatants understand and are bound by it. I mean, it was a strict rule on all American school grounds that one may not kick the other guy in the nuts during a fight, the kind everyone else circles around for its duration, the kind which was usually not spontaneous, but arranged earlier in the day. Now, kids mow each other down in drive-bys. Only in the movies and on television is there an aesthetic dimension to violence, only there are all fights dances, and even pyrotechnics are folded into those dances. The problem with violence in media is not a matter of quantity; it is rather that violence is always too beautiful. When violence attains an aesthetic dimension in life and sheds its vile beauty in media, the world will become less dangerous.

The genius of any culture centers on its maintenance of violent young males, a certain percentage of whom will always threaten "social stability." The trick is to do it without packing them off to wars; that entails stressing the aesthetic dimension of violence without muting in the adolescent imagination its consequences. Contact sports do that a little, but just a little, certainly not enough to save a culture from itself.

America is and has been for quite a while in the midst of civil war. Demographic shifts are cooling it off a bit, but the mortality figures from city to city, town to town, tallied up suggest strongly that we are at war with ourselves. Imagine that we got body counts every night on the news of each day's violent deaths. Imagine a grim-mugged talking head telling us the casualties of all the murders, accidental deaths with handguns, even traffic accidents, lumping them altogether, and solemnly reporting how many hundreds, thousands of violent deaths there were each day, as though, if only we had the national will, we could do something about it; we could stop waging war on ourselves. Our proxies could sign a peace agreement, because we are all combatants. A few years ago, a Japanese exchange student trying to find a Halloween party in a suburban neighborhood of Baton Rouge got blown away by a valiant homeowner. The entire nation of Japan was horrified. Not long after, a teenaged girl jumped out of a closet to surprise her loving father, who, truly surprised, shot her dead. Who hasn't known someone who died in a car? Never mind the kids on the streets doing business. We simultaneously vilify and romanticize them as though they are the quintessence of our violent natures, even as the No Man's Land of this great war runs down the middle of our own hearts, and they're not even on the front lines. America's sickness is that there are not two-thirds fewer violent deaths each day than there are. Some are inevitable, perhaps even healthful on the whole. But we are sick to be dying in such great numbers on our streets, freeways and street corners, in our bedrooms and on our lawns, in the soft lap of our neighborhoods and domestic spaces.

It is interesting that the most significant violent act committed by any Czech, at any time in Bohemia's history, was probably a young man named Jan Palach burning himself to death in protest of the Soviet invasion.

Followed so shortly by the slaughter of Tienaman Square, the Velvet Revolution seems in retrospect a blast of lilac-scented wind across the planet. Never mind that it was inevitable, and probably more than a bit contrived; it still smelled and felt good.

When Dick got drunk he would make Chuck and me do push-ups. He didn't want his boys to be "pussies." Once, soon after he got out of prison the first time, he glanced out the back window of wherever he'd dragged us, and noticed I was getting beaten by an older boy. He came out and rooted for me, on hands and knees, as the kid pounded me. When the kid got tired of punching me, indeed seemed to sympathize with me for having such an asshole for a father, Dick jerked me up, tore his belt off and whipped me for losing. I thank him for that. I thank that sick young man for doing that. For, years later, the memory of that event was all the information I needed about what prison had been like for him.

This, I said, is clearly the aim of the
law which is the ally of everyone in
the city, and of our rule over children.
We should not allow them to be free
until we establish a government within
them, as we did in the city, fostering
the best in them with what is best
in ourselves and securing within
the child a similar guardian and
ruler, and then let him go free.

Book IX 590 e

The first time I dropped acid I ended up in Tory Pines Canyon just as we began to come on (I assumed we were all pretty much synchronized). I was with seasoned veterans, so, at first, felt fairly secure. I'd taken a four-way hit of Orange-Barrel Sunshine. My good buddies, the seasoned vets of acid trips, had allowed me to take a four-way hit. No one, under any circumstances, should drop that much acid. As a responsible adult, a parent and a tax-paying, property-owning citizen and university professor (this latter I mention with no particular pride; I spend half of my time as a "professor" red-penciling comma splices and ignoring which/that confusion) I would caution against anyone ingesting drugs, even or especially hallucinogens. But if the kiddies are going to do it anyway, I want at least to be on record cautioning against a four-way hit of Orange-Barrel Sunshine, though I'm sure that like big-finned automobiles— or, more appropriately, VW vans— such massive doses anymore only rarely haunt the streets.

I peaked for ten hours. No one should peak for ten hours. I was eighteen and skinny, with a pretty face and thick hair puffing over my shoulders. I taught karate in people's backyards and mopped floors on the Coronado Naval Amphibious Base. On my eighteenth birthday, four and a half years after they'd adopted me, I'd moved out of my stepparents' house. I would later return a few days at a time, but I'd never live with them again. I'd gotten an apartment which cost sixty dollars a month, a small shed converted into something only an eighteen year-old male may occupy. I drove a '67 Mercury station wagon I'd purchased for four hundred dollars.

I was in Tory Pines Canyon with Marc, Steve, Bernie, and Darrell; it had been in the latter's garage bedroom we'd dropped the acid. As I peaked, I didn't speak a word. I was in a white place and no doubt certifiably insane. I just followed. After traipsing around the canyon, hearing the guys make what were perhaps jokes about the distances between the ledges they stood upon and the rocky and rough vegetation many meters below, I followed them back to Darrell's dirty-white Volvo. We crammed inside, and the blood-red seat covers were sticking to our skins and were therefore sinister. Darrell popped Rod Stewart doing "Old Man River" with Jeff Beck on guitar into the eight-track player, and we were off.

The journey lasted about nine minutes, or as long as it took to get to UCSD to meet a legend. As we walked across campus, though I actually at the time had no idea where I was, my trip intensified. I was beyond hallucinations. Those would happen much later, as I was coming down. As I followed my friends, those odd bodies I vaguely recognized, the discordant music of their voices laced with hoarse laughter seemed determined by a single trochaic theme, "Rodney . . . Rodney . . . Rodney . . . "

Rodney—I'd never heard his last name uttered nor over the coming couple of years would I hear it—was finishing a Ph.D. in Chemistry. Rodney dropped acid every day of his life, according to Darrell and Dirty Dave, Darrell's Hell's Angel brother (perhaps Dirty had only been an outrider with the Angels; whatever the case, he was definitely going through a biker phase, and himself dropped acid frequently, and ingested as well anything else available; he even "whooped" glue and other household products); for this, and the fact that Rodney was some kind of genius finishing a Ph.D. in Chemistry, and because according to his legend he was the source of most of the "good acid" in the Western Hemisphere, visiting Rodney, indeed having been invited to visit his dorm room, was a great honor. I was on my way to visit God, the Son-Of-A-Bitch who'd concocted the vile stuff at that moment making me nuts, making me wish I could be asleep, obliterate space/time, cease to be for the duration of that portable hell, that wickedly bright cast on the visible world.

He was so skinny he scared me. He had long, straight, greasy-blond hair, wore thick, black-framed glasses, had a scraggly beard, a few soon-to-be prolific zits, and his clothes, artfully mismatched and sleazy—a boyish horizontally striped t-shirt and maroon-paisley slacks—hung on him like eternal dread. He looked exactly as he was supposed to, and this frightened me deeply. Did my fear show? I was too fucked up for anything to show. I was an imploded personality. Surely nothing was registering on the outside of me, yet.

One of the guys told Rodney I'd dropped for the first time, and how much I'd taken. Rodney seemed mildly impressed, shaking his ugly, sage head slowly, flicking glances at me. He sat at a desk in his squat, cinderblock dorm room, pouring over equations, fiddling with a slide rule. He seemed mildly aware that we were in the room, and in fact gestured with his eyes to Darrell that we should all leave, or so it seemed to me. We'd been there three minutes or half an hour. God had spoken numerous times or not at all. As we exited single file, the others chuckled, but I had no idea at what. In the dreary hall of the student dormitory, the smell of dirty laundry meant there was indeed a zone of damnation, and it is a place I did not want to be, yet surely I was numbered among the doomed already.

The guys shook their heads and chuckled at what a divine puzzle Rodney was; they said he was a genius, that he knew things none of us was capable of ever knowing. They didn't say he was a god, though obviously they thought so. Like a god, he knew secrets mortals did not have purchase on. One of my buddies, probably Darrell, told a story about how he and Wink and someone else dropped acid and went to somewhere in Arizona. Rodney had appeared, just looked at them, and walked away. It had been a great joke, his driving all the way to Somewhere-In-Arizona to fuck with their heads, and it was something only he, only a genius such as he could think to do. He was, one of the other guys suggested, the true model for Mr. Natural. To know Rodney, Rodney the Genius, Rodney-Who-Dropped-Acid-Everyday-And-Did-Ph.D.-Work-In-Chemistry, Rodney a minor though not insignificant god, Rodney whom they hinted produced all the acid in the United States worth dropping, was to live inside a Zap Comic, which they seemed to think was a good thing. I was tripping eight time-zones the other side of Fuck Me I'm Dead, and did not find particularly attractive the thought of living inside a Zap Comic, though it would have been at that moment infinitely more desirable than where I was. Someone asked me if I was coming on yet. I looked at whomever had asked; I think it was Marc. I just looked at him for a moment, then I said yeah, and figured I had said it with such an inflection that the preternatural intensity of my trip would become immediately apparent. I was shocked that whoever had asked—Marc or Darrell—could so quickly fall into chatter about some innocuous horseshit after hearing the yeah I'd just uttered, an affirmation which winged beyond the horizon of mere linguistic connotations to swoop upon the scurrying heart's blood of some wild divinity.

I suddenly hated my friends. Yet I needed them desperately. What a terrible condition to hate what you need, though of course that is how it is, how it always is, I mused, brimming with profundity.

I had to take a piss. Outside, in the parking lot, on the way to the Volvo, I stopped, plucked out Ricky, and drained upon a tire. My friends paused as I did so, and stared at me. At first I didn't mind them staring at me clutching my One And Only, pissing on a tire, until someone, I think Bernie, said what the fuck are you doing pissing in a public parking lot; there are people everywhere. I glanced around, and he was right: people were coming out of buildings and walking down sidewalks and getting into their cars. Everyone moved in a very orderly fashion, with purpose and drab quotidian grace, and I was pissing on someone's tire in a public parking lot and didn't care who saw me, and my not caring was my glory, sad and profoundly frightened as I was, my absurd and wretched glory.

That evening I became a clown. I stopped peaking in the early evening; it was then that I was coherent enough to hallucinate, and that feeling of having a constant low voltage hooked to the backs of my eyes began. The hallucinations were simple and intense trails and distortions, nothing out of psychic wholecloth. I left Darrell's and Dirty Dave's garage (it was really Dave's, though Darrell seemed permanently camped there, stoned every day from light past dark) as the sky was darkening. Dirty Dave had begun to get on my sparking nerves, and I'd had to get away from him. He wore a cast on his right forearm from a gang fight, or so he said, and had dropped three four-way hits of the acid, an assertion I'd found incredible, and later realized was a typically boyish boast. I didn't dare drive my station wagon across town to my sorry hutch, so I walked, certain that the next cop who slid by would immediately spot me as some-one who was tripping.

Finally back in my pathetic little crib, I realized I'd go quite insane—or to a psychic Beyond, being at that moment surely insane— if I remained sequestered there, so prepared myself to reenter the wide-open world as inconspicuously as possible. I looked around, grinding my teeth. The room was half again larger than the bed, and everything I owned was under the bed in two small suitcases. There was no closet, except for the space in which the landlord had deigned to install a vile little toilet that never stopped hissing, and at the entrance to my hutch was a space bare-ly large enough to stand in where a hot plate and a tiny sink constituted my kitchen. I dragged out the brown suitcase, and fetched from it my "good clothes." It was at this point approximately nine in the evening, Saturday, early spring, in the year 1972. My hair was past my shoulders, very thick, luxurious. I put on a wrinkled white shirt and a tie, wrinkled blue slacks, a sky-blue Madras jacket whose sleeves were three inches too short for my lanky arms. I figured that because I was dressed thusly no cop would think of stopping me on a Saturday night. Oh, then before exit-ing my hovel, I put on shoes, my new shoes, my brand-new orange sneak-ers. All I needed was a red plastic ball to stick on my nose. It did not strike me how ridiculous I looked until I ventured half-way down Orange Avenue (yes, it seemed profound that the color of my shoes matched the name of the street down which they were taking me), and paused in front of the service station across the street from Ninth Street Liquor. A car was slowly ascending upon a hydraulic lift as another was coming down, and the hissing of the two hydraulics, and the sight of those two silver columns easing one into the other out of the ground, so lasciviously, gave me the first boner I'd had all day, and I realized that that day had been the longest I'd gone since I was five without popping a Bad Boy, and there I stood deeply aroused by cars going up and down on greased columns, and I looked down, embarrassed, and so gazed inadvertently at my shoes, my bright orange sneakers I'd bought on sale to work in when I swept, mopped, waxed, and buffed the thirty meters of tiled floor at the geedunk on the Amphib base every weekday (and that after stacking a hundred and thirty-six chairs on thirty-four tables, only to take them down again after cleaning the mop and pail and putting away the buffer). I stared at those shoes for twenty seconds or ten minutes, and was suddenly awash in my own excruciating absurdity, and was certain that any second a Coronado cop would see those shoes, perhaps from blocks away, for surely they shined like beacons of stupidity and guilt, and signified my deepest guilt, were incontrovertible proof of my guilt, the guilt I felt for leaving Joan, for making my passage in the world with an eternal hard-on, for doubting the existence of God, and for being at that moment on acid. Surely I was doomed. But I was also hungry. I looked in my wallet. I had three dollars, which was plenty, so I turned and walked across the street and down half a block to the Greasy Spoon, or the Night & Day Cafe as the sign above the door read. Trudy was on; Trudy was always on. I ordered a Three Egg Special for seventy-nine cents, and asked for extra hashbrowns, the additional price of which I don't recall. And water. Lots of water. I drank seven glasses of ice water. I was doomed, thirsty and hungry, not necessarily in that order.

"What you on, boy," Trudy grumbled.

"The stool, Trudy," I answered, and she just shook her head and clucked. She worked on two grills, and was cleaning one while the other filled up with orders. There were nine stools, and none was empty on a Saturday night for more than a few seconds. Everybody in the tiny diner was fucked up on something except for dyspeptic Trudy, everybody's stern mother until five in the morning. Red-eyed sailors in civvies hooked their wobbly cheeks on unsteady fists and thus propped stared at the grill; a couple of guys I knew casually, who'd graduated from Coronado High a couple of years previously and who probably were no less fucked up than I, chatted nonetheless with beachy aplomb about the prospects for the next day's surfing.

She was remarkable. She greased a spot on the grill and slapped yet another heap of shredded potatoes into the bubbling oil, then side-stepped to the other grill, ground in sweeping circles across its length a pumice stone the size of both her hands, then side-stepped back and cracked three eggs onetwothree, scooped three orders onto three preposi-tioned plates, wheeled around to the counter and dropped all three as though she had three arms and three hands, wheeled back, flipped the half-dozen orders of hashbrowns, messed with the eggs, sidestepped back and scraped the gray mess off the pumiced grill into the grease traps, side-stepped back and filled four more prepositioned plates and wheeled back to the counter and deposited them as with four arms and four hands, bussed three just-emptied spots, wiped them somewhat clean with a dubi-ous gray rag and put down silver and ice water before serving up what remained on the grill, which included my Three Egger, and then emptied the grease traps. Why is such divine competence not more frequently and loudly celebrated? She moved at the same steady pace for an entire eight-hour shift, and fucked nothing up. I'd never heard anyone complain about how his eggs were cooked. No one ever said, hey, I ordered these over easy. She always got it right. I am not a Catholic, but my mother was and ex-wife is, and I have watched High Mass, how busy the Top Dog Priest is during the whole affair. Trudy was busier, the ritual she presided over more complex, and certainly no less holy.

I stared into my empty plate, and could not recall having emptied it. I drank three more glasses of ice water, paid, and left.

The first cop I'd actually seen all day rolled by, and if he'd stopped I'd have either pumped my arms and knees, letting my new orange sneakers carry me somewhere dark and safe, or simply wept. The police car didn't stop, and I kept walking south, toward the Del Coronado, but turned west toward the beach, and was at the water's edge in a few minutes. I climbed onto the rock that Bernie, I think, had dubbed the Captain's Chair, and over it onto the flat surface partially hidden from the beach and, elevated roughly five meters, overlooked the Pacific Ocean. The wind was chilled and damp and exactly what I needed, and I lay on that rock looking out over the dark mild roar, and waited for dawn.

And as the sun came up behind me, I lay on my side gazing north toward Point Loma, and watched the surfers mount the waves of the new day. Still wired, still plugged into the trip, though it had now grown mild, I lay in my soaked silly clothes imagining the Perfect Woman, as young heterosexual males are want to do, and composed in my head the first lines of a poem about her. Maybe then I whacked off. I don't remember.

Those [desires] that are aroused during sleep,
I said, whenever the rest of the soul, the
reasonable, gentle, and ruling part, is slumbering;
whereas the wild and animal part,
full of food and drink, skips about, casts
off sleep, and seeks to find a way to its
gratification. You know there is nothing it
will not dare to do at that time, free of any
control by shame or prudence. It does not
hesitate, as it thinks, to attempt sexual
intercourse with a mother or anyone else—
man, god or beast. . .

Book IX 571 c

The last time I ingested hallucinogens was at the "Last Ride" (the poster commemorating the occasion still hangs above the downstairs toilet of the house I bought with and for Lois, and which she still occupies and is paying off). It was spring 1984, and the Ponchartrain Beach Amusement Park was closing down, an occasion for sad celebration in New Orleans, a city poised to celebrate genuinely just about anything at any time. I was a new instructor at the state university in New Orleans, whose campus on the lakefront was just a spit away from the Park, and had been hired in with a number of other instructors, of whom for several I've maintained affection. Some of us— all but I have gone on to greener academic pastures— decided to eat mushrooms.

I'd earlier in the day dropped some mild acid (I'd not taken any drugs for several years; for several years I'd not done too much of anything but write and read and be with Lois. . . oh, I'd drunk a little, toked a few, very few, joints, snorted a little coke when I was waiting tables; I was practically a Mormon); then I ate about an ounce of mushrooms a (now former) colleague had plucked from cowshit in Mandeville after a hard rain.

I don't think I'll ever experience another more beautiful night. I'll sum it up this way: The Drifters—old men by then—sang "Under the Boardwalk"; they sang it surely as they could never have sung it before. They sang it as though the boardwalk were *the* boardwalk, the dome of heaven, the Firmament, the Ceiling of the Infinite, and even though at that moment I did not feel Lois was the woman in whose arms I would die, if only because I could not conceive of such finality due to how my awareness of the world had early been determined, I loved her, exclusively, but in the indeterminate fashion of one who had never known any emotional permanence. I think I had begun to await the end of my marriage the moment Lois shrugged and chirped, "sure."

But that night was a fleck of eternity, and I loved her forever for a night. And I would love her forever for other nights, nights I waited at the bar for her to get off work and she was so beautiful and graceful moving about the darkened room with her tray of drinks, making people happier by her presence. I would love her forever nights we would occupy quietly the same space doing unrelated tasks, and days and nights among her friends who loved her for brightening their lives. And she brightened, I think, the lives of everyone who came into contact with her, and this is no maudlin misty recollection of Happier Days. I'm speaking of someone with a gift, a genuine talent for healing the souls of others, at least a little and if only temporarily, by her presence. There are asshole "professionals" getting paid bunches of money for what Lois, at least that woman I knew through the '80s, did for nothing, simply out of the sweetness of her nature.

I hate Romantic Love. The extent to which our culture doesn't work is the extent to which romantic love is a sick fiction which increasingly has more to do with selling soft drinks and tampons than establishing familial bonds. The genius of African-American culture, the genius of jazzbluesrock'n'roll and all of modern dance not infected with the insipid false classicism of Isadora Duncan, is that it recognized from the beginning the European lie of Romantic Love. It is the lie of transcendence, among other things a willful misreading of Plato, particularly the *Symposium*, which must be read less for what Plato's Socrates says than the context in which he says it, a wild party of beautiful buggering Greeks getting drunk with flute girls all around. And how many women's lives, particularly women's lives, have been made wretched by their worship of Romantic Love? It turns men into lying idiots, and women into pining or wrathful victims. I've read too much Freud to believe in Romantic Love, and too much Marx and Nietzsche and too much Western philosophy and history and goddamned literature to believe that Romantic Love is anything but a marketing tool, *the* marketing tool, as well as the primary means by which women—even lesbians, for often even among themselves women are susceptible to the lies of Romance; I have watched women break one another's hearts no less cruelly than men would, though always sans physical threat—are oppressed by and within the culture. To the extent that I am able, I will raise my daughters to be lusty, powerful citizens of the world, women whose lives are not determined by the search for perfect mates, but rather who, in their quests for fulfillment through work they love, find like-minded and like-hearted lovers.

Of course I've allowed my own life to be ruled by Romantic Love. But as I get older and uglier and more settled, joyfully settled into the daily rituals of parenting, of sharing the duties of parenting with a woman who, physically loving and sexually engaging, is also herself plugged securely into the dailiness of life (a woman who realizes that if I'd not impregnated her I'd not be with her as I know she would not have tolerated for so long my cowardice had I not through it all been a loyal parenting partner), I am very glad no longer to be ruled by Romantic Love. It's about obsessions; parental partnering is about necessities. I and Dom love one another out of a true necessity, and it is the only love I've known which has felt real and honest and enduring, enduring if only in the sense that by the time our girls have left our care, I'll be too damned old and certainly too damned ugly to find another woman who'll have me!

Parenting need not be the only realm of necessity defining a marriage. Past a certain age, the necessities cleaving to physical decrepitude also define it. In gay marriages this is true, though gay and lesbian marriages are also aesthetic constructs, as are childless marriages generally, those that last beyond the stage of obsession. Lois's model for marriage was certainly not her parents' (her mother divorced her father sometime after the fourth or fifth time he'd had her committed to the Mandaville mental hospital: she'd finally realized it was crazy to let him continue putting her away at his emotional convenience). Lois's model for marriage was the relationship between R and J, her friends from early adulthood.

I felt affection for R and J. After a while, they found me hard to take, and I don't blame them. I tried to conform to their social rhythms, to appreciate the unrelenting campiness of life around them. I even viewed them as teachers, individuals whose relatively unique perspectives on life, exhibited particularly through their subversive camp humor, could inform my own, which had been determined as much by the locker room as by literature and philosophy I'd read and misread. Lois, a classic New Orleans "Fag Hag" since her late teens, had been a friend to R as he was coming out in their early twenties. R met the seven-years older J, a comfortably trust-funded Greek and Latin teacher at a parochial school, not that long after coming out, and they almost immediately set up house. R spent the next decade moseying through a Ph.D. in French Literature, and during that time Lois was R's and J's constant companion. It didn't take me long to realize I was being tolerated by R and J, that as chummy as we all were I was the odd man out, the boring straight seeking, actually being forced to seek, gender enlightenment. Of course, compared to them, I was crass and socially inept, but they were actually more tolerant of me than I required them to be, and it was easy not to imagine what a male homosexual relationship entailed in its physical intimacies, so I didn't. I found the thought of male homosexual relations disgusting, as do most heterosexuals and self-loathing, self-denying homosexuals, this latter category comprising perhaps twenty-eight percent of the right wing of the Republican Party. I am now beyond such silly disgust because homosexuals are no longer exotic to me. Many of the people I work with are gay and lesbian, and we've all been together long enough to be thoroughly bored with one another, especially as sexual beings.

But R and J were, for the first several years of our marriages, exotic. Unapologetic in their domesticity, unshakable in their devotion to one another, they must now be dreadfully aware that their atypical devotion and monogamy likely saved their lives, literally. But they didn't, to their great credit, make a histrionic show of their devotion. They worked hard—especially J, by all accounts a truly gifted teacher—during the school-year week, and drank themselves stupid on the weekends. I couldn't keep up, though Lois usually tried. We all often ended up (after Lois got off work at the Chart House) in a gay bar, sometimes to see a drag show. R and J loved drag queens, and I developed an appreciation for the milieu of the Rampart Street drag bars. Of course I was terribly ill at ease in such places, but figured it wouldn't go over particularly well if I'd suggested we leave and hit the strip joints up on Bourbon. To participate in my wife's social life, to the extent that I did, I had to traipse with her and two gay men through some of the seedier gay bars of the French Quarter, and I don't at all regret that I did. I observed the gay world before the ravages of AIDS, heard the stories of outrageous sexual appetites, and observed men responding to mainstream American culture in most remarkable ways, with shades of irony I'd never experienced in or out of literature. I was tolerated, warily, but always with grace, as Lois's—the supremely gorgeous and feminine fag hag's—straight boy.

Both R and J, perhaps especially J, wore their Southerness on their sleeves as gaudily as they did their sensual predilections. J was from a small town in Louisiana, a proverbial stone's throw, but distinctively different in its Southerness, from New Orleans, R's hometown (he may have been born elsewhere, but, like Lois, claimed the city as his ancestral home). A couple of times I made the trip with Lois and them to J's modest small-town ancestral home, and viewed firsthand how the only male heir to three fairly well-off octogenarians tended to his future. He was princely and patient with his mother and her wealthy sisters, rather like a spider, I recall thinking, though I now realize I was judging unfairly. He genuinely loved them, and was probably more than a little sad that they necessarily viewed him as the future of their line, even as he lived his life such as to ensure he would be its end. His mother had to have realized something was—"wrong" is not the right word—not as she had anticipated. Why had he cohabited with a younger man for so many years, and obviously not just as a roommate splitting expenses? For one thing, J didn't for any financial reasons need a roommate, and, for another, R traveled with him everywhere, to the small town J was from, as well as on their annual summer trips to Europe which his mother knew J alone paid for. She even stayed sometimes in their house when she visited New Orleans, and of course even though on such occasions R and J slept in different bedrooms, that was the only concession they made; J's mother, with typical Southern Gothic grace chose to ignore the obvious, and certainly said nothing to the aunts, who no doubt hoped they'd live long enough to gaze upon J's progeny. What would they have said or done if J had gathered them and announced, "Aunty dears, I'm queer! Will you still leave me all your money when you die?" I don't know. Was J morally bound to tell them there would be no heirs? Of course most of what I know about his situation I gleaned from Lois, and I could be misremembering, and of course these matters are always more complex than they seem on the surface; J may indeed at some point have informed them that he was a confirmed bachelor, and maybe whether he would marry and have children was not as large an issue as I'm assuming here, but it seems likely that the old girls were giving their money not so much to an individual as to a wish, and he knew it. They wished, perhaps, for a part of themselves, their genetic codes, to drift beyond their own slow and fading, slow and drifting lives. Their money would be reinvested in subsequent generations, and therefore so would they be reinvested in a kind of fiscal reincarnation. J was screwing them out of—or unscrewing them from—immortality.

But with their money he would live a measured and responsible life, one which below the veneer of camp would have classical balance (with the exception of those times he was so shitfaced he passed out in public; I hear he's off the sauce entirely). As a teacher, he would be a fine father five hours a day five days a week nine months a year, and that's better than what most straight fathers manage. He would be a faithful mate, and together with his life partner pursue beauty and culture. The old ladies' money has hardly been wasted.

When we got together with R and J, the symmetry was obvious: J and I were the pitchers, and R and Lois were the catchers. But I could never live up to J as a husband, and though I didn't realize it, I was angry that Lois expected me to. For one thing, I didn't have any rich aunts. For another, I wanted kids. And for another, I wanted to have sex with other women. Being a cheating mate sometimes is simply an expression of personal freedom, a coward's expression of freedom.

I hope R and J remain well and happy for many more years. They have been good friends to Lois through some bad times. J was always fond of saying that there is nothing more tragic than a drunk middle-aged woman or an aging homosexual man. In camp parlance I think "tragic" means pathetic, because camp being a comedic vision of life may not admit the truly tragic, or perhaps I should say the classically tragic. Nonetheless, I hope R and J remain camp unto the grave. I hope that even as they become pathetic old queens, they remain wise beyond the tragic.

And such wisdom crumples Romantic Love as though it were a dried flower, a dead bloom of the Old Order, whose implicit codes no one may live up to but the insane and truly dangerous. From opposite ends of the cultural universe, Bruce Springsteen and Shakespeare, the former in *Born to Run* and the latter in *Romeo and Juliet* (this is an incredibly goofy pairing, but oddly apt) exploit the false tragedy of Romantic Love. It is false because tragedy is about dignity, and that, God knows, is the first thing Romantic Love sucks away, especially from the young, who generally have damned little to start with.

I'm not talking about mere courtship rituals. I'm not talking about bringing flowers home for the dinner table, or being generally thoughtful to someone into whose orifices you are often want to drain your procreative fluids. I'm talking about all that shit men tell women to get laid, all the lies, half believed by both parties. I'm talking about the dangerous loss of an ironic sense in the presence of the beloved. I'm talking about obsessions which are little more than distractions from mortality. Romantic Love is the essence of cowardice.

And I guess it had something to do with why Joan followed Dick, or allowed herself to be dragged along by him across the roadways of America, and I guess it had something to do with why he dragged us all across the Republic of Burma Shave. Joan, of course, was not innocent of all Dick's crimes. Clearly, she was an accomplice. What kept her out of prison, as Dick once angrily informed her soon after getting out the first time and even as he was revving up to start the whole ugly process over again, were us kids. For, though she herself never signed a bad check or bilked a car dealer or actually drove the car full of kids away from a Holiday Inn without paying all or part of the bill (sneaking out of motels in the predawn was my favorite family activity; it was an oddly affirmative, bonding experience. Even the youngest was always cooperative, uncannily quiet as we crept into the car and Dick pushed it at the door frame as Joan steered with her left hand, holding the youngest with her right; headlights off we crunched over gravel to the edge of the exit, and Dick jumped in and we sped away. It was thrilling), she was an accomplice.

And I don't recall her complaining. Perhaps she did. Certainly she wept numerous times, and numerous times expressed her weariness with life, and I recall once during a gorgeous sunset flanking the right side of the car she screamed at him that she just wanted a normal life, which was a clear indication that she was tired of living as we were living, but by my reckoning was not an unambiguous condemnation of Dick's illegal activities. Dick then promised her life would soon be normal, and that became the shining promise of my childhood, that life would soon be normal, and that of course is the great American promise, that hardships will soon evaporate and Happy Days will eternally be eternally here again, eternally. And those days are not exceptional life but normal life. I dreamed of the Normal as other children must have dreamed of the Extraordinary, and so did my mother, and so did the man, the boy-man, she must have loved. For only Romantic Love explains them. No other motivation explains how someone like her, quite beautiful (though I never saw it, I recall hearing that she had been on the cover of something called *The Navy Times*), with a terrific sense of humor (I've come to believe that a sense of humor is the only valid indication of non-mathematical intelligence), a young woman who loved to read, had a pretty singing voice (who sang "I'm Looking Over a Four-Leaf Clover" on Norfolk television), and who was by all accounts audaciously sociable (she and a girl friend sneaked into a hotel in Norfolk to meet Gary Cooper while he was in town shooting "The U.S.S. Tea Kettle" which was renamed something else

81

when it came out; they ended up interviewing him for their high school paper, or so I seem to recall her saying; he invited them to a hotel buffet and as Joan once told it the girls would go to the toilet to throw up so they could continue eating, the food was so good, and perhaps too because she never could hold her liquor, which Cooper, she said, plied them with. . . Perhaps Gary Cooper is really my father!); nothing but Romantic Love explains how someone like her could tether her life to such an obviously fucked up, pathologically lying pretty mama's boy as Dick was, a boy who'd been kicked out of almost every high school in Norfolk (someone, perhaps Al, once described how Dick at the age of sixteen had dangled a high school principal by the legs out the window of the top floor of a four-story building); who'd run away and tried, with some success, to join the army at the age of fourteen; who, the same year he'd dangled the principal, had had to marry a girl he'd "knocked up," but then had gotten the marriage annulled when she miscarried; who, by the time he met Joan, had pretty much exhausted the patience of the Norfolk police department; who, when he did work, always wanted immediately to be the boss, acted thusly, and got fired; who, having accomplished absolutely nothing of real value in his life still managed to find things to brag about, and he bragged constantly. Besides his good looks, what else was there of him?

Well, early on, he must have seemed damned exciting, but that can't be all, his good looks and audacity can't be all of it. But she obviously fell for him, was probably a virgin (though I'd like to think Gary Cooper got to her first), and committed to him with sufficient intensity to become what otherwise would have seemed wholly contrary to her nature, the passive accomplice to innumerable petty crimes.

Now the greatest punishment is to
be ruled by a worse man than oneself
if one is not willing to rule. I think
it is the fear of this which makes men
of good character rule whenever they
do. They approach office not as something
good or something to be enjoyed, but as
something necessary because they cannot
entrust it to men better than, or even
equal to, themselves. In a city of good
men, if there were such, they would
probably vie with each other in order
not to rule, not, as now, in order to be
rulers.

Book I 347 c

We spent half of my first thirteen years with Dick on the road, and the other half waiting for him to get out of prison. The first time he got out he had gone from a hundred and sixty to about two hundred and twenty pounds, all muscle. The Cuban Missile Crisis had occurred just weeks earlier; I recall being still a bit shaken by it. We had had the obligatory air-raid drills, the old duck-and-cover crap, and I recalled a *Twilight Zone* episode from a couple of years earlier (I hardly ever watched television when we were settled in one place, partly because the TV's we owned were terrible, but mostly because I was too busy ranging across surrounding neighborhoods on that pointless reconnaissance of prepubescent boyhood); in it, people fought over who would get to pile into a fallout shelter as Russian missiles swooped towards them. The very clear message was that whoever didn't have a shelter was fucked, and we didn't have one.

I'd asked Joan if I could build a shelter for us in the backyard, and she'd told me that Dick would be home soon, and we'd probably be moving into a better house "somewhere else," but if I really wanted to, go ahead. We'd moved out of the second-story apartment of the house that was across the street from the school and upstairs from my goat-fucking tormentor, into a dilapidated two-story house five or six long blocks away. At the new place, we had a huge pecan tree, and I gathered the nuts in season, cracked them with pieces of brick and peeled them, then filled pint jars with the brown meat. I sold those jars to neighbors for a buck each, a ridiculously low price even then, I'm sure. It was between two enormous root bulges at the base of that tree I planned to build the family fallout shelter. Using a battered shovel I'd found in a lot by the tracks (on weekends, I and other boys, black and white, gathered potatoes that fell from trains and dragged them home in burlap sacks), I started digging. Dick came home from prison just as I'd gotten about three feet down, five feet across. The previous year a box turtle whose shell was inexplicably whitewashed had appeared in our yard; we'd kept it as a pet along with Blacky, an all-black medium-size mutt that we had for over a year; the stray loved Joan and followed her everywhere, until a relative, probably Grandma King (Bula), decided we shouldn't have a dog, and one afternoon just took it away. But Whitey the turtle showed up one morning in my fallout shelter after having dashed away the previous winter. Dick, home—no, that's not the word—back only two days, yelled at me not for tearing up the yard, but for thinking I could save the family. Taking care of the family was his job. He told me to get rid of Whitey or he'd eat him, and make me eat him, too. I recalled the blood-smeared gray fur of those squirrels he'd dropped into the sink of the trailer we'd lived in when Arthur was born, and that he'd hacked at those little bodies for half an hour, rolling pieces of them in egg batter and then flour and frying them in lard. I took Whitey to huge-eared Scotty Caiton's house, and asked Scotty if he wanted the turtle, and he did but his mother didn't, so we dropped Whitey in the backyard of a family that had at least a dozen kids in it, figuring the odds were pretty good somebody there, none of whom we knew for some reason but all of whom we'd seen around, would want a turtle with a white-washed shell.

Things happened quickly. I was ten. *The Fly* was the hot flick in town. Dick yanked us out of school. We moved into a motel on the outskirts of Elizabeth City, and he immediately started drinking heavily. His tattoo, the Skull and Cross Bones five or six inches above his left wrist, was the only aspect of him which seemed the same. All that followed is a blur, the two trips to Hawaii, one with the whole family, one with just Chuck and me. He must have gotten caught soon after the second trip. I vaguely recall Chuck and me being escorted by FBI agents, very nice men who seemed genuinely concerned for us, and surmising from their talk among themselves that Dick, whom they'd actually had in their possession, had somehow gotten away from them. But before that, we'd taken our old circuitous route to Nowhere, pausing for as long as two months in Norfolk, where I don't recall if I went to school or not; if I did, I didn't go much, nor was much encouraged to. I remember it was cold, that husks of dirty snow lay scattered across the beach, and that I would walk the beach for hours, gazing upon the wild Atlantic swells of greenish gray flecked with white, hearing seabirds fight among themselves, and sneaking into the Ocean View Amusement Park which was closed for the season. I'd sit in the pastel cups of a ride that had a wheel in the middle of each cup, and turn the wheel that turned the cup until I was so dizzy I would throw up if I'd eaten anything for breakfast, which I never had. I got a library card and spent a lot of time reading books in the tiny branch library, mostly science fiction (Asimov's *The Rest of the Robots* was a favorite), but anything else I saw that struck my fancy. I probably did twenty times more reading skipping school than I would have had I attended. I wandered the Ocean View Golf Course, deserted in winter. I stayed away from the family as much as I could. Dick was drinking and being abusive. He moved us after a couple of weeks into yet another apartment, only a few blocks from the one we'd briefly occupy over three years later, when he would be slithering out of prison a second time, and soon thereafter would take Chuck and me to California in a stolen pickup.

Kennedy got shot while we were living in that second apartment in Ocean View, the one near the one we'd occupy in about three years. Joan and the five of us kids were out walking and, I think, shopping. It was a sunny, brisk day. A skinny kid with thousands of scarlet pimples all over his fair face and long neck came screaming out the backdoor of a drug store; he was wearing an apron and a name tag. He screamed that the president had been shot. Joan was startled, and told me to watch the kids. She ran into the drugstore. She was wearing a long black coat, some kind of fake fur. She came back out clearly stunned. We walked briskly back to the apartment that was shabbily furnished but had knotty-pine walls I quite liked, though perhaps the knotty-pine walls had been in the previous place. Grandma Irene had given us an old TV, and Joan immediately turned it on, tapping her foot as it took literally minutes to "warm up." Cronkite said that President Kennedy was dead.

Dick came home a couple of hours later. Obviously drunk, he said, broadly smiling and with no explanation, "I knew they'd get him." For nights afterwards I couldn't sleep. I was frightened. The dead president with the nice haircut whom everyone said was young to be president, though he looked pretty old to me, became the Chief Executive of Death, and all I could think of was death, of dying, of my own death, and of Hell but mostly of nothingness, and I didn't want to go there, into nothingness, where a man named Kennedy now presided. I didn't think much about Dick's comment; as was true for almost everything he said anymore, I didn't know how to take it. He would sit Chuck and me down in front of him in kitchen chairs; he would mount a kitchen chair backwards, with his arms folded over the chairback, and stare at us a long time. Then he would ask us remarkable questions, though actually I only recall one question: *How do you feel? How do you really feel?* He would ask over and over, and Chuck would cry, and I would tell him again and again that I didn't know what he wanted me to say, and he would grin drunkenly, and ask again how I felt, how I really felt, how did my not knowing how I felt, how I really felt, make me feel; how did my not knowing what he wanted me to say make me feel. And I sometimes too would weep, and he would sit there, drunk and grinning, but if we tried to get up and walk away he would yell for us to sit back down, and then he would ask us how his yelling at us made us feel; how did it make us really feel. Years later I realized that he had probably for whatever perverse reasons reenacted the group-encounter sessions he'd had to scam through to get an early release from the joint. If that had not been the case, he was sicker than I ever later imagined.

And years later I would realize, or at least guess, that in the joint (I think the Georgia federal facility had been the last one he'd occupied) he'd probably heard something about Kennedy, about the Mob or something. But clearly he'd assumed a conspiracy just hours after the assassination. I don't think there necessarily was one, or that Dick could actually have had any real inside information. But his was the first conspiracy—not theory but—assumption I'm aware of.

Then the road again for a couple of months, then Hawaii, then Hawaii again, then Dick was caught, then we were in the Projects in Norfolk, in the loving arms of LBJ's Great Society.

It is amazing to recall that as abusive and scary as Dick had been for the months he was out of prison, we all settled quickly back into our idealization of him, assuming that when he came home *this* time everything would truly get better. It's as though I, for one, harkened back to the younger man who had touched my face through the bars of that cell in Florida, and did not believe that the muscular monster who had made my life dark, confusing, and painful for part of the previous year would even bother to return. He clearly did not like any of us, not really, not even Joan. In my heart I was certain the first, whom I'd loved, would return, the one who'd fretted over feeding us, and when he'd not been able to had at least seemed angry and ashamed. Late at night the first one would start singing "Home On the Range" or "You Are My Sunshine" or the one that goes, "And he walks with me and he talks we me and tells me I am his own, and the voice I hear saying oh so clear, another has never known," and then Joan would start singing, and then the rest of us, who could, would sing along, and we'd sing, joyfully, yes, joyfully if quite horribly, verse after verse or just hum along, merging our vision with the beam of the headlights as we sang or hummed and rolled through the desert or between oceans of corn or wheat we knew were there but could not see. The second one didn't sing with us; he only mocked us. We'd all thought, so stupidly and pathetically, that the first one would return, even Joan.

Further, I said, is this not charming
of them, that they consider as their
worst enemy the man who tells them
the truth, namely that until they give up
drunkenness, overeating, lechery,
and idleness, no medicine, cautery,
or surgery, no charms or amulets
or anything of the kind will do
them any good.

Book IV 426 b

There is little malice in my heart. Like most folks who don't live defensively, that is, as though they are always playing defense, I have a half dozen enemies; I hate none of them. I have four or five colleagues who have done everything but poison my coffee and dynamite my office to blot me from their sight, but I have always won, and therefore they must suffer my smiles and little waves in the halls, the saccharine collegiality by which I mock them. Of course, winning or losing would not even have been an issue had I not pissed them off to begin with, but when I am in the thick of some bureaucratic ninny nest, one I would not have gotten myself entangled in were I not such a sucker for intrigue, the worst features of my nature, which love a little mischief, take over my life; and though at such moments as when I am being sucked down into the psychic murk, the nasty subterranean funk which is the collective unconscious of the tenured faculty of my department; and though when I am in that particular chamber of hell that is our muddled institutional memory, and that is less a matter of where one has stood on the defining pedagogical issues of a particular year or semester than who, figuratively and/or literally, screwed whom, how long and when; though at such moments I fantasize dragging, oh, five of them one by one over the levy behind the college and smacking them silly for a blessed, sweaty hour, in my better moments I actually feel grudging affection for them.

I am capable of killing. If anyone harmed my daughters, in any significant way, which is to say physically, I would end his or her life. I am capable of killing anyone to whom I am physically superior with my bare hands, choking life from anyone who harms my children. In this I am like most parents. But that's about it. I don't wish my enemies dead. I don't even wish them ill. It is in my nature to make up with people, which by midlife becomes a tiresome quality. One needs one's enemies, and one is needed by one's enemies. It is the symbiosis of loathing which marries two people for a lifetime, for one's true enemies are more faithfully what they are than one's beloveds may ever be. A beloved, a lover or child or soulmate, may desert or in some way transgress intimacy, may fail in the implicit conditions of intimacy, but a true enemy never can. He or she will always be true to the conditions of loathing, to the implicit contract mandating that two people will never cease striving to fuck up each other's lives and careers.

I'm a terrible enemy because I can't hate, and I'm serious when I assert that the fact that I can't hate is among my worst character faults. This disability may be the residue of adolescent narcissism by which I am indelibly stained. It may be a mutated version of Dick's assumption of absolute superiority; that is, though I do not assume myself a superior being, perhaps I am compelled genetically to display the haughtiness of someone who does, and perhaps what I then may have in common with monsters such as Dick, those who assume absolute superiority, is that though such a person may commit villainous acts, rarely does he do so out of true loathing, but rather in the sporting spirit of Lear's fly-swatting, wanton boys. Compounding the ill effects of my inability to hate is that I too often indulge in fits of temper. But after the raging, I'm okay. Whatever had triggered my anger no longer has any effect on me, or very little. In some ways I'm very lucky to be like this, except that my enemies, those who have elicited my righteous anger, too often settle into a life-long condition of unmitigated loathing. How does one do battle with people one is constitutionally incapable of hating? In a way, it isn't fair. Those who loathe constantly, those with the enviable capacity to hate, are made more vigilant by their loathing; whereas I must remain alert by force of will unprompted by strong feelings.

I assert with no irony that I wish I possessed the capacity to hate, just a little; of course I hate the Nazis, I hate the Right Wing of the Republican Party, I hate the NRA, I hate the John Birch Society, I hate the governor of Idaho (whomever he may be), I hate French and German tourists in any part of the world they may be found, I hate Skin Heads, I hate all men who batter women and children, I hate all pederasts, I hate poets who read too long at public performances, I hate MTV, I hate anyone who quotes Derridá (though I love Derridá), I hate Kant, I loathe Hobbes, I hate rich people who think they deserve their privileges (though I like rich people who are a little embarrassed by their privileges and act accordingly; George Soros is a kind of capitalist saint), I hate that stretch of I-10 between San Antonio and El Paso, I hate Pinochet and his secret lover Margaret Thatcher, I would hate Ronald Reagan except that he is too ridiculous to hate (and, recently, too sad) so I'll hate instead Ed Meese who is almost but not quite too ridiculous to hate, I really really really hate Jerry Falwell, I hate smug academic Marxists though I love Marx, I hate the Catholic Church though I tend to love most Catholics, I hate Christianity generally though I love that aspect of the Christian ethos having to do with forgiveness, I hate all those who advocate the destruction of Israel though I love those gutsy Palestinian kids throwing rocks at Israeli soldiers and the tenacity of their own people's will to exist as a nation, I hate Delta Airlines for cramming so many seats into coach and serving crappy food, I hate all Colleges of Education, I hate Greater Serbia, I hate Southern Baptists unless they're black, I hate "experimental art" because the science trope is and always has been deeply phony and besides whatever it is it's been impossible since roughly 1930 to do, I hate American poets who go to foreign countries— especially the small ones in Central Europe— and present themselves as being more famous in America than they really are (you sick bastards--especially the Poet of Hollywood who every spring slithers through Prague harassing students and bragging about humping the stars--know who you are), I hate junior high school English teachers who don't teach grammar, I hate that there are so many governing bodies in boxing and I wish I could hate Don King but I just can't, I hate Barbie dolls and grin with satisfaction as my daughters—even the three-year old—chant "Barbie sucks Barbie sucks Barbie sucks" when a commercial for the wretched icon interrupts Saturday-morning cartoons, I hate O.J. Simpson for not blowing his brains out during the low-speed chase and every white person in America who was "outraged" by the verdict, I really really really hate Amway, I hate Budweiser because I have drunk the real stuff in Bohemia and by comparison that piss water they sell in the States is but an evil and not even recognizable imitation, I hate young women who wear too much make-up though I am touched deeply by old women who wear too much make-up, I hate women who know the history of the women's movement and therefore what women of the past have sacrificed for them and yet still pull that old seduction bullshit with men to get ahead usually at the expense of other women, I hate middle-aged men who use their midlife power to get laid, I hate that such a sweet-hearted and brilliant and gifted person as Bill Clinton can be such a sick schmuck, I hate that my culture is so sick that his little sickness was such a defining national issue for so long, I hate that the world is on the verge of extinction, I hate that it is likely in my lifetime someone will blow up a major metropolitan area with a jerry-built nuclear device, I hate that it is likely a fair chunk of the world's population will be wiped out in my lifetime by a super plague that will probably be contrived by God-knows-what political/ideological forces, I hate grading freshman compositions, I hate that I am earning roughly ten thousand dollars less a year than the Southern average for full professors at universities, I hate smug trust-funded twenty-something expatriates in Prague, I really really really really really hate that stuck-up self-righteous asshole William Bennett and his being outraged that no one is putting people in stocks or dunking and burning women as witches any longer (I'd love to know the pretentious fat fuck puts on his wife's underwear when no one's around and prances about singing "I Feel Pretty"); all these things and people I hate, but more abstractly than viscerally. Visceral loathing of another human being I'm incapable of sustaining, and the more I think about it the more I'm convinced it goes back to the fact that I was, like every oldest child, supplanted by each subsequent sibling, and like every oldest child felt a primal loathing for those who had supplanted me, and yet also was a caregiver for those I loathed for supplanting me. I was the boss of the backseat of the car, but that often meant adjudicating and consoling, generally caring for those younger than I. In other words, the natural contradiction of loathing and loving that an oldest child feels was intensified for me by our circumstances—I couldn't get physically away, almost ever, from my siblings, and because Joan especially was such a casual caregiver I often at a very young age was compelled to nurture my siblings (as well as brutalize them) more intensely than is usual in families. I go through life therefore wishing to brutalize as well as nurture almost everyone I come into contact with in a competitive context. There is some level on which I can't help but turn my enemies into siblings I would brutalize for opposing me, and yet I am equally compelled to tend to them, hold them and coo that everything's going to be okay.

Oddly connected to this disability is my inordinate terror of thunder and lightning. That is, this fear is similarly structured psychically. Every time a typical ass-thumping storm grinds through New Orleans I am thrilled such that I desire to dance naked on the fifteenth hole of the City Park Golf Course, and yet simultaneously recoil such that I have actually dived under furniture at the crackle and roll of a loud but distant spike. I sometimes wonder if I would drop dead of fear on a thundering battle field without even getting hit by anything. In fact, I was wondering precisely that one day a few years ago in New Orleans. A generic, mid-spring blast of rain and lightning had just danced through the city, and had been particularly strong around the lake. I love the sticky sweetness of New Orleans after a real wet thumper has passed through, and as on all such occasions drove with my windows down from the lakefront to taste the newly scrubbed air. At a stop light, I happened to glance at a car to my left on the two-lane southbound side of Elysian Fields, and observed a kid packed into a late model American car with five others, all big guys in their late teens, toss an empty beer car out the window.

Without thinking, without recalling, certainly, the dross I'd over my teen years ejected from car windows, I yelled something truly ridiculous, something like what the fuck do you think you're doing, or, irresponsible punk. The large boy laughed at me as was perfectly appropriate. I'd been foolish to say anything. But I became enraged. A half hour earlier I'd been torn between ripping my clothes off, running from my office, through the glass doors of the college building out into the electric deluge, or just huddling in my office, almost whimpering in fear, and I'd chosen the latter. I was still hating myself for my cowardice. Also, by my silence I was lying to Lois, and hated myself for that. In addition, I was battling a perfectly decent woman who was then Chair of the department, and hated that I genuinely liked so much someone who was obviously—and I knew it was nothing personal—out to get me. I yelled something hilarious like do you punks want a piece of me. As the light turned green they were frolicking with laughter, throwing their torsos against one another and weeping with laughter, and I yelled something like pull over assholes.

They did. They shot ahead of me into a Shell station and got out, all six of them, huge strapping ugly white boys. One picked up a thick stick from in front of a trash can on the street that flanked the station, the street where they'd wedged their Mustang— it was probably a Mustang— between the rain-glossed sidewalk and the station.

I pulled into the station, popped out of my car, and was ready to die. I was insane. I was ready to wail into them and take as many of them down as I could. I was fearless. I was ready to kill. I was in a state I had trained as a kid in the Sasebo karate dojo to enter, but had in that instance entered it inappropriately. If those guys had been serious, if they'd been bent on destroying me, certainly, at some cost, they could have. But I saw fear in their eyes. They knew I was nuts. I was a big middle-aged crazy man, and they had girlfriends and homework and spring football practice and miles to fucking go before they'd sleep, and didn't need what I was offering, and piled quickly back into their car and sped away.

I fooled the youth population of Coronado into thinking I was a bad motherfucker. I'd received a black belt in karate in Sasebo primarily because Special Services needed English-speakers to teach the sailors (one of my "students"—maybe I gave the guy three elementary lessons—had been Kelly Hope, Bob Hope's adopted son who was a sweet-natured, dorky-looking sailor), most of whom were often out to sea and would come in to port a few weeks at a time and take lessons. As a military dependent, I was always in the dojo, so the sensai groomed me to teach the sailors. I was skinny and tall, fairly quick, worked hard, but was at best a mediocre athlete. I mean, there are athletes and then there are the rest of us. Some of us are good, but we'll always be just good enough to have dreams of grand accomplishments, only to fail when set against true athletes. I had a knack for teaching karate. I could work with someone much more gifted than myself and bring out the best in him or her. That individual would always assume I was physically superior to him, and I always found that fact fascinating, and useful. I had sixty tournament fights and won forty-eight of them, and came close to being the middleweight champion of something-or-other when about two minutes into the fourth or fifth fight of a big tournament I was kicked squarely and purposely in the nuts by a Japanese guy I was beating by a point. I writhed on the mat in front of a couple of thousand spectators, holding Ricky and his aching Sad Boys, and the ref actually peeled one of my hands from my nuts and raised it in victory as I squirmed and grimaced in abject pain on the mat, and the fellow I'd just defeated sauntered away chuckling. I'd made it thusly, by my opponent's disqualification, into the championship round, which was scheduled to occur in roughly twenty minutes, and upon engaging in that Fight of My Life I couldn't even raise my legs to offer weak front snap kicks. I got murdered, though with merciful swiftness. Barbara and Ray attended one tournament in which I competed, and it happened to be the only one in which I absolutely sucked. I was a better-than-mediocre fighter; I was six-feet one-inch tall, weighed a hundred and fifty pounds or so, was pretty quick, and could hit real hard for being so lanky. In fact, I had a hell of a punch; my punch, or really any kind of strike with my hands, either hand, was my small physical talent. I amazed my new friends on Coronado by breaking rocks and bricks and cinder blocks with my hands at parties. I'd get drunk and break rocks, bricks, just about anything. I was good at slamming my hand into extremely hard objects. Everybody was amazed. I knew it was nothing, or very little. Most of it was simply being willing to slam your hand into something hard, and the rest was fairly simple technique. That formulation would later inform my *ars poetica*.

Karate was a hot item. Dojos were springing up everywhere (I met Chuck Norris in the late '70s in his Chula Vista dojo—it was one of a chain— ; he was there to test someone, perhaps several students, for black belt. For all the hype surrounding him, he was obviously the real thing); Bruce Lee movies were hot; "Martial Arts" were in the air. Of course, everyone assumed that someone with a black belt was a killer. I'd gotten my black belt in Sasebo, but I knew I wasn't a killer. That my new peers on Coronado thought I was I didn't mind. They thought I was weird, but also someone not to be fucked with, and that was fine with me. Most of them grossly overestimated my prowess, and as far as I was concerned, that was their problem.

Coronado was packed with captains and admirals, admirals in all the flavors (including Jim Morrison's daddy whom I believe was a vice), rear and vice and retired, and there were even some retired four-stars around. The island is connected to the mainland by a sexy blue arcing bridge to the north, and to the south by a seven-mile long artificial strip of sand (so Coronado is technically not an island, though it once was), the Silver Strand, on which there is a four-lane highway leading to Imperial Beach, at the time a predominantly lower middle-class Mexican-American community. The huge North Island Naval Air Station occupies, still, the northwestern portion of the square-mile island, and the Amphibious Base, where among other things the UDT and Seal Teams trained, is tucked still into the "island's" southeastern part at the beginning of the seven-mile Silver Strand. The small, quaint city proper is always clean and understated in its considerable affluence. In the early Seventies it was as dense with drugs as any place on earth that wasn't a medical facility, probably even Berkeley, at least in per capita terms relative to its youth population. (Years later, *60 Minutes* would do an exposé on the "Coronado Company," a huge drug-smuggling operation headed by a Coronado High School Spanish teacher, quite a nice guy as I recall, and several of his former students.)

The children ("military dependents") of the men who had fought in the Second World War and Korea, and who were some of the major players in Vietnam, were consuming and selling vast quantities of every kind of illegal drug available in the continental United States. What seemed remarkable to me even then was how little control those powerful men and their almost always lushy wives exerted over their progeny. Even in the midst of widespread and by then quite protracted "youth rebellion," Coronado seemed the ideal space for parents to put their collective spit-shined shoe down. It was, the skinny Silver Strand notwithstanding, an island (no one had any reason to go south all the way to Imperial Beach unless she or he was passing through on the way to Tijuana, and that actually wasn't even the best way to go), a small, controllable space, one which kids were not quick to flee from given the availability of perfect beaches and often perfect weather, and relatively few outsiders visited because the bridge toll was fairly hefty. Yet the largely military, high-ranking-officer adult population of Coronado lived in another world of boozy affluence and profound funk over Vietnam, and seemed not to care what was going on among its Baby Boom progeny. Numerous times I ventured into the garage bedrooms (the fashion was to convert garage space into living space for male teenagers, thus getting them as far from the actual living space of adults as possible) of sons of U.S. Navy admirals, some of them deeply involved in the far-flung conduct of the Vietnam war, and purchased ounces of primo dope (at the time one could purchase an ounce of pretty good weed for ten bucks; I'm told it's quite a bit more expensive these days). Usually, the seller would pluck the already sand-wich-bagged green ounce ("lots of buds, dude, hardly no seeds") from a trash bag containing several pounds. Even then I wondered how the big brass daddies, those supposed Lords of Discipline, could allow such activities. It was as though they'd signed a pact agreeing among themselves not to do anything. It seems now to have been a community-wide sociological experiment conducted to answer the question, "What happens when a thousand or so teenagers, mostly from affluent military families, living on a paradisal island smack dab in the middle of the Counter-Culture Revolution and at the end of the stupidest war the U.S. military has ever been forced to conduct, are allowed to do just about anything they want to for the duration of their adolescence?"

I feel only contempt for that place. I love to return and wander its familiar, antiseptically pretty streets, so I should say I love the place and feel only contempt for most of those people who occupied it twenty-five years ago. I maintain from there one good friend, probably best friend, Bruce Donnelly; one intermittent friend, Marc Ward; and the rest are dross, even Buck, for whom I shall always feel affection but who perhaps better than anyone represents the vacuous spirit of Coronado.

Buck (of course this isn't his real name, and much of what I say about him here is correct in spirit but not in fact) has a prodigiously large cock. He, especially as a young man, was particularly proud of it, and would, among his male friends, as young men with fine animals are want to do, exhibit the thing and cackle wildly. I never had any problem with this behavior. I, too, was fond of my penis; it is certainly not as remarkable a specimen as Buck's, but I like it fine and covet no other. A man should have the same relation to his sexual organ as to an only child.

Buck was forever whipping out his cock and talking about it. I had no fundamental problem with the whipping nor the talking, except that over the years it got old. Buck was a star athlete in high school, excelling in baseball and basketball, and whizzed through UCLA mostly by getting his girlfriend Harriette—poor, severely pretty, warped, heavily mascaraed and emotionally abused Harriette—to do all of his work which didn't have to do with math and science. Then, with the Navy's help, Buck went to medical school in Colorado, only to get stationed at North Island on Coronado for a couple of years, after which time he bought into a lucrative practice which he fairly quickly bought out. The island was packed with several thousand aging affluent people possessing excellent medical plans. Buck, a very good proctologist, became the swingin' dick Prince of Assholes of Coronado, wheelin'em in and wheelin'em out. And he started to buy property, lots of property. But then, of course, the market went bust, and he's spent the last decade trying to pry himself out from under all that property.

Land-rich and cash poor, Buck worked his business even more furiously, and was constantly getting sucked into get-rich-quick schemes (Lois and I consumed dozens of bottles of Blue Green Algae because Buck said it was sent from God to keep us alive forever and because his cousin Biff— in trade for rectal work, I suppose— had done so much free work on Lois's teeth we just felt obliged to order and consume the foul substance). But through it all, the tedious hours of staring into the assholes of Valium-glazed widows and otherwise grasping at every foolish scam he attracted to his wildly enthusiastic and foolish regard, he never lost sight of his real dream, to be a pop-rock star. And it was in that enterprise more than any other, though also in all others, where he has been, to my eyes, not only the perfect representative of Coronado, but the quintessential American, that is, a being with seemingly boundless energy, ingenuity, raw talent, enthusiasm, confidence, a good memory for details, hope in abundance, and virtually—no, not virtually—absolutely no self-awareness. He is as vacuous as a puppy, and is the sort of individual doomed to remain so. Oh, he will suffer this or that spiritual crisis, and indeed I predict he will embrace religion, probably any minute, for religion is the last haven for the exceptionally self-aware and for the utterly vacuous.

Blond and Germanically handsome, with a singing voice somewhere between Jose Feliciano and Johnny Mathis (which is to say, not rock-'n'roll), he was a gifted drummer whose athleticism, whose quick hands and terrific eye-hand coordination made him a natural for gooey radio music. For twenty years I intermittently wrote songs with Bruce for Buck. They were terrible, but smart as pop stuff goes, especially musically, because Bruce is authentically talented and a trained composer, an honest-to-God professional. Why we hung with Buck so long neither of us can really say. When we get together we spend hours shaking our heads in wonderment at what a shallow twit he is. Smart, even gifted, but mind-less. He is incapable of abstract thought, and of discerning shades of irony. For twenty years, over which time we all pursued our own career goals and creative agendas, we would find ourselves congregating, at first almost every day, then every few weeks, then every few months, and final-ly every few years, but still we gathered to pay homage to Buck's dream of being a pop-rock star.

We, especially Bruce because he was the only authentic professional among us—I was the "lyricist," which meant I was absolutely worthless, because any idiot can, and does, write pop song lyrics; it is a sad com-mentary on Buck's character that he did not think he could compose lyrics and therefore needed me and others to do it for him—knew that Buck didn't have a rat's ass of a chance of fulfilling his big American dream unless he applied himself wholly to singing, playing, performing, and recording.

But year by year he continued to scope the crumbling rectums of retired admirals' alcoholic widows, to take out ridiculously huge loans to buy prime real estate that would soon devalue almost exponentially, and to talk talk talk about making it in music. He bought half a million dol-lars worth of studio equipment (much of which became obsolete within eighteen months) and started his own recording company, even did some pretty tasty stuff with old and venerable L.A. studio jazz men, and then of course did his own C.D. and tape. He even got some airplay. But the C.D., except for Bruce's instrumentals, was shit. Buck's voice had changed from pleasant mush to garbage, and no amount of studio magic could make it seem otherwise. He recorded songs written twenty years earlier, and they sounded like it. A forty year-old man was trying to be twenty again, and though he was still handsome, energetic, no less full of the Dream, he was pathetic, and so were we, a little, for having anything to do with him.

We hung with him out of love and admiration. We'd known him so long we had to love him, and we admired his tenacity, his unkillable enthusiasm for doing doing doing. On a faculty exchange for a semester in San Diego, I stayed with him in his huge, gaudy, expensive house which in a few years would be repossessed. The sluggish, brain-dead, gold-dig-ging, lazy, pill-popping, peroxide-blond, walking tit-job who was the mother of their twin infant daughters occupied one of the huge rooms upstairs; an ex-big-time-coke dealer, who was then training guard dogs, paid a thousand a month for another huge room upstairs; Buck occupied the master bedroom; and I was downstairs in the guest room, which was just off the Jacuzzi. I came home from teaching every night to Buck's sor-rowful monologues. He would slink into my room and shut the door and babble about the crazy woman who was pursuing him, whom he really liked and really liked to fuck but who had threatened to kill him if he did-n't drop his drowsy tit-job to be with her exclusively. Neither the tit-job nor the crazy would bonk him during that period, unless he gave them coke, which more and more he didn't want to do because now with kids he couldn't be blowing money on the stuff. The main problem was not so much that the crazy might murder him as that she was aware of the "creative" financing deals Buck had concocted for his properties, having contrived the schemes herself, and indeed it had been her brother who'd torched one of Buck's houses so Buck could scam the insurance company, and now she was threatening to make some phone calls to the banks, the police, as well as to the IRS.

I put up with his ranting because he wasn't charging me any rent, and because his life was even more pathetic than my own. At least I'd been fucked up between two extremely bright, soulful, decent human beings. He was squeezed between two California clichés: a Tit Job and a Killer Bitch, neither of whom had probably read a serious book between them nor even for a second considered the ramifications to their souls of having hooked their emotional wagons to a man so obviously incapable of adult relationships. I knew I wasn't talking to a peer, but to the boy I had met in school, the handsome, athletic, gifted, frenetic, adolescent whose greatest delight was exhibiting his horse's cock to his buddies. Of course, as a seventeen year-old boy he hadn't known much sadness, and now he was exceedingly sad, but now his ridiculous life with two women was his horse's cock, and he was wagging it in my face, and didn't want to hear about my life, and that he didn't was fine, because I didn't want to waste breath telling him about it. I still loved him like a brother, admired his vitality, his remarkable physical energy for getting things done, fixing the pool, tending to a work site where a house he couldn't afford was being erected on land he'd lied to a bank to purchase, peering into the sad anuses of the dying almost-rich and truly rich, and for dreaming into his forties of becoming a pop-rock star. He was beyond self-delusion; he occupied, I realized, another planet, another earth, one which was a physical overlay of the one upon which I breathed and moved about and lied and ate and fucked and fretted over my own mortality, yet one which—like in the Superman comics of our boyhoods—was in another dimension, like the Phantom Zone or Bizzarro World, and I had nothing, absolutely nothing to say to him about his life, because we no longer spoke even the same language, had the same cultural points of reference. He was swingin' Dick Prince of Rectums, the Cock King of a gorgeous dead place I still liked to roam within, to my heart a place that was as a well-kempt verdant cemetery of gaudy marble angels and illegible weathered markers. It was the place where I'd been a phony killing machine, and where I'd wanted so desperately to be accepted and yet, to the extent that I was, recoiled out of an instinct not to be absorbed into what from the very beginning, in late '69 as we returned from Japan, had haunted me about the place, a soulessness I would not experience again until Dom, Ema and I would spend six dissonant weeks in Innsbruck, Austria.

Coronado is where narcissism was cheerfully encouraged by every aspect of the vacuous social order; it was a place where, after a childhood on the road running from the cops, after the government housing projects, after Japan, I'd finally found the Great American Normalcy, and recognized it, eventually, to be if not a den of monsters, then certainly a place where authentic affection of any familial and/or erotic stripe was almost impossible. Yet I felt for Buck, who is a peculiarly American monster, a woeful affection as he babbled his absurd private hell, for it paralleled eerily my own. I felt kinship, and, even as I condescended in my heart to him, realized that what I felt most repulsive about him were conditions of mind we indeed had in common. He was simply more American than I.

> . . . we must observe how they face
> bewitchment. Like those who lead
> colts into noise and tumult to see
> if they are fearful, so we must expose
> our young to fears and pleasures to
> test them, much more thoroughly
> than one tests gold in fire. . .

Book III 413 d

I quit high school in the middle of my senior year. I decided to go to LA, where Bruce was attending USC and Buck was attending UCLA— Bruce music composition, Buck pre-med—to write songs with Bruce for Buck's album. Buck had signed a contract with an evil record company, an outfit which turned out to have been a one-hit wonder; that is, they'd recently had a hit, then mismanaged everything after that, including or especially Buck's project.

I was crashing on Bruce's floor, and sometimes Buck's; they lived in the same complex in the Silverlake district, pretty close to USC, one of those buzz-me-in secure apartment buildings with a game room, weight room and, of course, a pool and Jacuzzi. I got a day job selling herbal French cosmetics door-to-door. After a forty-minute training session I was dropped into a neighborhood and then picked up a few hours later. I was then dropped somewhere else, picked up, and dropped somewhere close to a bus stop. Two weeks into my job I discovered I was working East LA and Watts. The Black and Hispanic women whose doorways framed my skinny, hairy, ignorant body were all, all kind to me. No Black woman asked what the fuck I was doing selling Herbal French Cosmetics in East LA; I got odd looks I was not prepared to interpret, but every one of those women was kind to me or simply ignored me. In those neighborhoods I'd felt at home. Black women bought some of my cosmetics. Hispanic women actually looked at the product and said What is this herbal? One thought it was Mr. French's first name.

Then I got a job selling photographs. That is, I went from door to door, in parts of LA that may not even show on maps, saying I was conducting a survey. If the "lady of the house" could bring back the box top of her detergent, I would give her a special prize. The ones who fell for the line would return from their stinky kitchens beaming at me, holding the jagged box tops of Tide or Cheer or Whizz or Jizz or some other concoction of chemicals for a Better Tomorrow, and I would then, beaming back, inform them that a photographer would come tomorrow and take swell pictures of the whole goddamned family for FREE!!! She just had to give me a dollar for the film. So it's really not free, the smarter ones would say, crestfallen, as though they'd really expected me to come through for them, to supply some fundamental affirmation, some proof that the world was not a sausage factory. The dumb ones, alas, in the minority, gave me their crinkled Washingtons, four quarters, ten dimes, twenty nickels, or as happened more than once one-hundred pennies. I'd scribble the paper work, and the next day a real salesman (that is to say a heartless prick who'd been doing that kind of work for so long he was no longer human, no longer even in the animal kingdom, had actually descended to the organic level of viruses, not even lethal ones, just the kind that every few weeks causes lesions on one's genitals) would arrive, take pictures of the family, and compel those women not by reason but by sheer viral will to buy huge packages of photographs. That dollar was all I got.

One night while Billy T, who, though then he didn't even play guitar, would in a decade or so be one of the best blues guitarists and singers in southern California, was visiting from Coronado, I had an epiphany. Bill had a warrant out for his arrest in Coronado for punching out windows on Orange Avenue, and I was selling door-to-door in Purgatory, so, inasmuch as I'd ingested several white-cross hits of speed, smoked several joints, and put away a fifth of Jack Daniels with Billy in Buck's apartment, I figured it would be a good idea for Billy and me to stay up all night, then in the morning march into the Army recruiting office and enlist on the "buddy system." Billy was game. He was convinced that the numerous broken plate glass windows on Coronado's main street would be the last last last straw for the Coronado law-enforcement apparatus, a spunky, silly little operation probably better funded than the entire LAPD, but whose main purpose besides enforcing the island's insane twenty-five mile an hour limit and dealing from time to time with Billy's and Dirty Dave's shenanigans, was to spy on weekend keg parties and roust kids screwing on the beach. So surely this time, Billy opined gravely, he'd be severely prosecuted, and Judge Such-and-Such would lock him away for the duration of the '70s. So hell yeah, he'd join the Army with me.

I don't know if we actually made it to the recruiting office, or if we even set out the next day, which was a massive groaning hangover. We were probably counseled by a wiser head, which by morning would have been just about any skull cavity not containing either of our particular short-circuited brains. Somehow, we acquired the information that one may not join the Army when there is a warrant out for one's arrest, and so, if Billy couldn't go, I wasn't going either.

Buck's record deal had turned truly silly, and after working a concession at the Coliseum for a sold-out preseason Rams game, and that after ten hours of pushing a truly fraudulent product door-to-door God-Knows-Where in LA, I had another epiphany: College would be much better than this. So I packed it back down I-5 to San Diego, limped across that blue, arcing dream-bridge to Coronado, took Yoga and Folk Guitar in Night School, attended perhaps three sessions of each, and received my high-school diploma. That fall I enrolled at San Diego City College which cost almost nothing. It was there I met Louella.

She had a long, gorgeous body, the face of an exotic magazine model, with puffy lips and huge almond eyes one of whose green pupils pulled slightly away from her nose, so that sometimes, from certain angles, I couldn't tell if she was looking at me or not. I was eighteen, lied to her that I was nineteen, and was delighted for some reason I can't recall that she was twenty-two. She'd been married to a Marine who stopped having sex with her because he couldn't get the war out of his head; he was one of those poor guys who couldn't sleep unless he had a large floor fan on, approximating the sound of choppers. Towards the end of my relationship with his ex-wife I met him, and was embarrassed by what a noble, decent adult male he was, and how by comparison I was a sugar-headed boy.

Louella, too, had been a Marine, a secretary in a uniform, of course, but her hitch got her the GI Bill for school, and she enrolled at City College with some vague sense that she wanted to learn French. And she wanted to bonk. A lot. And that's pretty much all an eighteen year-old boy is good for. And we did. A lot. Sometimes seven or eight times a day, sometimes all night, sometimes outside, sometimes in rooms at City College, sometimes at parties, sometimes in my '67 Mercury station wagon, sometimes entire weekends we'd bonk and get out of bed only to eat and relieve ourselves in the toilet. Every straight male has a Louella, at least every male who got laid a lot; that is, he has in his youthful past a woman who, no matter how many times he'd bonked before her, was his first real fuck, his first serious assertion of heterosexual identity. Louella was a prototypical fatal woman, so feminine in her behavior, her every move and gesture, I sometimes just ached observing her, and would not again witness such a profoundly feminine human being until Lois, R and J would take me to the drag shows on Rampart. She herself was somehow meta-feminine, but not in the sense that she was a phony, a woman affecting a male ideal of femininity. She was what she appeared to be, and was therefore a social aberration, at least a little insane. Every guy at City College lusted after her, especially Cameron Crowe, who sighed, slapped my back and called me "swine" everytime he told me how much he wanted her, which was almost ever day. One morning he asked me in front of Louella if I'd like to accompanying him that weekend to his interview of Led Zeppelin. I laughed and said, "yeah, sure, Cameron." He was trying to impress Louella, but was being serious, and I was an idiot not to take him up on the offer. His sweet and bubbly mother was my counselor at City and believed deeply in past lives and reading auras and other such glorious bunk.

Louella moved out of her apartment in Ocean Beach and we got a place in Coronado, actually a nice little guest-house-behind-the-main-house pink stucco number, and it was there, perhaps two months into our almost uninterrupted fucking, that I discovered she was crazy, seriously suicidal.

I was taking a full load at City College, and so was she. I was also working at the geedunk on the Amphib base in the afternoons, and still working out somewhat vigorously in karate and giving private lessons to adolescent males who became disappointed that by the third or fourth grueling and repetitive lesson they weren't already certifiable killers. Louella baked bread and devoured French. She had a spry young French instructor, a petite peroxide blonde with jet roots, hairy armpits, and a thick accent who once shared a cab in Paris with Sartre. Louella, who'd never learned a lick of French and whose initial desire to study it was inexplicable, became enchanted by her instructor and by the language. She started talking with a French accent, which wasn't so bad during sex, but was otherwise annoying. The first time Louella slit her wrists was after a letter from her Bible-thumping papa informing her that she was going to hell for screwing me out of wedlock. She botched it pretty much, missed the arteries. I think she got some ridiculous counseling that seemed only to reinforce her resolve to become a corpse, a transformation she attempted the second time to achieve by ingesting numerous down-ers.

By this time I was nineteen, sexually exhausted, scared of, and in the parlance of the times really freaked out by, the strange woman with whom I was sharing living space and having ever more frenetic physical intima-cy. I also needed money, so when one of the guys I was teaching karate mentioned in passing that he was running twenty kilos of Panama Red to some place called Grand Forks, North Dakota, and that he'd pay me a fifth of the profits if I'd ride shotgun, which could be a thousand dollars, I said sure, a road trip would be nice.

Another guy was coming with us. He was called Spacy Fred because he'd ODed on Dramamine, of all things, several years previously, and had shaved roughly forty IQ points off of what had probably not been a triple-digit total to begin with. I didn't much like the idea of Spacy Fred, in his mid-thirties, coming along. He was incapable of conversing on any sub-ject for more than twenty seconds, and had scary eyes. But Tim, my karate student, informed me that it had been Fred who'd fixed the whole deal up, and that it was indeed Spacy Fred who'd fronted the cash for the kilos. I asked Fred where he'd gotten that kind of money sweeping and mopping the Sacred Heart School, and he just smiled and said he'd saved it up, and I said since when, '57? and he just kept smiling. I should have known right then that the whole affair was headed for disaster, but a thousand dollars sounded real good, and getting away from Louella for a while seemed like the sane thing to do.

Two events early in the trip presaged doom. First, insisting that he drive first since he was the one who'd set everything up, Fred stopped at a red light on Orange Avenue. The only problem was that it was two blocks away. Second, that night in the desert, upon waking from a brief nap, I noticed Fred taking a little snooze himself, behind the wheel. I of course could have had no idea how long he'd been that way, his eyes shut, his chin on his chest, his greasy hair framing his pudgy cheeks. I awoke him with a primal yelp. He shook it off and rubbed his eyes with one hand as he steered with the other, as though napping at the wheel was something one did. I screamed that if he didn't pull over and let me drive I was going to kill him, that I would beat him bloody and leave him to die in the desert. He pulled over, with shrugging reluctance.

From that moment I ate nothing but a banana for three days, and drank a quart of some foul-smelling liquid protein Tim had brought along. When we arrived in Grand Forks in just over three days, we stopped at a cafe for coffee before searching the town for Fred's "contact's" house. Tim got a local paper. The tall, black headline touted the capture of two Californians who'd tried to smuggle a dozen kilos of marijuana into God-fearing Grand Forks, North Dakota, and the article chronicled how they'd been caught in a sting, and would likely get life.

I'd counted on that thousand dollars, and so brought only twenty dollars with me. Back home, I had $84.39 in my savings account, and Louella had only the pittance she got from the government for going to school. Stunned sick, unable to lift my eyes from the doom-portending headline, I asked Fred some questions which should have been posed three and a half days previously, questions like who precisely was this "contact"; he'd casually mentioned in the car, somewhere in Idaho, I think, that he'd met the guy while delivering pizzas for Joey's; he used to deliver six or seven pies on a single trip to this guy and his buddies on North Island. I'd worked for Joey's too; every male under thirty on the island eventually delivered pizzas for Joey's, racing Joey's little VWs that had "hot boxes" where the passenger-side seats would have been, all over town, as well as onto the North Island Naval Air Base and the Amphib Base. It had seemed credible that a bunch of sailors would have befriended their regular pizza deliverer, and that then they may have concocted with him a scheme to make a little money when they got out of the service. It should immediately have occurred to me that anyone who would have judged Fred a reliable partner in crime would not be someone I'd want to do business with, even though I had allowed myself to get sucked into a partnership with him. We found Fred's ex-sailor friend's house, one he shared with another ex-sailor. He seemed mildly surprised to see us, but was hospitable. Fred went into the back room with his friend for several minutes, then came back smiling. He said he had to go to a bar on the state border, one which was strategically poised between a state whose drinking age was eighteen, and one whose drinking age was twenty-one, though I can't recall which state was which. I only recall that the eighteen, nineteen, and twenty year-olds of one state poured over the border to get drunk with their luckier compatriots from the other state, and that a lot of skin-headed new airmen from the Grand Forks Air Base, the ones under 21, were also there, and that rock'n'roll and shit-kicking country western coexisted loudly.

I assumed Fred would contact a buyer at that bar, someone who would take the 20 kilos—which we had crammed into every hard-to-get-at space in Tim's ancient Volvo—of very strong marijuana off our hands. But then I watched in horror as Fred went up and down the long counter of the deafening bar shouting Wanna lid? Got some real good shit. Need some dope? Got some great shit, man. Wanna bag of great reefer? Got some dynamite shit, dude.

I did not doubt that I would spend the rest of my life in prison, and imagined, horrified, sharing a cell with Dick. I grabbed Fred and dragged him into the bathroom. He was much older and larger than I, but he was afraid of me. I told him I was going to kill him, that since I was going to prison for the rest of my life anyway, I might as well kill him. After I calmed down, the odor of spunk and urine filling my head and guys jostling by me coming and going, the sound of flushing toilets and urinals ghastly in my head, Fred's spooky eyes, like those of a dead fish, before mine, I told my colleague I was going to take a pound, just a pound, sell it somehow, and get the fuck away from him, because he was definitely doomed.

I hitchhiked back to the ex-sailors' place and phoned Louella. She told me she was going to kill herself and there was nothing I could do about it. I said fine, and hung up, but was definitely shaken, because I believed her, and because I'd known this would happen while I was away, and still had left. I'd always been kind to her and had nothing to do, as far as I could see, with her wanting to off herself, but I felt responsible. I got wretchedly sentimental about all the times we'd bonked and about Joan whom I'd also deserted. I wept. Then I got a kilo from under the spare tire, split it in half and put roughly a pound of the rust-colored, powerful weed into a paper bag, asked one of the ex-sailors how to get to the air base, which happened to be close, and walked there, a pound of dope tucked under my arm. I sold that pound for a hundred and ten bucks to the second airman I propositioned, found the bus station, and got the hell out of Grand Forks, North Dakota.

We have, it seems, found other
dangers against which our
guardians must guard most
carefully. . . . Both wealth and
poverty. . . . The former makes
for luxury, idleness, and
political change, the latter
for meanness, bad work, and
change as well.

Book IV 421e, 422 a

Joan began to have dizzy spells and muscle spasms just about the time she met the first of two men with whom she had consecutive relationships. His name was Terry, or "Mr. Terry" as we kids were told to call him. Joan was thirty-two. Dick was in prison the second time, and something was definitely wrong between them, something they were working on through the mail. She'd always spent a couple of hours a day writing him letters, but now she scribbled to distraction; the household, always precariously tipping toward anarchy, now plunged into a brutal randomness. When I got home from school I fed the kids as best I could, rooting around in the nasty pantry, made nauseous by the odor of rotting potatoes. We spun around her, screaming, weeping, cackling, and she just sat at the wobbly little aluminum kitchen table, staring into the page she scratched on, looking feverish but not unhappy. I heated up canned beans, boiled a few potatoes (being careful to dig and scrape away the rotting parts), and maybe fried some baloney or olive loaf. The mess I created in the process was absorbed into the previous mess, which was but an overlay upon a still previous one, and of course there was below it all the ur-mess which probably dated to our entry into the apartment. And Joan was oblivious. Even Chris could not move her when he fell and broke his lip; she was absorbed in a task we, at least I, came to hold in awe, and when she finally finished that letter, which seemed to have taken most of a week, I don't know if she sent it to Dick or not, or even really that it was a letter, though certainly it was a task which was not a burden so much as an unburdening, and she snapped back, rejoined us, joked about how filthy the place was, but hardly moved to clean it but superficially, and that was just fine. Joan met Mr. Terry at the Pirate's Den or Pelican Club or some other such dive in Ocean View, a sailor hangout to which a neighbor, a single mother of a small girl, had finally convinced Joan to visit with her one Friday night. The neighbor, as I recall a sweet, rather pretty woman whom I'd seen escorted by numerous men who owned their own cars, loaned Joan some clothes, and Joan put on make-up and looked really terrific, and I hadn't seen her so happy in a long time.

I suppose she met Mr. Terry there, and invited him over the next day. She worked furiously to get the place in some kind of order, bathed the three younger kids, supervised Chuck's and my grooming, and told us a new friend would be visiting.

I recall Mr. Terry, a First-Class Electrician's Mate I believe, being an odd fellow, quiet and serious, and probably self-righteous. He tolerated us kids with some grace, though, and he tried, even, in small ways, to be a surrogate father. I wouldn't have anything to do with that, but I was coolly nice to him because I saw that it made Joan happy to have another adult around to talk to.

And I believe that's precisely what she was looking for, a man to talk to, not, at that point, anyway, have sex with. I imagine horny sailors flocking around her; she was, especially dolled up, quite beautiful still. She probably honed in on the one troubled, I'm guessing sexually dysfunctional swabby in the place, the one who wanted to talk about his two boys who were with his ex-wife in some other port city, and about his job and what he wanted to do when he got out of the Navy. He never spent the night, and Joan never was not home at night, so if they were intimate they'd had to have been so during the day when all of us but Chris were at school, and that seems highly unlikely, since the guy clearly worked nine to five. Besides, when she finally did have sex with Joey, she let me know in no uncertain terms.

Mr. Terry and his meloncholy and odd decency just evaporated; he one day simply didn't show up, and Joan didn't at all seem hurt or concerned; she might even have mandated his departure from our lives. But she soon hit the sailor joints again with the sweet, sleazy neighbor, and this time brought home a guy I really, really liked.

Joey was funny, laughed a lot, and joked all the time, and even cooked for us sometimes, and always brought us stuff (Mr. Terry, actually, had seemed a little stingy). He talked to Joan about books, and the movies he took her to on weekends, and he told me without blinking and never waivering from his story that he'd on more than one occasion seen ghosts, and therefore believed in them absolutely. He was a very reasonable man otherwise, or seemed so, and even when Joan chastised him for feeding me silliness he became uncharacteristically somber and said simply that he'd spoken what he'd witnessed and therefore believed.

More than a month into their friendship, Joan woke me weeping convulsively, obviously overflowing with Catholic guilt, for having been intimate physically with someone other than Dick. I, just turned twelve, was in a bed with my brother who did not awaken; the three younger ones were in the smaller room adjacent but separated by a door. My mother was confessing to me that she'd had sex with the man who'd been a good companion to all of us over the previous month. Joan had never told me about sex, and we'd never, as far as I can recall or even imagine, discussed it, but she sat there on the corner of my bed weeping, terrified and I think joyful, and she told her twelve year-old son that she'd "slept with" Joey, and babbled that everything was going to be okay, that she and Joey would be together, which at that point was fine with me because I was twelve and the worshipful love I had felt for my heroic, misunderstood father had curdled in my heart, and I said fine and hugged her and she went back into her bedroom to be with Joey.

But Joan got sicker. Her dizzy spells and little spasms—one arm would suddenly seize up and her hand would curl toward her throat and become rigid—became more frequent and severe. Her condition was undiagnosed for a long time, but it became obvious that something was terribly wrong with her, and as the sobering prospect of soldering his life to a very ill woman churned in his already-haunted soul—a woman with five kids, no assets, and a pissed off husband soon to be released from prison—Joey began to grow more circumspect, joked and laughed less. He quit the Navy and got a job selling Dictaphones; I recall the last time I saw him he was wearing a nice dark suit. It's odd that I recall his face and voice so vividly; he was someone I quite liked but not so much that he should be emblazened in my memory when my own mother's face and voice are apparitional.

Her affair with Joey went on for four or five months. It ended, Joe ended it—and he didn't, to his great credit, simply vanish; he said good-bye to Joan for hours at the nasty little kitchen table in the midst of the domestic horror he'd always been kind enough to ignore—just weeks before Dick got out of prison. And we, Joan and we kids, buried our affection for that happy, decent, haunted man under a gaudy hope that Dick would have changed, changed into someone like Joey.

As the day of Dick's return approached, we all became excited, and tried, all of us, Joan, myself, Chuck, Theresa, Art, and Chris, to believe that his arrival would mean wonderful things for all of us. We had a little party for him. None of us knew how to act around him, though, so the whole affair was rather awkward, coming down to a series of bad performances for him, as though he were a visiting monarch; I played some tunes for him on my battered tuba. I remember his saying again and again that he was going to take us out of that shithole, and I resented his calling that shithole a shithole because it was our home, a place that had nothing to do with him. And yet the promise of a better life was, as always, seductive.

That night Joan wept her confession of infidelity, and told Dick she was pregnant. Her screams were the black core of terror, and Dick, I believe by pounding her in the stomach, ended the pregnancy.

The next day, everything was fine. She remained in her room, but he strutted about, babbling about how things would be. Over the coming weeks her spasms got worse; her right arm would curl into a rigid hook, and she would lose balance and topple over pathetically several times a day. The doctors she had seen, for some reason, perhaps simply because we were poor, had not been able to diagnose her sickness. Finally someone did, and Joan was relieved, because at least what was killing her had a name. I remember her saying that at least it had a name. That week Dick moved us from the projects, promising a better life, delivering despair.

When we hear "the projects"—"we" being educated, progressive people anywhere on the racial spectrum—we roll up the mind's window and press down (if only slightly) on the mind's accelerator, glancing furtively at dark figures on the periphery, dark little statistics cavorting on chalked-up sidewalks, their teen mothers squatting on slab-cement porches rocking tiny, dark statistics. Down the block a little ways, on the corner of Liberal Guilt and Hard Cold Facts, peddling quick exits from pain and life-as-he-knows-it, a fatherless son tugs at his crotch, scattering vigilant looks all around; he's got more needs than we've got imagination, and he's armed.

I spent almost three years, formative years, in that housing project in Norfolk, Virginia. Indeed, by that time, what Joan had dubbed the Republic of Burma Shave had coalesced into a vaguely pig-like shape Dick would unfold and spread across the steering wheel, to trace with his pointing finger some bright-red line to a spray of red and yellow lines he'd jab with mysterious conviction. After so many years on the road and then three years in Elizabeth City, the projects were quite homey. In the mid-Sixties, the projects, at least the ones we occupied, were white on one end and black on the other, and there were many more white than black occupants. We lived at the very edge of the white section, bordered by a predominately black middle-class neighborhood of home owners. The situation was demographically delightful: a mostly white, public-housing neighborhood of American losers bordering a black community of American winners. My major source of income for the more than two and a half years we were there was from working in the yards of such homes, the owners of which, though always kind and fair, I was certain even then found delicious the irony of employing a poor white kid, and of course relished their neighbors glimpsing, in 1965 and 1966, a disadvantaged Causcasoid grimacing behind a push-mower so clotted with rust the green spears did not so much fly in its wake as flatten under its weight.

Several years ago, the eldest son of a thirty-six year-old woman who worked in the restaurant where Lois was working got blasted twice when he answered a knock at the door. He was nineteen, had grown up in the projects, and obviously had not resisted the allure of quick money and brief escape that participation in the crack economy affords, for, as his mother acknowledged, the shooting had been, in the official parlance, "drug related," and clearly just a warning, for the guy had coolly shot the kid first in a knee and then an elbow at close range.

Though we didn't have guns, the housing projects where I lived in no way approximated the ambiance of a Hollywood set for Wholesome City, USA. We hurt one another frequently, and seemed to possess only the slightest capacity for remorse. And the spatial relations of our environment were no less stifling than those of projects now, inasmuch as they are mostly the very same structures, and so are no less indicative of the purely abstract understanding the Problem Solvers in Wishington marshalled in response to the national need for low-income urban housing; the same housing project I lived in (I observed a few years ago when I was in Norfolk giving a reading at Old Dominion University), still stands exactly as it was when we lived there: cramped, boxy little brick and cinder-block domiciles stacked and strung together over a haggard terrain landscaped by a loveless fiend. I was struck by how small our apartment, on the end of a unit and facing the neighborhood of nice houses, seemed, much smaller than in my memory of it, and I wanted to go inside but was overcome by an uncharacteristic shyness, so did not knock on the door and announce that I had once lived there and that I desired simpy to stand in the living room and look around for a minute.

For me, ascendancy from the welfare class (before Dick came back we were scraping by, the six of us, on less than two hundred a month of which forty went for rent; it wasn't a hell of a lot even then) to the middle class was not the result of great ingenuity on my part. I simply got adopted into it.

Anger and a sense of being inferior were what I took with me from the projects, from life on the dole. But also I took with me a measure of resourcefulness and independence my Sasebo and then Coronado peers would seem not to possess. For one thing, I'd been largely solvent, in a kid kind of way, since the age of ten, and had even given Joan money from time to time. I flattened and raked lawns, washed cars, bagged groceries, ran errands, anything for a dime, a quarter, or—hosannas!—a greenback dollar.

I also tried stealing, but was terrible at it. Two of the times I tried I was caught, and for my clumsy stealth got only slow rides home in police cars. The problem was that, for whatever reasons, I hated stealing. But this is not to say I was a good boy. Oh, no. I brutalized half the kids in the neighborhood, black and white, getting into fights at the drop of a sweat-stained baseball cap. Actually, I was a mean-spirited little prick when crossed, and the couple of times I got my own ass whipped it was by guys who already had tattoos. Naturally, they became my role models. Like them, I carried a knife, and once when provoked, brandished it. These days, in most projects, even a pre-pubescent who acts cute with a blade gets laughed at, then shot.

It was in the projects I became that weirdest of social beings, a poet, for it was during that period I took to fucking angels, partly as the result of two events. I stole two books of poetry from a Salvation Army used-book sale; that is, I ran by one of the stalls and grabbed two books blindly, and they both happend to be books of poetry, one the *Complete Poems of Robert Frost* (if only they had been on the subject of high finance rather than poetry!). The other event occurred soon after my eleventh birthday, actually a few months before I'd copped those books. Neither Terry nor

Joey had been around yet, and Joan's sickness had just begun to manifest more than subtly.

Taking the garbage out the back door of the building, I looked around the dark horseshoe of units. Ours was the first unit on the right side of the horseshoe, the *cul de sac* of which extended inward some fifty meters. The little fenced-in duplicate yards of roughly thirty units, at the centers of which duplicate circular clotheslines (webs poised on silver poles) were ghosted to varying degrees, seemed less yards than cubicles of dirt upon which tufts of grass and drooping weeds jostled for light.

It was eightish, starry and moonless. To put it bluntly, I had what must have been a mystical experience looking at the starry sky and became a poet that night. I'll not describe it. I'd have to wax poetic, lyrical, the way writers describe their first sexual experiences, their first encounters with death, and, of course, those mystical experiences which herald their births as artists. Such rhapsodies are often quite lovely, a little moving, but also self-indulgent, and, finally, boring. Perhaps other people, architects, priests, plumbers find their lifes' work with similar cosmic gooseness, but I think such melodramatic entrance onto one's life project is usually reserved for petty dictators and lyric poets. When the youthful soul gets gorged with wonder, it burps its first foul, all-too-earthly and tender little ditties whose rank, celestial sentiments get wafted skyward by dint of hormonal propulsion.

Roughly twenty-five years ago, I got Mark Strand a reading at San Diego State. We were at a post-reading reception, and I was among a small cluster of admirers that had just spelled a previous squad. We made predictable noises, and Strand made predictable noises, but, as yet another cluster was swirling into place, I heard Strand mumble, "too many damned poets. . ."

Others have in recent years responded eloquently to the charge that there are too many poets in America, and though I respect and sympathize with many such as Strand who have made the charge (Strand has never, to my knowledge, expressed this opinion in print, and it is a bit unfair to use an off-handed remark sighed under his breath over twenty years ago, and which may not reflect his true and considered opinion now, as the primary representative of such a sentiment, but I will anyway), I choose not to despair over what is demographically obvious. I mean, it goes without saying that the unprecedented affluence America has experienced since the end of the Second World War, coupled with what at times has seemed a maniacal egalitarianism in "cultural" affairs, has encouraged a pervasive and largely uncritical any-boy/girl-can national attitude which has resulted in a swelling of the ranks in all the arts. This of course doesn't mean that a lot of really good art isn't getting made and consumed; it just means that there's a lot more of everything, wretched to wonderful, and it's impossible for Strand, me, or anyone to feel in touch with the community of artists in the same sense as was possible even two generations ago. Exponential growth in artistic activitity means greater fragmentation and a growing irrelevance of any institutional authorities. I could go to one of those Poetry Slams now in vogue and wag my *vita* at the audience and they'd just make farting noises and tell me to piss off. All the chancellors of the Poetry Society of America could march somberly robed before such an audience to wag their collective finger and they'd probably get literally pissed on. There is still something of a star system, but each year it grows more precarious, less authoritative, and more and more local "stars," really community arts activists who also deftly promote themselves as artists, are the real power in the arts. It's nice to get reviewed in the *New York Times Book Review*, but if Ringo Gomez, the President For Life of the Diablo Poetry Center and the author of numerous chapbooks and the editor of an anthology of poetry by gay Chicanos doesn't know who you are (and he probably doesn't bother to read the *Times* and there's no reason why he should), you'll not likely get a gig in San Antonio when your new book comes out. Ringo would probably know who Mark Strand is, may even have read many of his books, for Ringo is a true aficionado. But Ringo may also not give a rat's ass that yet another patrician white guy wants to read in San Antonio, and would rather give a thousand bucks of mostly public funds to his buddy Leroy Johnson, whose work he likes much better and who is more likely to pull an audience in San Antonio. The fact that Strand has an "international" reputation and Leroy Johnson is wildly famous within a forty-mile radius simply doesn't matter to Ringo Gomez, and I frankly love that it doesn't. Giving readings at every prison and junior college and even junior high school in south Texas he has managed to sell more copies of his last chapbook, *Rodeo Ringo and His Dream Horse Mikey*, than Strand did of his *New and Selected*, and when Ringo Gomez walks the streets of San Antonio people will often wave and smile at the Poet, and they wouldn't know Mark Strand or Jorie Graham or John Ashbery from Still Bill Whithers and his All-Girl Marching Band. I love Ringo's celebrity, and that his, rather than Strand's, is the model for the future. When Strand sighs that there are too many damned poets, he means there are too many Ringos, and too many me's, too many people defining themselves as social beings by the fact that they write verse, and are unwilling therefore, implicitly unwilling, to let Strand be The Poet. They may defer to his celebrity, his undeniable accomplishments, but they will not let him, in any room they also occupy, be The Poet.

How may there be too many poets? In the sense that any one of us wishes to occupy the rubric alone, no matter how much some may squeal about "community," about art as a process of "sharing," and other such mush. The role of artist, particularly of poet, is an extremely violent psychic field; Bloom, I think, largely has it right, and of course it all goes back to Freud. The poetry world much more resembles a family in which violent and endless battles between siblings rather than benign "community" is the more appropriate analogy for how we, who have in common this role of poet, relate to one another. And of course we have, for the most part, only each other to relate to.

Strolling with my beautiful Dominika in early October of 1989, several weeks before the "Velvet Revolution," through a massive housing project that juts from the flat landscape several miles outside of Prague, like a bad secret badly kept, I was stunned quiet as I rarely am, as though suddenly infused with a reverence whose symptoms approximate those of anemia. As we walked, scanning the huge, obviously poorly constructed towers—the cement was webbed with cracks and the joins between slabs seemed uneven—I was drained slightly of strength, and my emotions were not mixed so much as stacked, one upon another. That filing cabinet of human souls, that hornet's nest of gray conformity— though more imposing than the projects of my boyhood, and though isolated from the very urban context which largely defines public-housing life in the U.S.— seemed wholly and intimately familiar.

Twenty stories high and ten units broad, each building forms one side of a square, so that four identical structures enclose a commons where, obviously, healthy socialist children were meant to romp and grow. Besides the numerous play areas, there is an elementary school also in the commons and a small structure that appeared to be an infirmary. In addition, there are park benches, pathetic shrubbery, and a promenade leading nowhere. There were five such box-like installations and two more under construction. It seemed a perfectly rational structure for a space colony, or the first Mars station. It seemed utterly wrong, though, for the earth-bound spawn of a communist utopia. Everything was merely functional. There were no real grace notes, no attempt at majesty, humor, or, in any sense, beauty. The installation, no less so than the one I'd lived in, was constructed such that it could never be improved upon aesthetically by its inhabitants. It was meant to signify, as my projects in Norfolk were meant to signify, that the State disdains any aspirations you may have to know Beauty, because only the rich may have purchase on Beauty. In other words, the two States may have valued the rich with opposite regard, but agreed that Beauty was a province only of the independently wealthy. What was beautiful in Prague the communists tolerated warily, and were careful not to sustain too enthusiastically.

In a grim little beer garden attached to one of the box communities, Dom and I sat, sipped, and observed. She was a child of the city, of intellectual parents, and was herself an intellectual. She also seemed to me then typical of what I had observed, over the whirlwind week or so I'd been there, in others of her generation and class: she loathed "the system," (that is, the power elite preceding the revolution) and expressed an unabashed willingness to embrace the principles of capitalism and representative democracy. "Look at these people," she said, "they seem drained of life." I pointed out to her that they weren't killing one another and were obviously well-fed. "But what kind of life is this?" she asked rhetorically. Considerably more humane than in similar kinds of places in the U.S. I responded, yet my heart wasn't in the argument. Such comparisons seemed pernicious, inasmuch as to compare in such matters is to condescend.

As I and my beautiful Virgil rested, I observed from the top down; that is, I concentrated first on the old people, mostly old women, of whom there were relatively few in that complex inhabited by nuclear families. All seemed a little stooped, a little sad yet mysteriously resolute, like babičkas, grandmothers, everywhere. Most had transcended the aesthetic realm long ago, and having survived cataclysms of the worst kind, no doubt had transcended ideology. They carried their all-purpose bags draped from their forearms as though God had proclaimed they should transport their souls thus, outside their battered bodies, so that the transport to heaven might commence smoothly at a moment's notice.

The middle-aged men and women—those whose faces signified that each day a grain of lead got dropped into a pouch in each of their hearts— laughed occasionally over their beers, but sardonically. One sipped, chuckled, stared off as he sucked a cigarette, then slowly shook his head from side to side. Another mumbled something and stared at her beer. Was theirs a universal sadness? Did they think themselves sad? Perhaps there is a zone beyond sadness to which the excellent Czech pivo, beer, had transported them years ago. They are the generation which tasted the promise of "socialism with a human face," a promise flattened under the treads of Soviet tanks in '68, not to bloom again until November '89, which no one, least of all Dominika and myself, could at that moment have forecasted. On that October day in '89, as Dom and I sat and drank, bread in Czechoslovakia was cheap, beer was cheap, housing, such as it was for most folks, was cheap, and one worked, when one deigned to work, for the Greater Good of Communism. Indeed, the middle-aged laughed occasionally, but always a little bitterly, never full-throatedly.

The young men and women in the little beer garden laughed full-throatedly. They drank with ease. Their dress approximated that of their contemporaries in the West, but shabbily. A couple of soldiers on leave sat with siblings and friends, and they all practiced, it seemed, for a bitter, unfulfilled middle age.

The adolescents drew my attention the strongest. Of course, they ran in gender packs, possessed more hormonal energy than can be contained by the core of a nuclear reactor, and seemed unaware that life, alas, is tragic. A decade past, has the New Order delivered on its promises? Some by now are living beautiful lives. Some have had their lives circumscribed by a narrow range of prospects, and doused by delicious pilsner.

But then, in early October of '89, the color-coded towers in which their domiciles were stacked seemed citadels against Beauty; and I imagined that the starry sky would be as glorious to any of them as it had been to me, and that for eight or nine seconds on any given autumn night, having been compelled to transport garbage, one would shiver under a godless sky, almost weep, then spend a lifetime seeking words appropriate to that terrible glory, settling most often for a phrase that suspends some shimmering moment as though it were holy. As I sat there beside the woman with whom in a few weeks I'd conceive, accidentally yet willfully, a child in the midst of a small nation's joy, I wished profoundly that what I imagined would come true for one or more of those Czech kids, and still do, for there simply aren't enough poets in such a world as I have seen.

> The children of good parents they
> will take to a rearing pen in the
> care of nurses living apart in a
> certain section of the city; the
> children of inferior parents, or
> any child of the others born
> defective, they will hide, as is
> fitting, in a secret and unknown
> place.
>
> Book V 460 c

G's father was a Chief Petty Officer on the Ajax, a huge supply ship home-ported in Sasebo. He was out a lot. He was from Detroit, and was tall and very dark. He drank a lot when home, but was a pleasant drunk. G's mother was Japanese, and the family, which included as well a younger sister and brother, lived on the base in a Quonset hut that was too small for a family of five, but was comfortable all the same. G, half African-American (of course in '67, '68, and '69 this awkward term was not in wide use, but I can't recall if "Black" was either; did we say "Negro"? I really can't remember), half Japanese, like his siblings was physically very attractive and very popular at school. He was a good student, a talented athlete, and played in the only rock'n'roll band the small school had a sufficient talent pool to muster. He had been studying karate for a couple of years before I'd arrived, and got me into it. He was much better than I, and I didn't care, because he was so obviously the superior athlete. He had been in Japan, living on bases, all his life. He idealized America, and when he got his hands on a secondhand copy of Hendrix's *Are You Experienced?* he wanted desperately to go where such sounds were being inspired. Only in his mid-teens, he understood Hendrix. He was wildly excited by Hendrix's originality. He "got" it as few kids his age— especially those removed from the cultural context such a music signi- fied—were intellectually and emotionally prepared to understand it. Unfortunately, he didn't have much talent for the guitar nor much of a voice, though he had a good work ethic and became pleasantly mediocre.

I wasn't able to understand why then, but I got along so well with G because like me he'd spent his life longing for Normalcy. That was our bond. He was the most self-consciously American American I would ever know, and his America was the records he picked up at the PX, or traded for with young sailors and Marines. His America was what he gleaned from those who had been most recently there, and what he read in books and magazines.

Once I spent the night, and as he lay in his bed and I on a pallet on the floor, we talked in the dark. He spoke of what he would do when his family finally went back to America. He wanted to play in a band, of course, but he also wanted to be an Air Force officer, fly jets. I wanted to talk to him about something, but didn't know how. I wanted to tell him how different things were in Sasebo, in some ways better. I wanted to tell him that the way the white and black sailors got along, the way the black and white Marines got along, or seemed to, was different from how things were stateside.

But he seemed to know, and talked about it, with a sadness beyond his years. He talked about what his father had told him growing up in Detroit had been like, and about how it was just walking around Dragon Heights, where all the top officers lived, captains and admirals, and simply seeing that none of them was black. So that fifteen-year old African/Japanese-American kid knew his America was not America, and though he spoke longingly of the day he would go there, in his heart he was frightened of that day.

He told me that the Japanese were much worse than white Americans, and I didn't understand what he was talking about, and pressed. He said that his mother marrying a black man did not go over well with other Japanese, particularly her family, that she and G and the two younger kids were not welcomed in his mother's family's houses.

Soon after that conversation, I stole a considerable sum of U.S. government script, the funny money U.S. military personnel used instead of greenbacks, from Barbara's drawer. There was lots there, and I figured she wouldn't miss a few bills, and probably wouldn't have missed them had I not struck several times. Raymond was out to sea in his little wooden ship, his mine sweeper, and Barbara spent her days at the Officers' Wives' Club and playing golf. She employed a maid, Suji, a slightly stooped and nearly toothless "mama-san" who did most of the cleaning and cooking, so for all of Barbara's grousing, she had a pretty good deal. Much later I realized that her main problem had probably been not having sex for weeks, sometimes months at a time, but it certainly seemed then that she didn't have a hell of a lot to complain about. Of course she was extremely nervous for her husband's safety, but that wasn't something a fifteen year-old was capable of considering.

At first I used the money to go to bars. I was as big as a lot of the skinny young sailors, and easily passed for one. I began to drink a lot, and of course threw up a lot, too. Then I got drunk and propositioned a prostitute, a youngish, fairly pretty one, and had my first non-onanistic sexual experience. I liked it; I liked it a lot, so I did it several more times. Then I asked G if he wanted to come along.

We were drunk, and told the cabdriver we wanted to go to a "skivvy house." He laughed at us, and drove up a hill on the outskirts of the city proper.

Inside, we gazed at women, seven or eight, sleeping on mats on the floor. It was early afternoon, and the bright sun was filtering through shutters; the air was ghosted with motes, and big-blossomed yellow flowers drooped from a black vase on an otherwise bare table beyond them. An old woman rousted the women, who actually lined up, weary and wary, before us. They wore identical white robes, and were rumpled and distracted. After I gave the money to the old woman, we were instructed to choose, but before we did, the old woman took me aside, actually took me aside and suggested that I pick "the little one" because she would not sleep with my friend. I looked at the little one, and she seemed okay, but I didn't understand, and whispered, drunkenly and quite awkwardly, that I didn't, and she said simply, in a whisper but loud enough that G heard, "no like dark," and I got it, I got that she was saying that the little one wouldn't have sex with G because he was black, and that I should choose her to forego any embarrassment should G fancy her. So I did, and G chose the one with the largest breasts, and the other women lay back down on their mats, and G and I, even more puppy-like in our awkwardness for being drunk, took off our clothes and lay with the women we had chosen, on their mats, in the same room, and when we'd finished both women fixed the sashes on their robs and rolled over, and we left.

Barbara did, of course, discover money was missing, several hundred dollars, just as Raymond got back from a long stint off the coast of Vietnam. My disgrace was absolute; my guilt was a deep ditch straight to hell; my remorse was cosmic. I'd irreparably damaged the people who had saved my life. But if given the divine opportunity to change the past, I'd let that skinny, horny, ignorant and confused kid do it all over again. I'd let him have passionless sex with five or six bored women, get drunk in numerous seedy bars, and give his friend the gift of a few moments' guilty pleasure. For that boy was just a little more than a year out of the projects in Norfolk, Virginia, and was working very hard not to think about a woman he knew was suffering, and about three children he'd helped care for, if sometimes harshly and always awkwardly, and who also probably were suffering, at least emotionally, and about a man whom he had loved and sometimes loathed and was probably back in prison, and now that boy was in a very strange and beautiful place, attached to a family he didn't really know and who seemed increasingly distracted and annoyed and generally displeased, and who seemed not to understand that the past can't be officially changed, not on a birth certificate, certainly not in the heart where nothing is official but loss. I needed to talk about my life, my guilt, my confusion, but all that had to remain an official silence. I don't blame them. They'd taken on more than they could handle. Their sadness about the mistake they'd made was palpable.

Roughly seven years later, in 1975, I believe it was spring, but because southern California is so often paradisal it could have been almost any month in my memory, I stopped by the house in Coronado, though I don't recall why, perhaps simply trying to cadge a meal. Barbara was in her bedroom, lying on her bed reading a magazine. The door was open; we chatted about something, then she said, oh, by the way, Joan died.

I leaned on the door frame and stared off. She then said, "Don't act like you're deeply hurt." She actually said those exact words. I don't recall what I felt; I was trying that moment to pause and feel whatever it was I was able to feel, and her saying that was pure meanness. People who don't allow others their dignity, who take pleasure in subverting others' attempts to show, no matter how absurdly, dignified faces to the world, serve a useful if sad function in a world comprised primarily of fools. Barbara would not allow me any psychic room for sentimental response to the news of Joan's death. I had not sought Joan out. I could have traversed the continent and found her. I'd known for a couple of years she'd been physically incapacitated, completely so, and had feared seeing her, making any contact. As mean as Barbara was to say so coldly what she had said to me, and no matter that her motives were small and ugly, she was also, I would realize years later, morally correct. Her meanness, as vexing as it could be, was my reality check, my temporary stay against unabashed foolishness. She was, thankfully, the moral opposite of her brother; she was a relentless truth teller, and as much as I dislike her, indeed as repugnant as I often find it to be in her presence—an event that will never occur again as long as I live—I love her dearly for being a truth teller, for using the truth like a blunt object.

I stood before her, a twenty one year-old "poet," which to her was just another kind of bullshit artist, and that's precisely what she called Dick, not a con man, not a petty criminal, but a bullshit artist, and I, as far as she was concerned, was simply following in his footsteps. By her mean remark about how I should not respond to the news of Joan's death she told me not to feign feelings I wasn't capable of, and I was at that stage of my life so utterly self-absorbed I was incapable of feeling loss. Of course I hated her for her meanness, but her meanness, her inability to show affection, her lack of nurturing regard, were precisely appropriate to what I had become, and yet I don't know to what extent she, by her meanness during my adolescence, her insistence that I obliterate my past, encouraged my self-absorption, my turning in upon myself when there was no one, no familial presence (not even gentle-hearted Raymond who was so completely dominated by her), I could otherwise turn to. During my entire adolescence I was praised for nothing, and nor was Chuck. Every opportunity to criticize, and always with an edge of ridicule, was seized upon. The main thing I give that boy, that boyish man who was I, credit for was managing to maintain any self-esteem at all during a time of life when the internal mechanisms by which it is filled out and shaped, rather like glassblowing and just as delicate, were under siege by an authority figure whose *modus operandi* was to humiliate. By the time I exited my teens, I'd become numb to Barbara's vicious pettiness, and had been living outside her domain long enough that I only rarely suffered her dyspeptic nature. I wish I could love without reservation someone to whom I owe so much, and whom I respect deeply. I allowed her to be my mother, in my heart, for many years, but one of the more healthful of my psychic accomplishments has been to strip her of that role in my heart, so that she is no longer a mean-spirited, even ruthless mother, but simply a strong-willed woman who performed a noble and humane act in taking Chuck and me into her life, but then botched the job of actually being a mother to two adolescent males. She saw through my bullshit, as any mother sees through a son's bullshit, but instead of treating the illness she damned the symptom. Joan was my mother; Barbara, who brought my mother's death to me, rubbed my face in it, was the honest, severe father I never had, and did not require.

It was only a few months later I stuffed a backpack with most of what I owned, got the three hundred dollars I had to my name out of the bank, walked to a freeway entrance, and stuck out my thumb. Colleen had had a saline abortion a year or so earlier, and had immediately there-after run off with a Las Vegas card dealer she'd met in San Bernardino, San Bernardino where I'd gone with her to a cowboy/biker bar called the Sandpiper in which a guy, not knowing or caring that I was on acid, decid-ed to blindside me on the dance floor and bite a chunk out of my upper lip; San Bernardino, where I last saw the second insane and beautiful woman I'd be involved with over a three-year period, and where I would last feel the insane passion, the passionate insanity of my youth first begin to wither; San Bernardino, asshole of the planet, armpit of America, where all the foul odors of the world are manufactured and first tested, and where at four in the morning, coming down from acid, I had my upper lip sewn up by a tired Asian doctor named Li or Lu or Ly; San Bernardino, where I shall never again set foot nor show my face.

As I stood at the on-ramp I thought about Colleen, about a passion so intense it would eventually have killed one or both of us, and about the more recent relationship I was ostensibly running away from, and had no idea where I was going or how far three hundred dollars would take me. By chance, I'd seen Gary Snyder just an hour earlier on the San Diego State campus; he'd given a reading I'd missed, but as I'd walked away from him and the person who'd sponsored his coming to the campus, he'd said, "Have a good road!" and as I stood at the on-ramp I was glad to have had my trip blessed thusly by Gary Snyder, and I'd stood there only ten min-utes before a beat-up old Nash pulling a sorry little trailer stopped, and an ancient man said, Boy, the Lord has sent you, because I'd surely not be able to make this journey by myself.

God had told him to leave his wife and go to the Hot Springs in Arkansas to cure his cancer, and I was the angel God had sent to help him get there. I drove the first fourteen hundred miles, bought most of the gas, and got him as far as Dallas. When he wasn't babbling about God and his evil wife, he was sleeping, which was fine. Even angels have their limits, and I could not listen to him for more than forty minutes at a crack, which was about as long as he could stay awake. I was definitely not having a great road, but then Snyder had only blessed me with a good one, and even that Purgatory Mobile I was driving was good compared to, say, being stranded in the desert.

In Dallas he promised me he could make the rest of the way by himself, and I didn't believe him, but got out on the far side of town anyway and hitched a ride with a smallish truck that drove all night. The next morning the driver woke me up and told me to get out. I did, on St. Ann in the French Quarter. I'd known we were headed for Louisiana, but had not picked up that we'd make New Orleans.

I knew that Bernie had transferred from the Coronado Chart House restaurant to the one in the French Quarter of New Orleans. He and Marc had had a strong connection to the Gulf since working off-shore in the early to mid-Seventies; they'd trained to be diver attendants and had worked for Taylor Diving; they'd made pretty good money during the oil boom, until Marc got busted by Louie Dabdu (or Dabdeaux or Dabdoo or Dabdue), the same narc, he'd later brag while on probation into the next century, who busted the Grateful Dead, and Bernie simply preferred waiting tables, and I'd heard he was making a bundle as head waiter at the Chart House. I stood on the corner where the little truck had dropped me, and stared across the street at the dark-wooden and brass door of the Chart House, and figured I had nothing to lose calling Bernie, who in the cosmic scheme of things owed me a little assistance, having crashed a few years previously for several weeks on the floor of one of my sleazy apartments. I was surprised that the public phone only cost a nickel. I got Bernie's number and called him. It was six in the morning. He'd worked until two or three. He was only a couple of blocks away on St. Ann. That night I was washing dishes in the Chart House restaurant. A couple of weeks later, when she returned from an ill-fated vacation to California, I met Lois and was soon living with her on Dumaine in the French Quarter.

No aspect of my life has been planned, nothing truly important, anyway. Joan told us we had a guardian angel. She didn't make a big deal out of it, and didn't mention it often, but when I was very young and would get scared when the weather was treacherous and she and Dick seemed clearly worried about our safety in the car, she would tell me not to worry, that our angel would take care of us. As she told it, the angel would make us float down if the car skidded off an icy mountain road, or turn into a pillow and wedge between us and another car if one should swerve into us on a stormy night. I judged the proposition silly even then, I think, when I was four and five, but it helped. I imagined that if it did exist, it slept in the trunk, tucked under the spare tire, and simply jumped from car to car as we changed from one to the next. In the Republic of Burma Shave, contingency is divinity.

So one woman may have a guardian
nature, the other not. Was it not
a nature with these qualities which
we selected among men for our male
guardians too? . . . Such women must
then be chosen along with such men
to live with them and share their
guardianship, since they are
qualified and akin to them
by nature.

Book V 456 a, b

Thus far, my life's most exhilarating experience was kidnapping my oldest daughter in Prague and taking her back to New Orleans. I did this after Dom, Ema and I had occupied for eight months a small apartment half a block from Lois's and my house, a living arrangement that came to pass only after a protracted, volcanic scene. On the phone, before she and Ema flew over, I had told Dom that it would take some time for me to break away from Lois because she, Lois, was emotionally fragile, and I was deeply worried that she would destroy herself if I simply left. Lois had been exhibiting weirder and weirder behavior, had had episodes during which I was certain she was nuts. Of course, as I reassured Lois of my vast love and deep regret, she improved considerably, and during such stretches of time, between the day I returned from Ema's birth and that Christmas when Dom brought the four-month old creature to New Orleans, I and Lois in some fundamental ways got closer than we had ever been when married. We enjoyed one another's company, and hashed over the past, revising here, obliterating there. When I spoke with Dom on the phone during that time, I reassured her of my vast love and deep regret, and begged for time, assuring her that as Lois improved emotionally, as she got herself back together, as her mother's health improved and as Lois made the transition to another life, I would be with her (Dom) and Ema. I just needed time. I needed for her, Dom, to be patient. And from Lois, too, I begged for time, patience, forbearance. I wanted everyone to be very patient, because I was in one ridiculous situation with two women I cared deeply for, and I was telling both of them the truth which is to say I was lying to both, which is to say there were two truths, one for each woman, which means I was whale shit, a large clump of ghastly matter lolling on the ocean's dark and fetid floor.

Andrei Codrescu told me I shouldn't write about this aspect of my life. He didn't exactly say why, but did mumble something about unnecessarily making myself a target. I'm very fond of Andrei, have come to appreciate him as a terrific poet, one of the best (of his ilk) around, a judgment I don't make lightly. In his verse and prose he has managed brilliantly to appear to lay bare his life when in fact he's kept a fairly tight private zone intact; the persona with whom his fans, and I am one of them, feel a friendly intimacy is very much a public one. So I have no idea if Andrei has ever been a rogue and therefore is pained a little to see something of his own darker self herein. My guess, though, is that most men who have ever been rogues, and who have then been forced by circumstances to stay put and witness the psychic damage of their roguery, upon being reminded cannot avoid tasting again, like a kind of acid reflux, the bitterness of their own duplicity. The rogue as a public figure is attractive, a delightful mischief-maker; as a private being he is a tiny destroyer. I started out as a rogue and became simply a fool living in the moment because the future was terrifying. I was not worthy of the affections of either woman whose life I was poised to damage, but neither would cut me loose. Dom of course had the practical consideration of a child, but why Lois did not immediately sever her affections from me I cannot know. All I know is that even as I was the agent of Lois's sorrow, I was the only person she would confide in regarding that sorrow. Suddenly all the friends whose lives she'd brightened lived at a distance. She was, I think, unspeakably embarrassed for her friends to know that her marriage had failed. Night after night I would listen to her weep how she felt about her mother, whose life could be snuffed out any second, and about our marriage, which had been snuffed out and yet seemed still to haunt us, to exist as a thing, apparitional yet pungent, binding us even as "we" had been legally ripped asunder. I became a caretaker to my ex-wife, and as such after deserting her could not desert her. Surely if her mother had not been ill she'd have handled her psychic pain much differently; her mother could have been an ally and source of strength, the confidant she so desperately needed. But I was her only confidant, and in that role I would say anything, absolutely anything to relieve her pain. Andrei Codrescu is right; I shouldn't write about this aspect of my life, except that not to would be a lie of omission, and though I am telling many such lies herein (this funky little universe is littered with black holes) this is one that would suck whatever truth I am managing all the way down into its indeterminate core. To those who may charge that I have no right to reveal Lois's private life simply because it was tethered to my own I would point out that she never complained, in fact was obviously delighted, when I chronicled in books of verse some of the more private aspects of our lives, even in a couple of instances events I would not here dare to repeat in the bare-bulb bluntness of prose. Shared time, shared joy and woe, shared life, is not community property that gets split down the middle or otherwise negotiated. Only when revenge is the motive does the revelation of shared private life become tawdry.

Dom arrived with four-month old Ema, whom I'd not seen since the day after she was born, and I fell in love all over again with the child, and

Dom was radiant, strong and bright and poised. I couldn't take my eyes off the baby, couldn't get enough of her. Lois was convinced that everyone would be civilized, that we would all be friends and work everything out. Dom wasn't particularly interested in being friends with the ex-wife of her child's father, the man who had told her unequivocally that he wanted her to have the child, and that he would take full responsibility for the child. To Dom, this meant quite simply that I would marry her and be a proper father to Ema, and I gave her no reason to believe that that was not exactly what I had in mind. I wanted to marry her and be a proper father. I also wanted to continue living with Lois and affording her the security of our long-term relationship (we occupied the house together out of economic necessity; I lived upstairs, she down, though we ended up sleeping together more often than not. We were not very good at being divorced). In other words, I wanted to stick my face into a deep-frier cranked up to five hundred Fahrenheit and feel only a mild and refreshing tingle. I felt truly responsible for the first time in my life, and it was for the three people sharing Christmas in my house with me: my ex-wife, my four-month old daughter and her Czech mother. When I moved Dom and Ema that late afternoon over to the apartment a half block from Lois's and my house, the whale shit hit the fan.

I am happily married to Dominika, and we have two big, beautiful daughters and live in Prague 4 near Vyšehrad. I am faithful to her because I am too weary not to be, and because kids change everything. Dominika is the best friend I have ever had, not only because she is smart and funny and wise and we see the world in remarkably similar ways, but because she is the only person with whom I have had, and will ever have, serious and protracted conversations about actual shit. Any parent knows what I'm talking about. There are some men who seek other intimacies precisely because they feel the need to bond with someone other than the women with whom they have gazed with that odd parental pride into soiled diapers, and actually commented, in all seriousness, upon what one finds there. For me, such discourse is the ultimate bond, signifying an intimacy far deeper than any other. A Czech woman we know is pregnant with a U.S. Embassy Air Force Lt. Colonel's child; she is strong and smart and much better than what he deserves, and he is back in the States now with a childless wife he was always rather vague about and calls his pregnant lover often, sometimes swearing devotion sometimes ranting in despair. From our friend's reports, her Lt. Colonel is even more fucked up than I was, if that's possible, but I just read to Ema and help her with her homework, and tell Annie Big Bear stories, and bathe my girls and feed them and take them to the park and tickle them and scream at them and laugh hysterically with them and their beautiful mother at almost anything and our pregnant friend and her crazy Lt. Colonel have my sympathy, his wife has my sympathy, the whole world has my sympathy, because I have been whale shit, and when one has occupied the heart's murkiest depths, shifted about slowly by its deepest, coldest currents, one everafter abounds in sympathy for every idiot man and every idiot woman who has ever loved badly, a subset of humanity indistiguishably smaller than humanity.

Dom and Lois had been quite civilized during dinner, had been remarkably charming, and as they chatted I grinned like an idiot and fantasized all four of us living together as a remarkable family. What I didn't see was that Dom and Lois were positioning for battle. It was understood that Dom and Ema would stay in the apartment down the street, and I was fairly certain that Dom understood that I would sleep not over there with her, at least not at first, but in the house as I had been. Of course, when evening was coming on and it was time to show my little Czech family to their quarters, the first volley boomed over my head. As I showed Dom around the nicely if sparsely furnished apartment, she seemed satisfied. When I kissed her lightly and said I'd be back later to tell her *dobrou noc*, good night, she seemed a little startled. Tell her good night? Be back later? Of course I'd be spending the night, wouldn't I? Yeah, of course, what was I thinking. I'd leave for a while, but come back and stay with her.

Back at the house, seventy meters or so away, I helped clean up after Christmas dinner and gift exchanges. Predictably, Lois had gotten Dom something quite nice, whatever it was, and seemed pleased with herself. She'd come a long way emotionally from that evening in Dom's Prague apartment when she'd expressed repeatedly, chanted, the fervent desire to hack my balls off with a chunk of broken glass, and had seemed fully prepared any second to realize that desire. She was contented that everything was going to be okay, that she and I would be remarried in "the Church" this time, and together we would help raise Ema. Her side trip, alone, to Majagoria while in Europe had, I suppose, reinforced her quirky faith, her self-concocted feminist/existentialist Catholicism. Yeah, that's right, in the Church, I said, sure, but I think I should stay over there tonight, being that it is their first night here, and being that it's Christmas, and, well, I think Dom's a little scared.

Back at the apartment, I tried to explain that perhaps it would be better if we waited for the next night; if I stayed in the house that night and then started staying at the apartment after that, you know, emotionally Lois. . .

Back at the house I explained that, well, you know, Dom really is disoriented and. . .

Back at the apartment. . .

At around midnight Lois expelled at least temporarily from her heart the holy calm of that little town in Bosnia and started breaking furniture. She destroyed two lamps and a chair, and was going after another chair when I'd decided that she'd won. I told Dom, look, she's nuts, loco, out of her ever-loving mind, and I'm probably going to have to have her committed tomorrow, so please, let me stay over there and tomorrow we'll get this all worked out. Dom, much less volatile—she was, after all, a mother of an infant, and therefore had vastly different priorities than Lois—

informed me that she could pitch a fit, too, and that my place was with my child and her mother.

The neighborhood in which I'd purchased my house was a typical Ninth Ward, working-class, racially-mixed one. I liked living in a neighborhood as black as white, as gay as straight, and I'd even liked how truly weird some of our neighbors were, especially the family comprised largely of actual idiots whose backyard bordered ours, and whose front door faced the apartment I'd rented for Dom and Ema. On one of my numerous shuttles back and forth that afternoon and evening I'd seen them lurking about, and recalled Lois's having told me of once hearing the old woman shout to a car full of teenage girls, "I'm not your fucking grandmother!" Lois'd not heard the sentence to which the witch had responded, though imagined it to have been something like, "Bye, grandma," to which the extremely ugly, filthy old broad had felt compelled to correct a factual error, though perhaps she'd simply forgotten that she was in fact their grandmother. She and her son, in his late fifties, were the only ones in the house, which sheltered five humans and a couple of addled hounds, who were not mentally retarded, or at least by contrast seemed not to be. One of the "boys," probably in his late thirties, spent almost every hour of every day acting out extremely strange fantasies in the backyard of his house, which unfortunately I could see from the window at the top of our stairs, and when he jerked off, and he did so often, he'd cackle during the entire episode. Once he cackled loudly for over an hour and I was trying to get some work done; I was almost ready to help him out, throw him a pair of Lois's underwear or something, anything to stop that horrible sound.

Dom had glimpsed that whole weird brood over the course of the late afternoon and evening, and simply didn't want to be left alone in an apartment across the street from them. They sat on their front steps late into the night—the addled dogs, the grandmother, the son, the two late-thirties "boys" and a thirtyish female with buck teeth and a stare so vacant it was almost beatific—everyone but the dogs smoking cigarettes, not talking, the three actual idiots rocking their torsos while they puffed, no porch light on. They'd have made a wonderful poster for Dan Quayle's next election bid; "Family Values with a vengeance" could be the caption. But they scared the hell out of Dominika. It seems they had no corollary in Czech society she was aware of, even among Romas, gypsies, the most destitute of whom by comparison were simply exotic.

Back at the house, I told Lois, again, that Dom was scared. She broke something else, though I can't recall what. She told me that if I stepped out the door again, we were through. There was no way she could have known how beautiful that ultimatum sounded.

Five minutes after I'd returned to the apartment, she was at the door. She wanted to talk to me. Back at the house, she said she'd give me another chance. I told her I didn't require another chance. Or maybe I said, swell, but we'll work it out tomorrow, right now everyone's tired; it's after two; get some sleep.

I don't recall where I slept that night, and do not wish to trouble Lois's or Dominika's memories on the subject; I do recall that the third or fourth Step Out The Door ultimatum finally stuck, and I was living, for the most part, at the apartment. That is, Dom would have me even though that next day I'd compelled the two women to sit down together and compare notes while I left the room with Ema. After they did, and thereby discovered (like they didn't already know!) what a lying, duplicitous creep I really was, they spent about an hour in wonderful solidarity. It was beautiful! They stood shoulder to shoulder, their arms crossed, the Light and Dark Eve's of my life, calling me vile names and shaking their heads. It was glorious. I grinned idiotically, oddly, and only momentarily, unburdened. Finally, Dom said something like okay, asshole, come over and help me take care of your daughter. But then Lois said, okay, you're a vile prick, but I'll give you one more chance, and I couldn't believe it; they were back at it, ripping me to pieces. From the depths of my guilt I bucked up for a moment, and said something like wait one fucking minute, I *tried* to tell both of you the fucking truth, but you wouldn't fucking hear it. You both have been fucking jerking me around, so fuck both of you, or maybe I just whined like a whipped dog. Yeah, I was a whipped dog. But at least now that they knew I'd declared my love and loyalty to both of them, that I'd been insane in my feelings of responsibility to both of them, I could proceed in truth. Yeah, I thought, now everything would be better because everything was out in the open.

I can condescend to the child I was; I can condescend to the adolescent and even the young adult I was, but that schmuck who actually thought "things" would get better was I, and I'd like to reach back, the way Dick would reach back over the car seat, and smack the hell out of him, not for what transpired, but just for being so goddamned stupid. That all of this silliness, all this low comedy has to do with my not having mourned my mother is too obvious even to mention, so I'll not again mention it.

I got good at parenting, really loved it, though things were not going well with Dom. Lois started playing the Other Woman, quite subtly at first. She needed help with a lot of things she'd never needed help with before. And she absolutely needed me to drop her off at work in the Quarter on Fridays and Saturdays. Ema was the only sweetness occupying my days, and as I delighted in her I despaired for the two women in my life. The poet William Matthews—the last time I saw him was a couple of months before his death; I hailed a cab off of Celetna in Prague for him and his lovely companion; in my introduction to his reading a couple of nights previously I'd called the speaker of his poems a "postmodern gentleman," and Bill was that, a genuine and graceful man whose love for the truth in beauty, especially when the beauty was not immediately apparent, was profound; he was one of our very finest singers—wrote that the price of bigamy is two wives. I was paying the price. Though I slept with Dom, I was functioning still, in everyday affairs, as Lois's mate. Of course Dom was angry and had every right to be. Though Lois is constitutionally incapable of consciously manipulative behavior, unconsciously she can be extremely controlling, and regarding her ex-husband and his weird little family she had her unconscious on cruise-control. I let Lois play me like a blues harmonica, bending and distorting every gloomy batch of wet notes. Besides, I'd let Lois's lawyer chew both my legs off in the divorce settlement. I'd agreed to give Lois stuff I wouldn't have in thirty years, half of everything I'd ever have to give, including, I think, organ transplants. She owned me, pure and simple, and if she ever pressed for me to honor our settlement fully, I'd have to steal outright to do so. I reminded Dom of that, and she responded appropriately, calling me a fool for allowing the lawyer and Lois to destroy me like that. I tried to explain the guilt I felt, to which she told me simply to look at our child, that Ema should always put my petty guilt of betrayal in perspective, and I knew she was right, but felt no less guilty, exquisitely guilty, deliciously guilty. I wore my guilt like a pair of gaudy orange sneakers. I was a cosmic fool, that very clown who had walked Orange Avenue in orange sneakers on acid, indeed, those very clowns who'd jumped out of a box and crammed me into it. I was cramming my actual life, my real and palpable life back into that box, but I couldn't wake up. The cosmos was telling me I was doomed, and the beauty of my condition was that I was the agent of my own wretchedness, though my doom was predetermined. I look back now and wonder at what point I became such a fucking Puritan.

Lois and Dominika came from very different kinds of broken homes. Lois was the oldest of four, and was often the surrogate mother for her younger siblings, especially on those occasions Lois's Willy Loman-like father shuffled his wife off to a mental hospital (the only thing that was ever wrong with Lynn was that she had an artist's heart and was married to a sanctimonious and sentimental automaton; her troubles began on a beach in Acapulco when, on a business trip there with hubby, she ripped off her clothes and ran naked in the sand; to some, mere exaltation is insanity); Lois's father was the puppet of his own maniacal father, the real patriarch in Lois's life, the authority against whom she rebelled. He lived in Oklahoma, had some money; his politics were eighty yards to the right of John Birch, and his sensibility was vintage Redneck, or what Redneck becomes when it acquires a fair chunk of money. He'd been prepared to pay Lois's way through Tulane if she attended on his terms, and she, to her great credit and very stupidly, told him to piss off and got disinherited. When Lois's mother finally left Lois's daddy-beaten daddy, she and Lois got apartments in the same building on Dumaine in the Quarter, and became like, acted like, looked like— Lynn was and is a dish— fooled around and even giggled like sisters. That what Lois desperately wanted but never had was a nurturing mother, and still I think wants to crawl into Lynn's lap, is a fact of her life she has negotiated with typical grace. She became her own mother's mother in so many ways, and was always a mother to her siblings, and was independent of any paternal or patriarchal authority from the time she was seventeen and working in the Quarter. She became the Queen Bee to her own mother and siblings and friends, the latter of whom were mostly gay and lesbian.

Dominika's parents broke up when Dom was ten, but her father, a beautiful rogue who had two other children, besides Dom and her brother, by three subsequent marriages and I'm guessing innumerable affairs, remained actively involved in Dom's and Filip's lives; a civil engineer who had published several novels under the old regime but has pretty much retired from writing as well as engineering, he's a happy, sardonic Czech intellectual who now loves to baby-sit the girls. Dom's mother is former vice-dean of the law school of Charles University and one of the leading law scholars and professors in the Czech Republic. Dominika grew up in the same apartment all her life, spending weekends at the same "chata" or summer house twenty minutes outside Prague in Dobřichovica, and though one of her earliest memories is of watching Russian tanks roll through the streets outside her building, her life was as stable as life could be, even as her father flitted about with a sexual agenda that precluded his staying with her mother, but which otherwise did not exclude him in any significant sense from her life. Next door to Dom's ancestral home, the three-room flat on the third story of a nondescript building in Smichov, was a two-room flat where Dom's father's divorced mother and father resided for most of Dom's childhood, together. The authorities let them divorce, but wouldn't let them live apart, that is, wouldn't let the old coot, a former "industrialist," have his own flat. So babička and děta, grandma and grandad put up partitions and lived, divorced, separated by a wall, sharing the same toilet, tiny kitchen and bath for many years. Dom would go next door to visit grandma, say good-bye, then walk into the other room and visit grandpa. Lois was the product of a culture in which most men cheated and when they got caught were condemned in biblical terms; Dom was the product of a culture in which almost all men cheated and its occurrence was treated with the same aplomb as that with which the Czechs greet most of life's unavoidable disasters. In American terms I'd been a cad; in Czech terms I'd simply been a man. The truth is somewhere in the middle, out in the gray Atlantic, lolling and decomposing on the ocean floor.

So several months later Dom and Ema went back to Prague; I would come over in a few weeks. I told Lois—and I swear I don't know how the thought came into my head; I don't know at all where my head was, as we used to put it—what the hell, let's get married again. She insisted that we do it "in the Church," and I said fuck the Church, fuck especially the pope and all his buggering bishops, let's just do it the way we did it before. The fact that after everything she still wanted to be married to me meant that I had to marry her again. That's how insane I was. So we went down to City Hall and did it. Then I went to Prague and told Dom I was going to stay with Lois, but that I wanted to do everything I could to parent Ema. Of course, Dom told me to fuck off, that I would never see my daughter again outside of Prague. I'd remarried my ex-wife. Why after everything was I going back to her? Because she needed me. Dom was strong and independent. Actually, Lois was strong and independent, but in a different way. Didn't I love her and Ema. Yes, of course I loved her and Ema, and I wanted to remain in their lives. Did I know I was insane? Yes, I knew I was insane. But if I knew I was insane, how could I be insane? Maybe, then, I wasn't insane. But wasn't everything that had transpired insane? Yes. Wasn't putting Dom and Ema up in an apartment only seventy meters from my ex-wife's house insane? Yeah, it was a little insane, but it was also convenient. Convenient for what? Further insanity. For giving Lois the opportunity to use me like a husband who just happened to be living with his child and the mother of his child. For wearing my absurd, bourgeois guilt like a pair of orange sneakers. For getting myself into such a situation in my personal life that colleagues treated me like a sloppy road kill they did not wish to look at directly.

But wasn't I a good father? Yes, I was a good father. Didn't I try to keep everyone well? Yes, I thought of others, and I did my job well, when I wasn't pissing off senior faculty. I even managed to write another book, and it had been accepted by a university press. Wasn't I a good friend? Yes, I was a good friend, an attentive mate. But I'd just married my ex-wife, and had been told by the woman I should spend the rest of my wretched life with but now couldn't that I'd never see my daughter again unless I came to Prague to see her. That meant that Ema would be a Czech and not a Czech-American, which meant that I would always be something foreign to her, and would not get to father her as I wanted to, that is, intensely and with vast affection and humor and stern and daily guidance. In New Orleans, Dom had told me to decide what I wanted to do, that she wasn't going to live that in-between bullshit any longer. I had had to do something, so I remarried Lois, who should have told me to fuck off when I suggested we drive over to City Hall. I'd made a decision, an insane one, the absolutely wrong one, but it was a goddamned bona fide decision after months of spineless waffling, months of self-pitying guilt-wallowing insane indecision. In fact, doing something decisively, even though as I did it I knew it was absolutely wrong, had felt good. Taking action, some kind of decisive action had felt damned good. Saying, Come on, Ex-Wife, let's go down to City Hall and get remarried had felt good. As the decrepit and probably (that is, typically) corrupt New Orleans judge had droned the ceremony, I'd stood there telling myself that the last thing I wanted was to be married to my ex-wife, that I actually preferred her as an ex-wife, but I'd made a goddamned decision, a real suck-up-your-balls-and-deal-with-it kind of decision, and it had felt good. So there, in Prague, still flush with the personal victory of having made a decisively insane decision, I made another one, and kidnapped my year-old daughter. I was on a roll.

All I wanted was to force Dom to accept my participation in raising Ema. When I got off the plane in New York, the cops nabbed Ema and me. But Ema was a U.S. citizen. There was nothing they could do. I then bought Dom a ticket; when she got to New Orleans, I looked her in the eye and said, Do you promise that no matter what happens, I can be this child's father? She said yes, and I handed her our daughter. Much shilly-shallying silliness insued, but Dominika was dignified and patient. Lois was dignified and increasingly impatient, and her inevitable blossoming out of the humiliation of our ridiculous second marriage finally finished. Dominika and I married in Prague's Old Town Square with Ema, three-years old, looking on in the midst of Dom's extended family and our Czech friends.

It seems to me that a fit body does not
by its own excellence ensure a good
soul, but on the contrary it is a
good soul which by its own
excellence ensures that the body
shall be as fit as possible.

Book III 403 d

On a writing fellowship to the University of Virginia I learned that angel fuckers are by their very nature cowards. Those who do not fuck angels live under bare bulbs in smoky rooms drinking cool coffee waiting without distraction and with nagging headaches to die. Those who do not fuck angels and do not believe in God or Love are the true heroes of life. I did not come to these conclusions because of anyone I met at UVA. Rather, I learned these truths feeding, and wiping the asses of, dying children.

The year I was in Charlottesville, I read, wrote, bonked; I also worked three or four days a week at Bloomfield, a home for crippled children, most of whom were dying of MD. I worked there because my roommate and erstwhile fiancée insisted that we live in a lavish log house thirty miles from the campus—I mean, the "grounds"; one said "Mr. Jefferson" and "the grounds"—and my fellowship money simply wasn't enough to supplement her new-faculty income. I'd gotten the fellowship probably primarily because I was cohabiting with the hot new poet-in-residence, who at the beginning of our stay in that lavish log house started talking about us getting married. I no more wanted to marry her at that stage of our relationship than I wanted to shove a toothpick into the roof of my mouth, but I went along with the idea. I knew she no more wanted to marry me than I her, but she, inexplicably, persisted in the fiction that we would actually get married in Charlottesville, and actually wrote a lot of folks, many of them well-known poets and fiction writers, announcing our intentions. People wrote "us" back, congratulating "us" on the wonderful news, which to anyone who knew "us" was so silly as to be almost frightening. Philip Levine, at the time (and I have to admit that to some extent he still is) my favorite poet, wrote "us" a sweet letter of congratulations which, I'm ashamed to say, thrilled me. I would later stupidly but somehow necessarily piss him off as a kind of daddy-slaying gesture. We officially hated each other for about a decade, though recently changed our regard for one another to cool acceptance. Life is truly too short to hate someone officially whom you actually respect and rather like, and besides, I have heard with what acid humor Levine can in conversation burn those who have pissed him off, and feel lucky that after a decade my ears are not scorched petals hanging by bloody tendrils from the sides of my head.

Mercifully, Ca started bonking the Brit Marxist lit crit guy who was very well published but untenured. That freed me up to bonk some of the honeys in town. I went through a brief period of jealousy, about eleven and a half minutes, then started bonking some real sweeties. Of course, I can't recall any of their names, though do recall that each was attractive and bright. But the childish intrigue and gratuitous, narcissistic humping meant little, for I was spending twenty or so hours a week taking care of the physical needs of children who were dying and knew they were dying. I was only a part-time caregiver; most of the people who worked at Bloomfield lived on or near the grounds of the huge, white converted mansion, and were deeply committed to those children. One in particular, a skinny handsome Vietnam vet who, like Louella's husband and so many other guys who'd risked their lives in Southeast Asia who couldn't sleep unless the room was filled with the sound of a large fan, was a truly gifted nurturer of such children and loved his work.

I'd never wiped another human being's ass before. Even as a boy taking care of my siblings I'd never been called upon to perform that task. But at Bloomfield I learned to bathe nine through eighteen year-old, forty to one hundred and thirty pound kids who were incapable of moving, some of them, any parts of their bodies but their heads and faces, and to place them on toilets and, wearing a plastic glove of course, wipe their asses, and then dress their bedsores, often a half-inch deep, and unfold their bodies to exercise their fragile limbs, working each arm and leg like something just oiled, and then pull up the covers exactly the way each desired— some wanted just the sheet; some wanted the blanket just up to their chests and some to their noses; Harry wanted his head covered— and then turn off the light. I also learned to feed them and to laugh at their jokes about death. As should be generally true in all societies but isn't in ours, at Bloomfield the oldest and therefore closest to death were afforded special respect by everyone; they were royalty, and the two princes of Bloomfield were Harry and Judd.

Harry was sixteen and weighed forty pounds. He was warped, like something thin that had lost its true shape in drying. He was ugly and mischievous and worked hard for each breath he drew. He would call me terrible names and cackle. He had to be strapped to his motorized chair, but could move, barely, two fingers on his right hand, so he could manipulate the little joystick on his right chair arm. He often terrorized the other children by coming up behind them and slamming into their wheelchairs which were not motorized.

Judd was eighteen, almost nineteen. He wasn't emaciated like Harry; in fact, he was even a little hefty, probably around a hundred and thirty pounds, but was clearly zeroing in on death more efficiently.

He started dying in earnest three days before the '79 World Series in which his beloved Willie Stargel would be playing for his beloved

Pittsburgh Pirates. We kept a twenty-four hour death watch in his room, and he labored for each breath. Twice on two different shifts twenty-four hours apart I'd been certain he would completely deflate. That second shift, around three in the morning, he started asking, rasping, every twenty minutes or so, for me to hold a mirror up to his face. He certainly wasn't a vain kid; he just needed to see himself. He could die any minute, any second and just wanted to see himself. It made perfect sense.

He hung on through the Series, receiving reports every afternoon or evening about each game. When Game Seven arrived, we were all going nuts. We knew we were witnessing some kind of miracle of the human will, that we were witnessing the goddamned greatest baseball fan on the planet, one whose greatness, whose sweetness and purity and love of a game he had never been able physically to play transcended any accomplishment of Ruth, Cobb, Shoeless Joe, Paige or Mays or any other player who had ever graced a ballpark. In my memory what transpired was wholly my own initiative, but if anyone else was involved I beg forgiveness.

Without thinking I called an operator who hooked me up with another operator who patched me into the ballpark. I babbled to someone about Judd, and somehow I got routed to the dugout, and goddamned if Willie Stargel didn't get on the phone. Yes, this is an autobiographical novel, though I'll have to call it a memoir, and like anything comprised of words, of symbols, is a kind of intricate lying about the truth the more it claims to tell the truth, and yes, I have, herein, for all my posturing about others' mendacities and implicit insistence upon my own veracity, edited considerably the details of my life for the purpose of achieving thematic unities which are as imposed upon the narrative as organically emerging from it (nothing is "organic" in that which claims to be art, Coleridge's elegant assertions to the contrary notwithstanding), and yes this dated and sloppy little metafictional gesture is as suspect as any other vile posturing of "sincerity" I've to this point inflicted upon the reader, but Willie fucking Stargel got on the phone, and we got Judd into his chair and to the phone, and I or the sweet Vietnam Vet held the phone and Willie Stargel talked to Judd, and then Judd stayed in his chair for the Seventh Game of the 1979 World Series and witnessed Willie Stargel hit a single, a double, a triple, and a homer, and he witnessed his beloved Pirates become World Champions, and Walt Disney was surely whacking off in Heaven—for, yes, there was a God and a Heaven and Hope for a couple of hours, but then they evaporated—because everyone present had to weep, and once again I'd lived in the midst of the miraculous, and Judd died an hour later, according to the Vet who was his closest friend and I think the only one present, with a smile on his face.

We must then again enlarge our city.
That healthy community is no longer
adequate, but it must be swollen in
bulk and filled with a multitude
of things which are no longer
necessities, as, for example, all
kinds of hunters and artists, many
of them concerned with shapes and
colours, many with music. . .

Book II 373 b

August 18, 1990, eleven days before Ema was born, the Stones played Prague. It all started three months or so earlier, when Dom's twenty-four year old brother, trained as a lawyer and just finished with his mandatory army service, decided it would be a swell idea to have the Stones visit Prague on their Urban Jungle tour. Filip was selling "good Moravian wine" on the Charles Bridge in the first flush of entrepreneurial activity, and he and his shifty-eyed cousin hashed over the idea, and started making phone calls. For the important phone calls, however, that is, the phone calls to England to speak actually with the Stones' corporate operatives, they needed someone with much better English, and Dom was and is one of the best Czech English speakers anywhere.

Somehow they'd actually gotten a huge office in the Castle to run their scheme, a testimony to how hip Havel is, and when the big chips were on the table they called Dom in to do the talking, which means, considering how innocent those two young guys were, she pretty much put the deal together talking off the top of her head on the phone.

I love watching her work. She's so professional, so good, and she takes such modest pride in her language skills. When she's dolled up and on the job, her beautiful face and voluptuous ass are irresistible. Especially when I watch her work, I'm reminded of how fiercely attracted to her I was upon seeing her, and how attractive, how drop-dead beautiful and alluring she still is to me. I love how practical she is, how quick-witted and graceful, and I love how stubborn she is, how immovable when she has decided something should be a certain way.

I cabbed with her to the Castle that day in July because her brother had begged her to come and help them out with a particularly delicate bit of negotiations with the Big Boys in England. She was huge with Ema, was working every day, and was pissed at her brother for hooking her into doing work she was in no mood for. She yelled at her brother and cousin in Czech for several minutes, then got on the phone and took care of business. She looked like a mountain with a beautiful face and appendages, and she improvised the whole deal right there. Three young Czechs, a few months after the Velvet Revolution, when there were virtually no commercial laws yet by which such huge entertainment enterprises might be accomplished, winged it with seasoned corporate Big Shots in England and put together the largest popular-culture event in the thousand-year history of the Czech lands.

On August 18, Dom didn't think it would be wise for her to go to an open-air concert at which there would be over a hundred thousand people. So I went alone, with her blessing. The whole tram system of the city had been rerouted for the event, and I jumped on one where I'd usually caught the 9 tram, and went all the way up the hill to the Strahov stadium, which the communists had boasted was the "largest stadium in the world." Maybe it is; I couldn't tell. It's certainly huge, and by evening when the pyrotechnics and music actually began it was packed with Germans who'd poured over the border for the relatively cheap Czech tickets, as well as with Czechs who'd paid what was for some the equivalent of a week's salary despite the Stones' organization's attempt to keep the prices as low as fiscally possible. Filip, who in a couple of years would be one of the Czech Republic's top entertainment and commercial lawyers, slipped me a free ticket. I arrived while it was still light, and into the opening set I heard several Americans say they'd spotted Havel dancing behind bullet-proof plastic. I didn't see him, but nor had I scanned the stands looking for him. I kept riveted on the show, feeling the specialness of the event, though feeling also utterly bored with the greatest rock band in the world. They were, simply, a bunch of middle-aged white guys, guys pushing fifty, doing music which made different promises than their bodies could keep. They're slick, smart, ironic, and of all the white bands that ripped off black musicians to become multi-millionaires, they're among the most original and interesting. And the spectacle of it all was gaudy and gorgeous. And though a light drizzle persisted the entire evening, the hundred and twenty thousand or so people seemed impressed and happy. Jagger got in his aerobic workout, and his voice, as far as one can tell through all the electronic filters, was on. Richards was impressively sleazy. They were fine, predictable and fine, and I was jaded, bored with rock-'n'roll, bored with all popular music, bored with spectacles, bored with Western popular culture, the greatest colonizing agent ever devised, and I was certainly bored with my own youth, not too much of which still remained. I left early, before the finale, and occupied a tram car with others who had for their own various reasons decided to leave early, and among them were two beautiful teenage females, one American and the other Czech. I gathered from their chatter that the American's parents had been Czech, and gotten out after '68 and prospered in California. The Czech was her cousin whose English was weak but functional. She strained to understand the vacuous chatter of her fashionably outfitted and glittering American cousin, whose voluptuous woman's body contrasted starkly with the childish idiocy pouring from her mouth. I was

strongly attracted to my fellow American; she was sexy the way a beauti-
ful young woman is when she is just beginning to understand her new
power of attraction, yet does not yet fully comprehend its gravity. Her
innocence made her dangerous, and therefore that much more alluring. I
was also repulsed by her, because I recalled how a few months earlier
Czech kids her age and a bit older had been the heart of the Velvet
Revolution, working together with humility and maturity, not just march-
ing and chanting, but cleaning up after the demonstrations, forming
childcare units so young mothers could participate in the demonstrations.
I'd never seen young people act in great numbers with such grave yet
happy diligence, and yet with such adult pride in their actions. The most
moving sign or banner jutting from the massive crowd on Wenceslas
Square had been one that Dom interpreted as WE WHO WERE STU-
DENTS IN '68 ARE PROUD OF OUR CHILDREN. And as the tram
rocked gently through the evening, I listened to the American beauty
chatter to her lovely but rumpled cousin about malls and clothes and boys
and money, and knew that the American beauty assumed herself superior
to her Czech cousin, and it was an assumption as deeply rooted in her
nature as the knowledge of her own beauty and national identity. It was
an assumption based on knowledge that was to her incontrovertible and
therefore unchallengable. She was superior in her own soul to her cousin
and to everyone on the tram, for surely she assumed herself the only
American on that tram, and superior to the entire city and country. I
found her revolting because I knew I was no different, deep down, that I
too had been conditioned to believe, despite Euro-pissyness and the
nationalistic sentiments bubbling in the heart of every non-American I'd
ever known, that my Americanness made me superior to others, even as
I knew otherwise, even as I grew more humble in the midst of those
remarkable people who had conducted a revolution of laughter, who had
laughed with such vigor at the silly gangsters who had vexed them for
forty years that the old farts simply wafted away.

Yet I knew myself to be not an American so much as a citizen of the
Republic of Burma Shave, those great highways and all their supporting
industries and dangers. America was the place I'd always wanted to get to,
for America was a condition of Normalcy, and the Republic of Burma
Shave was the spastic journey sometimes from It, sometimes longingly
and pathetically toward It, but It was as that liquid-seeming flag of trans-
parency wavering above hot asphalt in the day-time distance which
diminishes only when the sun's light dims.

My kinship with the Czechs, not including that mysterious and
wondrous one still lolling in Dom's body, was that they too dreamed of a
great American Normalcy, a simple affluence and popular-culture heaven
of dazzling distractions. I gazed up to where the statue of Stalin had once
loomed above the city, and where now there was a broad banner declar-
ing the Rolling Stones. As I got off the tram, the girls worked real hard at
ignoring three strapping German boys. I crossed the Vltava, came upon

the Jewish Cemetery, and paused to stare a moment through the bars at the weathered headstones which were only crooked shadows in the darkness.

I thought about how in a few days I would hold my child, and about the hundreds of corpses, all now bones and dust, stacked on top of one another in a sloppily-organized filing cabinet of eternal repose. I knew Rabbi Loew's dark tomb was in there, and I knew the tales about his Golem, his sacred avenging robot fashioned of the river's mud, and about how the great rabbi would animate his Golem by putting pieces of parchment with prayers written on them in its mouth, or by some accounts the name of God. And I said under my breath, I don't believe in you, God, but don't take it out on my child. Please be kind to her or him. Amen. And then I walked the rest of the way to Dom's apartment, and marveled at her beautiful face as she rocked in a chair and read, stroking her stomach from time to time and cooing in Czech to whomever occupied her. And I said inside myself, God, I really don't believe in you and never shall, but please be kind to this woman, and to the one in New Orleans, and while you're at it, forgive me.

At the core of my wretched sentimentality is a quaint religious impulse. In the Republic of Burma Shave, a God which does not exist presides over a universe wracked by ubiquitous Evil allowed to exist for reasons Reason quakes to reckon.

Why did Dick chop their tails off? There were five puppies. I was four, or five. I've no idea where we were, though I recall we occupied a real house, a little one with a large back yard. I don't know where he got them. But they were black and tiny, and for some reason he was compelled to chop their tails off. I recall those little tails curled in the grass, and I recall, or at least I think I recall, or I imagine or dream, those tiny babies squealing. When we hit the road again a few days later, we took one of them with us in the car, and I've no idea what he did with the other three or four. I recall awakening one morning in a motel, and calling for my puppy. I called and called, and looked in the bathroom and under the dresser, then under one bed and then the other. He was way under, and I reached, stretched to reach him, and I pulled him out from under Dick's and Joan's bed and he was stiff dead. I screamed hysterically, and Dick awoke and got up and wrapped the carcass in newspaper and threw it away. That Christmas we stayed in another house and Dick got us toys, even a tricycle, then he packed us up just before New Year's and took the stuff we'd gotten for Christmas, at least the big stuff like the tricycle, back to the store (obviously he was getting some kind of refund, though considering that he'd bounced a check to get them, I don't know how). We waited in the car and watched him tote Christmas back into whatever retail joint he'd bounced a check to acquire it from, and then we kept going. We kept going. We kept going.

Rock'n'roll is the fascism of youth. It doesn't account for the terror and sadness of being young; it doesn't account for loss. Ema and Anna, darlings, if you ever read this, know that your Tata loves, loved, you ferociously, even as he expressed his love with as much gentleness as he could manage. Babies, I want the world to account for you, and I want you to love the world with a regal tenderness. I recall a man, a young man who got drunk and decided it was necessary to chop the tails off of infant beasts he'd acquired as a grotesquely worshipful gesture to Normalcy, a god who tormented him. My darlings, I shall never again myself chant prayers to Normalcy, and as you grow into your own odd circumstances, Ema and Anna, I your father shall sing odd songs of qualified praise to whatever is the source of his, and your, abundant blessings.

So too with sex, anger, and all the desires,
pleasures, and pains which we say follow
us in every activity. Poetic imitation
fosters these in us. It nurtures and waters
them when they ought to wither; it places
them in command in our soul when they
ought to obey in order that we might
become better and happier men instead
of worse and more miserable.

Book X 606 d

In a motel somewhere, an old-fashioned kind of place that tried to look like where one should live permanently and not just sleep for a night, soon after Dick got out of prison the first time, I got attacked by Jesus. There was no TV in the cheesy but perky little kitchenette, but there was an oval reddish-brown wooden radio that got only one station clearly, and that evening a choral version of "Good Night, Irene" crackled from it, and Dick got sentimental and sang along horribly because Irene was his salty old Greek mother's name. There were two folding cots in addition to the two big beds and blood-dark couch, and I got to sleep in one by myself, and Chuck got the other. We all went to bed at the same time that evening, and there was running water outside somewhere, a sound I found pleasant. The moving small water, perhaps it was a fountain, a little cement fountain at the heart of the drab installation to convince passers-by of a native civility, that gentle constant lapping and falling put me to sleep, yet I wasn't asleep; I was still in the room on the cot, and I knew I was dreaming but I was awake, and I even looked around the room at my siblings and parents and I could hear everyone breathing, even when Jesus walked out of the bathroom.

I wasn't frightened. He looked exactly like the picture on the lectern of the Baptist church Joan had made Chuck and me attend summers in Elizabeth City because the church fed us lunch; He walked over to me, glowing a little, and looked down at me and smiled.

He kept smiling, and his smile changed, slowly, into first a scowl, then the most hideously contorted mask of hatred and contempt I could imagine, and his face began to lower towards me, until all I could see, shocked paralyzed, were his gleaming teeth and glowing eyes and he opened his mouth so wide he took in my entire face and I awoke screaming. I couldn't tell anyone about the dream. The kids howled and wept in sleepy fear, and Joan tried to get me to tell her what I'd dreamed, but I just whimpered and sat there in the lamplight until Dick got fed up and ordered me to lie down. I don't think I slept, and certainly didn't sleep well for several nights. Jesus had gotten really really pissed off at me, and I didn't know why. He had tried to eat my face, chew the skin off my skull, and I certainly hadn't been *that* bad! But perhaps it wasn't Jesus. Perhaps it had been the devil making himself look like Jesus! I was reassured, slightly, by the thought that the devil and not Jesus had wanted to eat my face, but it had sure looked a hell of a lot like Jesus, the white flowing robe, the brown hair and cropped brown beard and blue eyes and serene expression, especially that serene expression, and I just wasn't sure. I have never since been able to consider Jesus without recalling that image of his contorted face coming at mine, and perhaps therefore I have never been able to consider good and evil as bifurcated, but rather have always considered them dovetailed and singular. Maybe that's why I thrilled to Freud's writings when I started college and read ravenously everything but what was assigned in my courses, and why the Frankfurt Marxists, particularly Marcuse and Adorno, thrilled me as well. Evil suddenly had a structure, a face, and it was the same one that was supposed to be good. I looked around and saw that everything was a sham. Religion was a sham. The university was a sham. All authority was a sham. Even my desires were a sham, though only to the extent that I might try to express them in a vernacular that was a sham. I was liberated from all responsibilities, because responsibilities were cast in the structure of sham authority.

For example, I got a job in the Special Collections of the university library a couple of hours a day. I didn't do squat; I just read. There was a collection of small-print-run poetry books, a couple of hundred maybe, and I read them all fairly quickly. Most of them were crap, like *Code of Flag Behavior* by a brilliant phony named David Antin, a guy with absolutely no hair on the uncovered parts of his body (I'd had cocktails with him and some other folks from UCSD a couple of times) and whose scholarly interests are in modern art, I believe. I can't recall what he was doing in that first book of his I read, but when I later waded through *Talking at the Boundaries,* I laughed and laughed. The guy talked to an audience, recorded what he said, and then had it transcribed and printed in a book. He says that if Eliot and Lowell were poets, he doesn't want to be one, but if Socrates was a poet, well, then he'll allow himself to be called one, or some such horseshit. Never mind that Socrates was largely the gleanings of Plato's selective memory and imagination (Does anyone believe the old bugger died of hemlock poisoning as peacefully as he does in the *Phaedo*?), and never mind that Eliot and Lowell are easy targets for no-talent avant-garde bullshit artists.

I even read some of the special collection of books and journals on orchids. Orchids, of course, reminded me of female genitalia, so I moped through the stacks with a hard-on from gazing at flowers. I have never much enjoyed porn; oh, I whacked off as a kid over centerfolds, but I've never sought the stuff out, especially after I started getting laid with considerable frequency, but I loved those orchids, and had no guilt about getting a hard-on gazing at them. Besides, I was reading Freud and Marcuse and Fromm and Norman O. Brown, et al., and guilt, especially about sexual desire, was boring.

Nor did I feel guilty about ripping off the library. Oh, I didn't steal; stealing was boring unless one had to do it to acquire absolute necessities, like food and water, maybe pot, and then it was simply revolutionary *praxis*. No, I ripped off the library in terms of time. It was in the midst of converting to a system that would keep people from stealing books. The library got a state, maybe federal, grant of some kind to hire students to thread strips through the spines of all the books in the library so that a buzzer would go off if someone didn't have the strip first deactivated by checking the book out at the desk. Most large libraries have similar systems these days, but I have to think someone's come up with a more efficient way to mark the books.

They hired scores of us to spend three to five hours a day each threading the spines of books, until a few months later we'd finished the entire library. The only problem was that they still had a tiny bit of money left over, so whoever was administering the program told my boss in Special Collections that they'd go ahead and pay me for two months of part-time work in the Special Collections over the summer, and of course, already paid, I would show up every day and fill the humidifier and then sit and read. Sure! I'd do that! It was summer, the beaches were packed with beauties, I had stacks of books to read in my little hovel, and yeah, right, already paid, illegally, unethically, stupidly, by a petty bureaucrat who simply didn't want to give the money back to the government, because if he or she did the government wouldn't fork over as much the next time, I would show up somewhere and do absolutely nothing for four hours a day. Forget that I had lied and said I would show up. Hell, I was helping them out by taking the money. I even showed up a couple of times, several days apart, and no one even noticed that I hadn't been there for several days! That next year I got vague looks of disappointment from the weird little guy who presided over the Special Collections—my beloved orchids—a fey little fiftyish guy who seemed unable to smile, that is, it seemed his face lacked the necessary muscles to form one. But no one ever said anything. I think I got seven hundred dollars.

But those hours actually doing the work, threading the silver strips through the spines of books with thin metal rods, had not been all that bad. My crew had been a chatty one. We sat in a circle in the stacks with carts of books we worked through at a leisurely pace, attaching the six-inch sticky metal strip to thin pliant rods and goosing the rods through the books' spines where the rods stuck. I recall none of my colleagues' names, those fellow student workers, except for one, whose nickname I recall because I gave it to her; we called her Apple because she came from New York, was New York tough and sassy, and cursed unabashedly. She was the first woman I'd ever heard speak openly, even lovingly, about her pussy. In her thick New York brogue, she'd complain about a yeast infection, suddenly blurting out while keeping her eyes on the spine of whatever book she was threading, that her "pussy itched." She had a darling face, pert and pretty, and her body was a bit thick, but she was altogether attractive. I had sex several times, twice in the library, with a quiet and pretty biology major in our circle, and had lusted after a marketing major whose boyfriend dropped her off and picked her up at the library; the latter had enormous breasts, almost grotesquely so, and Apple used to look her square in the eye and say that if she, Apple, owned those tits she'd "rule the whole fucking world." The boyfriended one took it as a compliment, though I couldn't understand why. She certainly wasn't ruling the world, and was being told that accompanied by superior intelligence and talent and moxie those tits could be of much greater material, perhaps even spiritual, value than they presently were.

Apple liked me. She would greet me with a big, contagious smile and How ya doin', Fuck Face. She was constantly telling me she was too much woman for me, and I would cheerfully agree. I liked her a lot. I loved talking and joking with her. But I couldn't get Ricky to stand at albeit-crooked attention for a woman who talked so openly, so lovingly, about her pussy. That, of course, was my problem. And I thought about it: I like Apple, and she's quite attractive, and she's more fun to be with than any other woman I know, I'd tell myself, so what's the problem? You'll bonk all the others, stupid ones, even a few ugly ones who happen to have great bodies, so why can't you bonk her? I'd ask myself. I just couldn't get beyond how she talked. She had a beautiful mouth, and I used to try to imagine getting head from her, but always in my fantasy she'd say something like Don't fart while I'm down here, and I knew that that indeed was what she'd probably say. And of course I could expect absolute honesty. She'd tell me I was a bum fuck and it would be true. Apple was definitely too much woman for me. Besides, I felt that after six weeks of working with her every weekday, I knew more about her pussy than I did about the pussy of any woman with whom I'd been physically intimate. She said her pussy was tight with big lips and a clit the size of a cat-eye marble. I suggested that perhaps she was getting a little carried away, so she offered to show me, so why didn't we just make a little wager about her clit, then she'd show me; I backed off. I laughed and happily admitted my cowardice, and confessed that I'd indeed grown wary, even frightened of her pussy, such that even the prospect of gazing upon it sent chills up my spine. This made her roar with laughter, and from that moment forward I was under constant threat from her pussy, which any second, when I least expected it, might appear, suddenly, in all its velvet glory, to suck the eyes out of my head and the coins out of my pockets, or, Medusa-like, simply turn me to stone. Upon graduation, Apple secured a job as a collections agent for the IRS, and I could not imagine her making a more nearly perfect career choice.

As a car dealer, my brother Chris had made the perfect career choice, and in fact according to reliable sources had thrived at it right up to the time he ripped off his boss and got bounced. After Dick had taken over making payments on the truck and I was sucked in to visiting him every couple of months I was in the U.S., Dick hired Chris to work for the little company Dick's wife Peggy owned. As far as I could gather, the company worked for insurance outfits, going out to rural locations and drawing blood, taking blood pressure, weighing, and performing other such duties related to determining health risk and insurability. A registered nurse, Peggy was qualified to perform such tasks, and Dick had actually gotten certification in the joint to do such things. Chris, I guess, took a short course of some sort and got hired.

On one of my trips to Quinsey, a woodsy rural parasite of Tallahassee, thirty miles or so from the Florida State campus which dominates north-central Florida, Dick contrived to get Chris and me "back together," which I assured him was futile since we'd never made any adult connection. I made it clear that if Chris showed up while I was there I'd hit I-10 back to New Orleans, kick his ass, or both.

Chris rolled up the dirt road to the trailer with his "new family," a pretty, nondescript woman in her early thirties, and a boy of eleven. I tried to be civil to the woman and boy, greeting them politely, and then simply asked Chris why he had come, knowing I'd no wish to see him ever again.

Dick loved it. He'd arranged everything, insisted to Chris that he come over and reconcile with me. But I had no desire to reconcile with him. He'd suckered me once before, told me numerous lies and stolen from me, and there was no reason for us to reconcile. It had nothing to do with forgiveness; I had plenty of that. I just didn't want to see him or talk to him. Our lives, tragically or not, had taken different paths and simply had nothing in common, except weird familial circumstances we could only come to terms with separately and alone. When he'd stayed with me and Lois in New Orleans, it'd been obvious that, like Arthur, he thought I could make sense of his life, that I, the mildly successful, at least respectable (if one simply overlooked the quagmire of dung my private life had become) older brother who could make connections, remember things, figure it all out and tell him why his life had been so weird and difficult, lacking in structure and lacking in familial love and compassion. Maybe when it had become apparent that I could give him no knowledge about his life, that I was no Delphic oracle of familial mysteries, he'd felt compelled to rip me off for material things. But it doesn't matter. I didn't deserve to be hurt by him, and I owed him nothing. And when it became apparent that though I had no problem verbally forgiving him I still didn't want to spend any time in his presence, he packed up the new wife and her kid and roared away in a swarm of dust.

But that night he returned, a little drunk, with the boy. He banged around the trailer as though he searched for something, mumbled that he'd left something out back. It was after midnight; I'd taken a couple of Sominex pills on top of a couple of shots of whiskey to sleep. I stirred from a dull half-sleep, pissed and blurry, and yelled out the screen door to know what the hell he was doing. Again, he mumbled about looking for something. I asked him why in the world that boy was in the truck, and he told me to fuck off it was none of my business. I said that he was correct; it was none of my business, except that as a responsible adult I take notice of all matters regarding the health and safety of children, and yelled to the boy to come in. Peggy and Dick were up by this point, and Peggy took the boy into her bedroom. Chris began to insult me heartily and challenge me to a fight. I am six-feet and almost two inches tall, weigh two hundred and thirty pounds, and bench press over three hundred pounds on a good day. Since getting middle-aged and slow, I have bulked up. Though I'm twenty pounds heavier than I'd like to be, I am pretty strong, and still pretty quick with my hands, though my legs are mush. Chris is about one hundred and seventy pounds, five nine or ten, and not in particularly good shape. Part of me wanted to pound him, and part of me wanted to protect him from himself. I tried to calm him, but he took a couple of shots at me, missing, and I fired back a couple of stiff jabs, busting up his nose a bit. Then I walked away.

He yelled that I was a pussy, that he'd taken my best shots and I was just a big pussy. He followed me onto the screened-in porch attached to the trailer, chanting that I was a pussy. I turned, took two quick—they were probably lumbering but in my memory they were quick steps and pummeled him for about ten seconds. I bloodied his face and bruised him up pretty much. And when I pulled away I was ashamed not because I'd been violent, but because my pounding him was precisely what he'd wanted. He'd wanted me to kick his ass to even the score. Now he didn't owe me anything, in his own mind, and I knew he did, but it didn't matter, because now he was free and clear by his own warped karmic accounting system. I'm sure he thought that after kicking his ass, after evening the score, I would settle into being his big brother, the Oldest of the Five, and as such do my duty of making sense of his life. He kept chanting, even as he bled, that I was a big pussy, and I told him yes, indeed, I am a big pussy, because though my anger flares quickly, I do not enjoy causing pain. I didn't say this to apologize; I was simply confirming his observation. I felt no satisfaction. And he, banged up a little bit, could go forth with the knowledge that he'd taken my best shot, which he hadn't, and his oldest brother was just a big moose of a pussy, which I am.

> . . . is a bed any different if you
> look at it from the side or from
> the front or from any other point?
> Or is it not different but appears
> different, and so with other things?

Book X 598 a

When I returned from Grand Forks, North Dakota, Louella had not killed herself. Instead of lying drained of blood on our bathroom tiles, she was screwing a French lounge singer she'd met in the hotel bar he played piano and sang in. I acted hurt that she was bonking another man, and being young my ego was crinkled a bit, but in all truth I felt like the beaten and barely conscious member of a tag-team match, stumbling blindly for my corner as the crowd howls, flailing my arms before me to touch the outstretched hand of my partner, and though I never met the guy, I felt as though I'd tagged up, and now Louella was his problem, because I was definitely getting the hell out of the ring and the arena.

I was essentially homeless for the next year. One of my most loyal karate students, a sailor who owned a house at the northern end of Orange Avenue, towards the bay, let me stay in his shed off and on for a few months, and it *was* a shed, a gray-plank tool shed I cleaned up and stuck a battered mattress in and fixed up in generic hippie decor. When I wasn't there, I crashed with Colleen in her room, a lovely little room in a quite lovely house just a block from the golf course that rimmed the bay. When her stepfather passed out in his car after miraculously weaving home from the Mexican Village bar, I felt safe for the night, and I therefore felt safe most nights, because the poor guy passed out that way, still in his business suit, almost every night, but always the next morning made it to work on North Island where he was a well-paid civilian contractor.

Colleen was a gorgeous, petite Latin beauty with large breasts and a simpering sexiness. She was extremely bright and passionate and moody. She was seventeen when I met her.

I'd been working at the Ninth Street Liquor Store, and she and her girlfriend had come in often to purchase soft drinks and the like. I'd been immediately struck by her, and tried to converse, but she always acted nervous and distracted. She had a hard time looking me in the eye. I discovered later that her demeanor was school-girl coyness, something quite extinct in the courtship jungle of early-to-mid-seventies Coronado. Finally, she spoke to me. I asked to see her. She said okay. I said let's walk on the beach in the evening. She said okay. She was disconcertingly passive. Everything was okay, until I suggested, a few days later, intimacy. She balked at first, but then that was okay, too. I fell hard for her. She took me home to her parents, a youthful and strikingly attractive mother who owned a successful chain of beauty parlors, and a stepfather who was a successful civilian contractor and a wildly more successful alcoholic. About a decade ago, fifteen years after I began my relationship with Colleen and thirteen and a half or so after it ended, I could walk past that house—two owners later—and still see the faint prints of my bare feet on the garage door, which was just below the tiny balcony off of Colleen's bedroom window. Hanging from her balcony by my fingertips, dangling before dropping to the pavement that graded up to the garage door, I could glance in the soft light of the blue arcing Coronado bridge the slow-nodding palms of the first tee of the Coronado golf course.

When I heard her father bouncing from wall to wall then pause in front of Colleen's door, I'd wriggle into my clothes, dash for the balcony, climb over the rail, and, bracing my feet against the garage door as I hung from the ledge, listen whether he had pushed on to his room, or opened the door to hers. A couple of times he had opened her door just to check; both times I dropped to the pavement as soon as I heard the click and saw the faint light pouring across the floor. One time, I'd fallen asleep, and he shook me awake. Thankfully and inexplicably, I was wearing my clothes under the sheet, and he quietly, with a calm and civil slur in his drunken voice, told me to leave.

It is odd that when I think of that time in my life, I'm not overcome by memories of the passion I experienced with that gorgeous young woman, nor even am I filled with sadness regarding the saline abortion she had near the end of our relationship, or after that dropping acid and chasing her to God-forsaken San Bernardino where in a cowboy-biker bar called the Sandpiper a guy bit a piece of my lip off after jumping me on the dance floor; rather, I am filled with sadness and affection for that man, that lonely middle-aged man who fell asleep almost every night behind the wheel of his poorly parked station wagon. He did not approve of me, nor should he have, but he was never unkind, and tried, really tried to accept his life and all that had been poured into it, even a twenty-year old long-haired skinny kid who studied poetry in college and worked some-times at a liquor store, sometimes giving karate lessons. He loved his lit-tle family. He obviously felt he'd married over his head, a feeling I've since myself become more than a little acquainted with; he was plain and straight and boring, and his wife was lovely and vivacious, even glam-orous. He'd helped raise Colleen from the time she was three or four, and she was a real piece of work, a drop-dead beautiful kid who was extreme-ly bright but wholly uninterested in anything but putting on make-up and fantasizing about someday having her own kids. He obviously felt very much like a father to her, but was always being reminded in pernicious little ways by both Colleen and her mother that he was not her "real" father; that her "real" father happened to have been a creep who'd never shown any interest in Colleen seemed of little importance. Perhaps Colleen and her mother didn't mean to hurt the man, and even then, as emotionally ignorant as I was, I knew they hurt him; perhaps their little barbed asides, always delivered with innocent smiles, were unconscious. But that man was lonely, lonely to the core. He required familial affection, and received from his wife a cheerful and vacuous friendliness, and from his daughter, whom he loved unconditionally with a nurturing regard he didn't know how to express except with quiet kindness and despairing patience, he received contempt and hostility, and only occasionally the respect and affection he deserved.

There are a few casual acquaintances in our lives we would like to pull into the present, lives in the margins of those which had directly determined our own, marginal lives we would pull from the dark still waters for a moment that they may hear, dripping atrocious nostalgia, words our former selves had not had the wisdom to speak. To Colleen's father I would say You are a decent human being, and I have known very few. I would say You are a humble man, and I have known very few. Or I would simply go to his car at midnight, open the driver's-side door, and help him into the house, that house on which my footprints will remain for several years, and in which he is a stranger among two women he loves.

If someone then comes to a man
in that condition and gently tells
him the truth, that there is no sense
in him and that he stands in need
of it, but that it cannot be acquired
unless one works like a slave to
attain it, do you think it will be
easy for him to listen in the midst
of so many evils?

Book VI 494 d

Whatever gym I regularly attend becomes my church. A few
years ago, it was called Total Fitness, or otal Fitness as the sign
outside the building read. It was adjacent—alas, it is now
defunct—to Regency Park, a gated community in New Orleans East, a
part of town Dominika calls a Culture Free Zone, occupied primarily by
lower middle-class black people, and yet for whatever reasons failing to
project the vitality and rich communal expressiveness of African-
American enclaves elsewhere in the city, and indeed throughout the coun-
try. It is as though a predominately black network of neighborhoods, even
as the individuals comprising them lived as black Americans participating
in and enriching black culture, collectively somehow took on the
demeanor of a community of Swedish immigrants. It's an eerie place, New
Orleans East, the only part of New Orleans with absolutely no character;
in fact, it is so characterless, that is its very charm. Living there was some-
thing of a respite from unrelenting Big-Easy panache. The exhausted
shopping centers and fast-food feedbags, the planned ugliness of the
place, suburban Anywhere USA but with the Big American Hope ratch-
eted down five or six clicks. I found the section of town—quite near the
university and therefore convenient, and particularly my little gated com-
munity of mostly middle-class blacks— quite comfy; in fact, I have always
felt comfortable around middle- and lower middle-class black people, and
I don't mean to sound ridiculously self-congratulatory by acknowledging
this fact. I've always felt that I have more in common with most of them
than they can know by looking at me.

For example, in otal Fitness, I was in the racial minority, and that
was just fine. Most of the guys in that gym were black guys my age or a
bit younger. One guy, Melvin, was my hero. He was 64 and cut like a kid.
He looked like a 40 year-old man who worked out earnestly. Besides run-
ning a couple of miles or so almost every day, I worked out for forty to
sixty minutes just about every day, at otal Fitness and in my Prague gym
which as far as I could tell didn't have a name. Of course, I was less com-

fortable in my Prague gym than I was in otal Fitness. In both gyms, as is still true when I work out, I didn't waste time. When I work out I don't chat much; I don't socialize; I pump. I'm not a gym rat. I don't enjoy working out anymore than a sane pious person enjoys praying. For years I've wanted to take my workout to the proverbial "next level" so that I get more cut and look less like a retired professional wrestler. But I pump iron more out of spiritual duty than physical necessity, and figure I owe my spirit no more than fifty minutes or so of physical pain each day.

I loved the middle-aged black men who came into otal Fitness. We nodded and smiled and groaned, and though we didn't talk much there was respect and sweetness among us. Most of the middle-aged guys, black and white, who worked out there, who prayed in otal Fitness were cops or worked for Federal Express, and they were muscular with protruding bellies. We were all ten to twenty pounds heavier than we should have been, but we were also strong. There were guys in their forties who bench pressed over four-hundred pounds, and I am contrite, subtly, toward those who are stronger than I. I didn't talk much as I worked out in otal Fitness, but I did listen.

In the couple of months before I moved out of Regency Park, out of the Culture Free Zone of New Orleans East, I did my work out in the morning, and the gym at that hour, usually around eight, was dominated by two young black guys. I mean, they worked out together at that hour, and were large and exuberant and worked hard every minute, cheering one another on to greater physical accomplishments. One of them, who had huge muscles but was about forty pounds overweight, clocked in I'm sure at around two-sixty, each day laughed when he saw me enter the gym. He laughed and shook his head, his sweat-beaded head. He told me I looked like I should ride a Harley. I was honored that he thought I looked like a biker. I was a 41 year-old English professor, which didn't mean much in the grand scheme of authentic life, and he found humorous the presence in his church of a fifteen-to-twenty pound overweight, fairly muscular white guy with thick long black hair and a beard. I prayed with him. Well, we prayed at roughly the same time. He and his buddy got there before me and left after, but the core of our workouts were temporally contiguous.

What kind of horseshit is "temporally contiguous"? It's the horseshit of someone who grew up feeling inferior, and who when he was a child felt the linguistic distance between the materially blessed and wretched. I have always fought the desire to sound smart, if only because at an early age I realized how ridiculous I seemed when I failed, which has always been too often. But I never tried to sound smart in otal Fitness, and when one of the guys asked me what I do, I'd tell them I'm a teacher, and if he asked what I teach I'd mumble English, and he'd probably think I'm a high school teacher, which is fine, because most of us at urban universities, when we're not teaching in that heaven which is a graduate seminar or an advanced course in our field, are glorified high school teachers who don't have to put up with all the pettiness public school teachers must tolerate from the semiliterate bureaucrats vexing their professional lives.

I offer here a solution to the education crisis in America: shut down every goddamned College of Education on the continent, and throw out every certification program ever concocted. From first grade to twelfth, hire people with proven skills in math, science, writing, et cetera. Give them a standard two-week orientation, then throw them into the classrooms and leave them alone. Don't check their lesson plans, and don't sit in on their classes unless they invite you in. Tell them the classroom is sacrosanct, virtually all theirs, and give them vague targets of accomplishment. Let them talk to one another on-line, and thereby create their own communities of professionals even as they redefine professionalism. Let them go through tenure peer reviews, and encourage them to publish in their fields. Don't insist that they publish, simply encourage them to. The most important thing is that individuals are encouraged to feel they are mathematicians, scientists, scholars and artists who are teaching, and not math teachers, science teachers, and writing teachers. Pedagogy is passion and curiosity within a subject area; someone who simply "loves to teach" and whose love for a subject or activity has primarily to do with teaching it may be beloved by students, but isn't really worth a rat's ass. No one can teach someone else how to teach what either truly loves. In that regard, real teachers are uneducable. Only individuals who love what they teach should be allowed in the classroom, and so if nothing else of what I have suggested gets done, the Colleges of Education should be shut down.

In otal Fitness I was the white English teacher who looked like a biker to some of the black guys. No one asked anything about dangling participles, split infinitives or misplaced modifiers in otal Fitness; they took me on my word that I was an English teacher, and when I did butt in to some conversation I did so quickly and obviously knew what I was talking about, even if I was wrong. I was certain, for example, that Foreman beat that German kid, the one who looked like the fair-haired lad who sang "The Future Belongs to Me" at the end of *Cabaret*, only older and pumped up. I thought and still think Foreman took most of the early rounds, albeit narrowly, a couple of the middle rounds and drew at least one of the later rounds. The kid beat him badly in maybe four rounds, but not badly enough to get ten/eight scores (if they even allowed ten/eight splits when there were no knockdowns; I can't recall what rules they were using). So, though old George got the worst of the fight, he did win it, and shouldn't have gotten booed. The guys talking about the fight listened, and one agreed, but the other laughed and said we hadn't seen the same fight, that Foreman got wupped by the kraut. The guy who agreed with me just smiled and winked and popped another set, and I did, too, and so did the guy who thought the German had won, and that was that.

I can't recall where we were when Clay fought Liston, but I was still "getting to know" Dick after he'd gotten out of prison the first time, and he was doing things like making Chuck and me have push-up competitions which Chuck won because he weighed less than a gnat and was indeed strong for his size. Watching fights with Dick in motel rooms was great; he'd be just a little drunk as the fight got started, and talked about his storied boxing career, one in which he'd lost but one amateur fight, and was lightweight Golden Gloves champion of Norfolk. Of course I believed his martial boasts, and the part about actually losing a fight made it all seem that much more plausible, though when I pressed about that loss I discovered it was because Dick had been disqualified for knocking the guy out a split second after the bell ending the first round.

I don't know why I blurted out that Clay was going to win. Dick laughed at me and said Liston was an animal, and that he'd kill that "smart-ass nigger." I stood my ground. I repeated my belief, based on nothing but that I thought Clay was funny when he talked on TV, that Clay was going to win.

I remember thrilling to the fight, round by black-and-white round. The reception in whatever dive we occupied that evening was terrible, and Dick rose often from the foot of the bed to jiggle the rabbit ears, but I knew Clay was pulling it off, even when his eyes got messed up, and Dick cursed and mumbled that it was fixed, and when Liston stayed on his stool I gloated a little for having picked the winner, and Dick simply ignored me and said the Mob had rigged the fight, that Liston had thrown the fight because the Mob had paid him to, and that that was the only way the "queer coon" could have won.

I was dejected. I'd won, beaten him, and he wouldn't let me have it. I'd picked the winner, and instead of letting me enjoy it, he made me a kind of ignorant coconspirator in foul play, or some kid who didn't know how the world really worked. I was sad for a while, and finally got around to asking what the Mob was.

I actually saw Dick on two occasions between the time I was eighteen and twenty. The first time was just before Christmas after my eighteenth birthday. He rang my little garage apartment and said he'd buy me a ticket to come see him in Canada, in a small town just north of Detroit. I thought about it and said okay, if you're paying for it. He said yeah, yeah, of course he'd pay for it; he was rich now. I could go ahead and write a check for the ticket and he'd reimburse me.

I'd not had any truck (ugh!) with him for five years. Surely he wouldn't rip me off. Surely he was in Canada, doing fine, and just wanted to see me for Christmas. Wouldn't it be wonderful if he'd straightened out his life, actually parlayed his looks and charm into big bucks! Maybe he knew how Joan was doing, though I was deeply frightened to know anything about her condition, and didn't know that I was frightened. So, like an idiot, like an eighteen year-old boy/man with delusions and confused loyalties, I wrote a check and got a ticket, and of course I didn't have the cash in the bank to cover the amount, not nearly enough, and I'd told Dick I didn't, but he'd told me not to worry because by the time it cleared, after the weekend, I'd be back with the cash he'd give me, and he'd give me much more than just the cash to cover the ticket. Hell, he might give me enough to get through college! I actually believed I might return wealthy to Coronado in three days.

I took a cab from the Detroit airport across the Canadian border. Dick paid the fairly hefty fare in small bills, peeling each one slowly off a wad as if to impress the cabdriver and me with his fortune. He lived in a run-down cabin with a stuttering old alcoholic who was dumpy and kept her teeth in a glass of water. He drove a pickup that looked remarkably like the one he'd stolen to take Chuck and me out to California from Norfolk, but couldn't have been. I recall nothing of that trip but disappointment. He obviously had some money, and I figured that somehow he got it from that sad old stuttering hag. He had lots of food and liquor in the cabin, and the land surrounding the cabin, which he assured me he owned as far as the proverbial eye could see, "right up to the fucking North Pole," was quite lovely, but he looked terrible and talked nonsense. Of course he wrote me a check to cover the airfare, and of course it bounced. Several frantic phone calls resulted in his actually wiring me about half the cost of the ticket, and I was grateful to have gotten that.

The second time I hooked up with him was over several weeks when I was twenty. I was living in a house with two other guys, going to San Diego State, teaching a little karate, working again at the geedunk on the Amphibious Base a few hours a day. I think it was a little before I moved into the shed on Orange Avenue, worked at Ninth Street Liquor, and started up with Colleen. Again, Dick contacted me, this time from San Francisco. I ran some dope up to Berkeley soon after that, and figured that as long as I was close I might as well see what he was up to.

Again, he was with a worn-out old alcoholic, but the place where he lived, that is, her house, was nicer than the cabin had been, and she had a large family of grown children who were around a lot. I stayed a couple of days, and studied how Dick interacted with them. Clearly, he'd told them nothing of his past, which is to say he told them many whopping lies. Once, one of the older sons—there were five kids, three males and two females—took me aside and tried to grill me. I smiled and neither confirmed nor denied Dick's whoppers.

A couple of weeks later, Dick decided he would drive down to see me, as well as visit Barbara and Ray. I was surprised that the youngest of the second hag's daughters, who was married to a big dumb guy I rather liked, had come down with Dick and his "wife" (he never divorced Joan, and she was not yet dead). The young woman was blond and pretty and she quickly made it clear that she'd come down to be with me. So I was with her. She spent the night with me rather than at Barbara's and Ray's house with Dick and Dotty or Dinky or Dowdy or something like that, and Dick became very angry, and came over to get the young woman in the morning to take her back, but she didn't want to go back right that moment, and I didn't particularly want her to hang around, but Dick stood in the street and threatened me, and I stood and stared at him, and said, without premeditation blurted, that if he took one more step I was going to kill him. And I was indeed prepared to fight him, and fight him earnestly and for as long as it would take to make him stop moving. And he knew it. He got back in the car and drove to Barbara's and Ray's. A couple of hours later, my guest walked the four blocks to the house, and left for San Francisco with her mother and Dick.

It had not been a Pyrrhic victory, but nor had it been a decisive one. I'd backed down a phony, or perhaps his backing down had been an apology. I didn't know, and still don't. It was all quite silly. By then all the affection I'd ever felt for him as a child lay buried under the knowledge of his petty nature, his life of lies. And so having contact with him I was no better than he. In some ways I was worse. On both occasions of my contact with him preceding Joan's death, he'd floated vague promises of material gifts I knew, in my heart I knew, he would never, could never make good on. I had tried to con a con, a fool's game.

Those beautiful old black men who waited tables in the French Quarter could not be conned. They believed nothing, except the formality and habits of their lives. I worked with them after marrying Lois and leaving Ca, unfortunately in that order; over the next three years, when I wasn't doing graduate work in Fayetteville, Arkansas (I owe both Jim Whitehead and Miller Williams a lot; they were terrific teachers and were patient with me), and then Iowa City (likewise Stan Plumly was a terrific teacher and very patient), I was bussing and eventually waiting tables in the Court of Two Sisters, Begue's in the Royal Sonesta Hotel, and even, finally, in Broussard's.

The Chart House, where I'd worked the summer of '76, had hired people in their twenties, usually college kids, almost exclusively. There were of course the peripatetic Chart House waiters who became addicted to the "life style" (among other things), moving from Chart House to Chart House, working pathetically into their mid-to-late thirties waiting tables in Hawaiian shirts and hitting on cocktail waitresses receding each year further from their decreasingly randy and increasingly desperate grasps. The Chart House shtick was scrubbed and Aryan Pacific youth, though in New Orleans they adopted a Creole element as well.

In early 1980 I began to work indigenous New Orleans restaurants, and it was then I came under the influence of the beautiful and cryptic, laconic and skeptical old black men. They seemed to move slowly, and yet everything got done. They wore tuxedos with pride, and yet they were not proud of their work, except that they did it exceedingly well. They were tolerant of the younger waiters, especially of the college boys just passing through, yet their tolerance was edged with a disdain for everyone who took themselves more seriously than the jobs they did, and that of course included all the young waiters, especially the college boys, like myself, just passing through. They didn't want to be anyone's daddies or uncles or wise mentors. I'm thinking here of five or six geezers my life brushed against over a couple of years of faking it in a tuxedo, of pretending I knew about wines when in reality I knew squat, of pretending I cared about the general happiness of the rich and almost-rich, of living the great lie of Fine Dining. Those old guys had been working in New Orleans restaurants for at least forty years each; the oldest, a service-bar bartender paused once, flicked his eyes toward the ceiling as he counted under his breath, then answered that he'd been waiting tables and tending bar for fifty-seven years. I'll not name them because one stood out no more than another, and though they were distinct individuals, they were singular in professional demeanor. As young men they had lived under American apartheid, and as old men they themselves imposed a spiritual apartheid upon the world. Dignity was not a word any of them would use chatting with their younger colleagues, black and white, and yet that is precisely the aura quavering off the surface of every gesture they made. Whether polishing silver as they set up their stations, or presenting menus, or explaining house specialties, or lighting cigars of the pretentious little men who plucked them from the maitre d's humidor (always with matches, never lighters), or corking wines, or ladling flames down the long spiral of an orange peel in the preparation of Cafe Brulot, or giving directions to departing clients, or standing in lines in kitchens with white towels folded over their forearms as they waited silently for their orders and as we, the young, screamed and wept and conjoled and begged and cursed and threatened death to those evil bastards working behind the silver counter separating their Realm of Evil from our Realm of Desperation, the old men were the essence of weary tolerance and mute dignity. They were lovers of Pure Form, I think, believing in nothing but the efficacy of formality, seeing in the formalities of Fine Dining a good and necessary lie, a false civility one may occupy with authentic grace. I believe they all had come to a Zen-like station of advanced consciousness, and were a little holy. Each of them seemed to look through me, know my self-deceptions immediately, and yet were kind to me, as they were to everyone, if kindness may be a quiet, even gentle disregard. I would aspire to be as they, but could never occupy silence with such aplomb as they, could never live as they within the unqualified assumption of the world's meaninglessness and remain sane, much less gracefully functional. Such existential dread so beautifully managed would be impossible for one such as I.

Now this capacity to preserve
through everything the right
and lawful belief as to what
is to be feared and what is not,
this is what I call and define
as courage, unless you say
otherwise.

Book IV 430 b

My brother Chuck was years ahead of his time. When everyone around us was proceeding on vague, poorly understood counter-culture ideology, a set of values which in most cases did little more than license irresponsible behavior, he courageously refused to follow this common course of youth. I mean this. It took courage to be a right-wing fanatic in the late 60s and early 70s if you lived in Coronado, California and were under seventeen. He and I would argue endlessly in our mid-teens, and I of course would cheat, never allowing him his intellectual due. In many ways he was much brighter than I, and I simply was unable to see that my being larger than he did not mean that I was superior in every other way as well. I think we have spoken only once or twice in the past fifteen or so years, and probably no more than half a dozen times over the past twenty, and I doubt we will ever reconnect, if only because despite years of intimate proximity we were never really connected, except by common experiences we processed in radically different ways. For one thing, for reasons I don't understand I have never felt compelled to deny my past. Oh, I have my dirty little secrets, my hidden trophies of shame, but I have never felt compelled to obliterate my weird origins. Chuck, on the other hand, perhaps not out of shame so much as despair, obliterated his weird origins, and was encouraged to do so by our stepparents, especially Barbara.

I made friends easily in Sasebo and then Coronado; he didn't. He was a sad, nervous boy who had odd little ticks and made annoying grunting noises as he twitched. He was lonely, and suffered more than I. He was good-looking, and had a dry, quite sophisticated sense of humor, but possessed no social skills appropriate to peer bonding.

Part of the process of adolescent peer bonding, especially for individuals who are forever newcomers, and therefore interlopers, but actually for all who seek intimacy, is a willingness to share a narrative of one's life up to the moment of engagement with the individual, individuals with whom one seeks relationship. When kids, especially boys, tell their lives to prospective new friends, what issues from them is mostly false. That falsity is the real poetry of youth. I told my life to the guys I would bond with, and though the details I shared were largely accurate, because my motive was self-aggrandizement, my narrative, in the telling, was a lie. I didn't mind telling my new buddies about my criminal father and my weird peripatetic childhood because I knew it rendered me exotic in their eyes, and because the gist of the popular-culture times was that outlaws were cool. But I didn't tell my weird life to my friends only to impress them. In a sense, I had no choice. I spoke, I narrated my early life out of a necessity I couldn't understand, yet somehow trusted. When I told G in Japan, and then Bruce, Buck, Bernie and Marc in Coronado the odd details of my early life, I was acknowledging blessings. I was saying, yeah, it was difficult, and people around me suffered, my mother in particular and atrociously, but I am here, now, for reasons I don't understand nor ever shall, and I am full of wonder and enthusiasm for life, even though everything I have seen and felt tells me life is a curse for most, and that I am a fool, a clown for assuming it is not also a curse for me.

Chuck needed, desperately needed, to obliterate his past. Barbara told everyone she met in Coronado she was two or three years older than she was, and even, I discovered, invented childhoods for Chuck and me wherein we'd been birthed and raised by her exclusively. She felt, I suppose, Chuck's need to obliterate his past, to create a different one, and by encouraging and indeed facilitating such a process accommodated him emotionally, but it was much more her own need to deny our pasts, of which she was ashamed for reasons I don't fully understand, which determined her behavior. Her relationship with Dick was a complicated one, and centered in so many ways upon the loss of their older brother, about whom I have never heard her speak unless prompted and only then tersely, almost dismissively. How their parents dealt with that loss, which I will never know, is perhaps the key to both of their pathologies. She hauled around in her heart a ton of silly guilt regarding her criminal brother, and regarding the familial conditions—surely determined by her parents' inappropriate response to the oldest son's death—which had propelled Dick on his petty career. Whatever her motives or motivations, she insisted that Chuck and I keep secret our childhoods. Though I wasn't able to articulate my outrage, I felt offended that someone was telling me that I could not speak my life as I understood it. Of course I understood it inaccurately, even inappropriately, but goddamnit it was mine. It was also Chuck's, and there's the ethical rub. In telling my life, in choosing to tell my life to peers, I was telling his as well; I was making a decision for him, one he was loath to make. His temperament was such that he had to obliterate his past to move on with his life, and mine was such that I had to disclose, and in the process mythify my past in order to proceed from it. Our interests, our psychic interests were in genuine and irreconcilable conflict.

I fault Barbara for not recognizing that my need to disclose was no less real, no less valid and a matter of psychic health than Chuck's was to conceal. But I also credit her greatly for the depth of her commitment to both of us, and for intuiting that Chuck had, for whatever reasons, been more damaged than I by events, and that therefore his need for secrecy, his need to obliterate, was a more desperate one than mine was to reveal. She was extremely mean to Chuck, emotionally abusive at times, but at her core she wanted to protect him. He needed, much more than I, simply to be held, to have someone show him unqualified affection. Barbara took him on, fed and clothed him and gave him structure, of sorts. But she could not be gentle with him. She couldn't daily sit down and patiently listen to him stutter what he felt, compel him to grunt and stutter what he felt about his life. She couldn't touch him, stroke him, show him gentleness. I didn't need gentle camaraderie from her; I'd gotten plenty from Joan. But Chuck needed it desperately. He was bright, sensitive and extremely proud, and was ashamed of his origins, and he needed someone to tell him that though his life had been odd, its oddness needn't mean that he should forever be an outsider, an interloper.

Some nights, in our separate beds, Chuck and I would sing in the dark. We both had sweet voices, but his was particularly sweet. We would argue throughout the day. I would by turns dismiss and torment him, condescend to him and laugh with him. But at night my brother and I would sing the songs we'd heard on the radio, or had learned in the Coronado High School Choir. I swear to whatever gods there are, and there are none, that as I compose these sentences a Czech band has just begun playing "House of the Rising Sun" in the bar of a funky hotel up the road from our country cabin in Dobřichovice. I'm drinking cheap Czech whisky and pounding on my Apple, and a band of country-bumkin Czechs is oozing "House of the Rising Sun" in Czech, and "House of the Rising Sun" is the song Chuck and I harmonized on most nights we broke into muted song in the dark of our room in Coronado, and the House of the Rising Sun, according to Darlene Jacobs, Lois's and my crusty yet decent, quite successful landlord (and one of the leading trial lawyers in New Orleans) when we lived through the mid-'80s in the French Quarter, was the apartment between Bourbon and Dauphine on Saint Louis which she owned and in which we resided. A superficial Freudian with sympathies for feminist critiques of key features of Freudianism, I believe that much of what Jung posited was merely fanciful, even, or especially, his synchronicity shtick. But one must marvel at all the tiny, weird convergences of lived life and memory, the spine-tickling coincidences.

The last time I saw Chuck was in the House of the Rising Sun, that is, in Lois's and my high-ceilinged apartment our landlady Darlene Jacobs insisted was part of the original brothel, which had occupied the entire building, known as the House of the Rising Sun. The Navy had sent Chuck to some special six-week training program in Pensacola, and so, passing through New Orleans, he looked me up on a whim. We tried to be civil, but politics crept into the discussion, and predictably we both went bullshit. He occupied, as he always had, the ideological far right, but unlike our father, whose politics I would not discover for years, Chuck was smart and thoughtful and relatively well read. He was also deeply sincere about his convictions, and, certain I was an unrepentant commie, spoke with as much pity as contempt. I don't recall if I tried to explain that I was not a communist, that though I'd been influenced by leftist thinking, I did not, for example, accept the authority of the Communist Part anywhere, and pretty much thought that communism everywhere had collapsed into petty totalitarian structures which were generally pernicious and dangerous. Nor did I tell him that I believed, albeit in wholly sentimental terms and following Comte's lead, that the goal of humankind should be the achievement of maximum individuality within maximum community, a ridiculously fanciful yet profound paradox for which neither communism nor post-industrial capitalism had adequately accounted. I did not tell him that I believed communism cannot accommodate its winners, and capitalism cannot adequately accommodate its losers. Instead I attacked the American Right, and he loved it, because the conversation, for him, fell into a clear confrontation between ideological good and evil, and he had memorized all the media-drenched comebacks, and so our brief hours together withered into the silliest exchanges, the most superficial and worn-out ideological exchanges, when what I should have said was screw it, Chuck, neither of us really knows what he's talking about, and everything we're saying is because we were damaged as children, so I'll turn off the light, and you lie down on the couch, and I'll lie down on the floor, and we'll sing, little brother, we'll sing "House of the Rising Sun," because the woman who rents this place to me says it's the House of the Rising Sun, and though she's probably wrong, it doesn't matter; let's lie in the dark and sing, because that's how we used to heal ourselves, if only a little, between darkness and day light.

They look down always with their
heads bent to the ground like cattle;
at the banquet tables they feed, fatten,
and fornicate. To get their fill of such
things they kick and butt each
other with iron horns and hoofs and
kill each other. The are insatiable
as they do not fill the real and
continent part of themselves with
true realities.

Book IX 586 b

For four Mardi Gras's Lois and I held open house at the House of the Rising Sun, and many of my colleagues took advantage of our central location. Mardi Gras is democratic, extemporaneous theater for which the tyranny of play space has been obliterated. It is an occasion when everyone's primary narcissism is set spinning across an urban dreamscape from which the usual psychic threats have been temporarily cleared, and so it is an occasion for laughing at death. The rituals of reciprocity, the throwing of beads and useless baubles, imitates quantum reality, or at least that version in which quarks are comprised of strings which quaver between the past and future, and by their very natures explain away, for some, Einstein's vexation at "spooky action at a distance," that supposed phenomenon by which Schrödinger's boxed cat remains in a state of life/death until someone deigns to open the box thus collapsing the wave-function of a photon in that box and releasing the creature—in time—to its fate (of course I don't really understand this stuff; I just like reading about it). The reciprocity of Mardi Gras is also a highly ritualistic enactment of sexual orgy on a breathtaking scale ("breathtaking" is my favorite cliché); it enables a couple of million people to screw symbolically, and symbolic screwing is precisely what New Orleans is about, for, as the wonderful and wise old novelist Vance Bourjailley once slurred to me on the balcony of the House of the Rising Sun—he was wearing a tux and making wretched noise on a sexy new trumpet, unaware that he was serenading the abode of Al Hirt directly across the street from us—people talk about the sensuality of the Big Easy, but fail to notice that it's gastronomic rather than sexual. So, except for that engaged in by the boys swarming Lafitte's In Exile and the other gay bars, there is less wholesome Give It To Me Big Boy, and Lift Up Your Dress And Pull Down Your Panties And Put Your Hands On The Table Baby 'Cause Here Come Freight-Train Freddy, down and dirty fucking at Mardi Gras than one may imagine, and

I think it was like that before the AIDS plague. The symbolic fucking of exchanging baubles publicly is certainly more Catholic, and less messy.

My colleagues came to the House of the Rising Sun primarily because it was a convenient place to take a piss. Most of them I liked quite well, but I considered it a sighful professional fate to have ended up among people for whom I could muster but tepid affection, and for whom I felt so weak an affinity. They were, are, decent and hardworking folks; in fact, I can say that I admire and respect them greatly as a collective, though a few individuals seem to me rather small and scared. The bitterness of four or five is palpable. Yet they are decent. Almost all of them seem concerned with some overarching idea of fairness, what it means and how it is achieved. Some, I discovered with shock, are extremely active in church life of one kind or another. We have staked out, all of us, political positions which we are more or less tethered to for life, though to have done so seems sillier and sillier over time. I am of course talking about most workplaces individuals occupy for long periods. Mine is no different. I knew more satisfying collegiality working in restaurants than I have known slogging away in academia, but it is wrong to think that one must get along with one's fellow workers. One must coexist, that is all, and do as little damage as one may in the process.

On the balcony of the House of the Rising Sun I coexisted with my colleagues who needed to piss in my toilet and drink my cheap beer and gaze out over the street where drunk tourists and dazzling drag queens weaved from the Rampart-side of the Quarter toward Bourbon at its heart, and I know now that I was enjoying my life too much and too unabashedly before their eyes. I was having small successes with my little poetry books, books that were making my name a household word in dozens of homes across America, and I was very happy to have my name be a household word is dozens of homes across America, and I stupidly, boyishly, let my enthusiasms blaze forth. I wanted to talk about books and gossip about writers I knew and play tennis with ideas I did not even half understand, but many of my colleagues simply wanted to talk about restaurants and movies and golf and jazz. I was stupid not to realize that it was bad form to enjoy my life so openly when I was having small successes, successes easy enough to dismiss for people who knew themselves smarter and more talented and more deeply read than I, people who themselves wanted to have their names be household words in dozens of homes across America. But they pissed in my toilet and swilled my cheap beer and stood on my balcony, my big blue balcony with the generic black-lace grillwork, and gazed out over the heads of hoi poloi, symbolically fucking with them, tossing and catching the baubles and plastic strings.

I remember only two individuals of the tens of thousands who over those four Fat Tuesdays passed beneath the balcony of the House of the Rising Sun. One was a drag queen decked out in a puffed and flowing dress of millions of red, blue, green, and gold sequins, and whose headdress, literally three meters high, branched out into an inverted candelabra whose outer prongs brushed the opposite gutters of the street. As she passed in all her enormous glory, she glanced up at Lois and said, "Got a pin, hon?"

The other passed during my final Mardi Gras in the House of the Rising Sun. He looked emaciated, and was obviously shitfaced; he had long blond hair and a handlebar mustache. He was gauntly handsome and shabbily dressed, and held a half-empty bottle of Jack Daniel's by its neck. He paused and requested that one of the women on the balcony show her tits, a common refrain at Carnival. Then he looked up into my eyes and said, "I've got cancer up the ass," and stumbled on. He might as well have said, You are a fool to enjoy your life so much, for you are doing so improperly. Your delight should not be in the absurd condition of having your name be a household word in dozens—maybe in reality not quite a dozen—homes across America, for that is anonymity of the loneliest sort. You should delight, while you may, that you are not me. For I am death laughing at itself, and you've a life, a perfectly fine life to laugh at, and laughing at life is the only honest joy that does not involve eating fine food, conversing in utter truth, fucking humbly and feelingly, or holding a child. There but by the grace of Whatever stumbled I.

The truck finally got repoed. Dick had paid off all but about two thousand on it though, so my credit, which had always been good, more because of Lois's diligence than mine, got smacked around a little, but not devastated. I ended up cashing in an IRA and paying it off, though the truck by then had been auctioned off or something, and I was mostly paying some ridiculous penalty fees. Once again, and for the last time, Dick had conned me. He stopped making payments because I wasn't calling very often, or visiting at all. I wasn't calling very often because I was getting tired of the implicit threat that if I didn't he'd stop making payments. I was weary from prostituting my familial affections to the stupid, vapid man who was my biological father, and I was tired of his lies, like the one that I owed him money, money he forced into my hand and which I thrust back at him and he insisted that I take, because I was obviously sucking wind financially, making my numerous trips to Europe and taking care of two households during those months Dom and Ema were in the States. When I drank, I drank the cheapest Canadian whiskey, the kind that comes in plastic liter containers, and otherwise did absolutely nothing for myself, so I should take the four hundred dollars, and then in a couple of weeks four hundred more, and I thought about the clothes he never paid for, the thousands of dollars of college loans I'd paid off entirely by myself, the vital necessities he'd never paid for, and I said okay, sure, I'll take it, but someday I'll pay it back, along with the thousand I got for that old Continental he gave me as a typically weird present, and certainly planned to pay him back the eight hundred or eighteen hundred, as soon as I won the lottery or scored an NEA. But soon my life's details thickened further, such that it was impractical to drive seven hours to Tallahassee, hang around with bible-blathering idiots for a day, then scoot back for seven hours; as soon as it became apparent I could no longer live the lie of constant verbal contact with him over the phone, he stopped making payments on the truck, the truck on which he'd tucked away over eighty thousand miles doing his and his wife's business, before they sold their operation and entered upon blissful white-trash retirement. He'd gotten his money's worth out of the thing, and frankly I think he still wanted to even the score from when I bonked the married daughter of the ditzy old alcoholic from San Francisco and was subsequently prepared to beat him to death if he'd taken one more step toward me. But I don't know. It could be that in some ineffable sense I'd become his own father, Charley, who had dismissed him. Indeed, I was dismissing him in similar fashion as it seems his own father had dismissed him, not even bothering to critique Dick's wretched life to his face, not having the time or patience to engage Dick concerning his mendacities. I am certain that Charley, a hardworking and loyal man who'd lived a weird life before settling down and who'd never recovered from the death of his eldest son, simply lost all patience with his youngest son, and summarily dismissed him.

All I know about Charley, all anyone will tell me, is that he came from a fairly well-off family in the tobacco country of North Carolina. It seems his mother, a grand old matriarch, beat him mercilessly, and he ran away. He married a wealthy widow when he was sixteen and she was in her mid-thirties and remained with her until she died. I guess he got some of her money, and I've heard that he had a sister who bought in heavily to Coca Cola very early, and became wildly wealthy. So rattling back there in the ancestral closet with the bleached bones are some gold coins, it seems. As a black sheep, Charley was disinherited from quite a bit of tobacco money, I've been told, but don't really know. I've no desire to sift through the ashes and bones of my ancestors, not yet, anyway. All I know is that as an adolescent Dick lost his older brother, Charley Jr., to pneumonia, and that the entire family was devastated, especially Charley Sr. No one talked about that loss, not honestly, except, weirdly, Dick. And he did so when I was five, not quite six.

I recall watching Liberace light the candles on his piano and play something thick, sweet, and busy, and then the TV being switched off. For some reason, Dick and I were alone in a room; he didn't speak directly to me. Rather he spoke to himself unconcerned that a child was listening. It was dusk, I think autumn, and in a place where autumn is particularly dramatic. We were staying in a small two-bedroom apartment. The sky which had been overcast all day was tilting into dusk, and dogs suddenly began to howl all over the neighborhood. I recall my young, handsome father peeking through white-gauze curtains, parting them delicately with two fingers and peering out; then he said, in a low, matter-of-fact voice that someone had died somewhere, that dogs howl when someone dies. A moment passed, then he said, still peering out, that when Charley died dogs howled all over the neighborhood, and that the first thing he thought when his mother informed him, nine or ten years-old, of

Charley's death was that now he, Dick, would get his room and all his stuff. Dick was confessing this to the window, to the gray and darkening sky, to the howling dogs, and his five or six year-old son just happened to hear him say aloud that the first honest, conscious response to news of his brother's death was that he, Dick, would acquire all of the dead boy's earthly belongings, and there was sadness, perhaps even remorse in my young and handsome, wildly self-deluded and self-consumed progenitor's voice. I am certain now that he had never been allowed to mourn, that his loss, which he'd immediately translated into material gain as a canny compensation, had never been acknowledged, and that he'd somehow been made to feel guilty for his brother's passing, for even being alive after his brother's death.

I'm pretty sure he was nine or ten when Charley Jr. died, and Barbara was five or six. I recall stories of how no one spoke at the dinner table in that house, that Dick was backhanded if he said anything. I've heard that Charley Sr.'s response to events or utterances not to his liking was "Ain't that cute. Ain't that funny," repeated sometimes more than once. I've heard that he drank a pint of Four Roses every night, religiously. I've heard that he was laconic, and needed silence around him always, not just at the supper table. I've heard that Charley Sr. helped out most of the folks in the neighborhood during the Depression, because for some reason he was okay financially during that time and believed in the concept of civic duty. I've heard he was a Mason, and was pretty high ranking. I've heard, over the past thirty-five years, very little about my fucked-up father's father, but I've heard from several sources that he held me weeks before he died, when I was a weeks-old infant, and predicted good things for me, and he was right, my life has been good. I've heard that he worked for Otis Elevator for thirty years without missing a single day's work. I feel him in me, the desire to be apart from others, and the desire to help those I would be apart from. I feel his need for secrecy, as he joined a secret fraternal organization. I joined the most secretive club of all, the tribe of angel fuckers, whose collective purpose is to obfuscate the ugly truth of human woe toward a clarity some may call transcendence, others healing play. I feel also his sense of quotidian duty, his need to rise each day with a purpose. From opposite generational ends of Dick's life, he, Dick, suffers contempt. His father and his son have looped across time in relation to him, and Charley's contempt is heaped upon mine, and yet I am chastened by Charley's contempt, because his contempt, his disgust, was not earned. That is, he did not suffer his son's soul sickness, as did I and everyone else whose life Dick contaminated by his presence, his self-aggrandizing lies which are his essence. That man whom I loathe, who is the young man I loved unconditionally, is as damaged a human being as I have ever encountered, and Charley, with whom as I grow older I feel, appropriately or not, greater affinity, was as much as anyone or anything the cause of that damage. All the silent and untouchable fathers have damaged all the lying and searching sons, and we are implicated, singularly and generationally. The world needs a new kind of father.

Then, for the rest of time, we
shall care for, and worship at,
their graves as at those of
divine spirits. We shall follow
the same rites for anyone of
those who have been judged to
have lived an outstandingly
good life, whether they die
of old age or in any other way.

Book V 469 b

When I visited Joan's grave in Elizabeth City a few years ago, I also visited her mother, who was in an old folks' home dying of Alzheimer's. Bula looked quite lovely, and it was difficult to believe she was in her mid-eighties. She was tall and thin and her skin was translucent and seemed smooth, though when I drew closer I saw how all her wrinkles, thousands, were tiny closely-packed tributaries. She smiled serenely, like the complete idiot she was. I patted her hand and she continued to smile off, and I recalled how I'd never much liked her, how one New Year's Eve when we'd been visiting her while Dick was in prison the second time, I'd awakened just before midnight, and for some reason we'd found ourselves together going through things in her attic, looking for something familial and long past, and how when the bells started ringing and sirens began to shriek, she asked me to kiss and hug her, and I wouldn't. I recall that for a moment she'd seemed deeply hurt, and for some reason I hadn't cared, which was unusual, because I had not been a distant or undemonstrative child. She had pissed me off fundamentally, and I just didn't like her. I tolerated her, was coolly nice to her, but I wasn't going to hug and kiss her. I think she was the first person I'd ever heard say bad things about Dick. Or perhaps it was because of a Japanese doll in a glass case trimmed in black wood she'd kept by her bed in Seattle where both of her sons had bought her a house and where she'd lived for several years before returning to Elizabeth City. There was a steep hill in front of that house in Seattle, and Chuck and I when we were very small loved rolling down that hill the couple of times we visited. When I was four and Chuck almost three and Joan was filled with Theresa and Dick was zig-zagging us across the continent, we stayed for a few days with Bula in Seattle. That doll, I'm sure gifted to her by Mac her merchant-marine eldest, was beautiful to me; it was one of those cheesy painted-china geishas wrapped in intricate folds of shiny fabric, red with golden figures, I think tiny dragons, from neck to foot. She held a white fan spread upon her breast. I wanted to sleep with Joan and Bula, as Chuck did, so I could be near that doll. I wanted to go to sleep near that doll and be close to my mother's body, but I had to sleep with Dick on the couch, and I hated doing so. Bula was scared I'd mess with the doll and break the case, and Dick was upset that I wanted to be near the doll, so I slept on the narrow couch with him, and he threw his leg over me and snored, and I felt wretched in the dark, and blamed my wretchedness on Bula.

The evening of the day I visited Bula in the old folks' home, I stayed in her house, which she'd shared with Mac, her eldest son who is a merchant marine with the IQ of a house pet. Mac had arranged for me to get the key, and Chris and Arthur came down from their respective entanglements to visit. I was a couple of months away from Chris's fateful visit to New Orleans, so I did not assume him anything but a car salesman, which is to say green scum on jagged rocks protruding from the great Free Market ocean, a professional liar, but not someone who'd rip off a brother. And Arthur simply scared me, gave me the creeps, though I admired and even liked him a little. We rifled through everything we could find, especially photos and papers, and came across very little, though a few things we found over time have resonated with denser frequencies. Irene's brief obituary, clipped from the *Norfolk Pilot*, I guess, was among pictures of family I knew little or nothing of. I still find it quite odd that Bula would even have taken notice of Irene's passing, inasmuch as they'd hardly known one another and as far as I could tell had held no opinions, good or bad, of each other. Though I could be wrong. They could have had at some point a very complex relationship; they could have been lovers, for all I know, or bitter enemies. Bula could have blamed Irene for all of Dick's faults, and therefore for all of Joan's suffering, though I don't think Joan really suffered in the early years; I think she thrived. I think she rather enjoyed the freedom her crazy young husband craved.

I also found a letter from Theresa to Joan. A fifteen year-old girl wrote her mortally sick mother from a state-funded home for adolescent girls, and was witty and bright and sounded more mature than her years, and I was affected, deeply, because I'd never as a boy given Theresa much attention, had never shown much concern for her. I could tell from her letter she was very bright, and wrote extremely well. I admired how she used humor to lift Joan's spirits, admonishing her not to hustle the young doctors. Joan, at the point in time the letter had been written, could not, Arthur told me, have moved any part of her body, except her eyes. Nuns had read letters to her. Theresa promised to visit Joan as soon as she could get away.

I don't know why I didn't phone or write to Joan when I returned from Japan. Between the ages of fourteen and eighteen I'd harbored some vague notion that her disease was not necessarily fatal, and that some people who had it even after a while got a little bit better. In my mid-teens I projected some indeterminate future when as a grown man I would find Joan and take care of her, but I managed quite nicely otherwise to file her away emotionally, at least consciously. Theresa, Arthur, and Chris had not had that luxury, and Theresa especially, as a female, a bright girl-becoming-woman, no doubt felt a particular emotional obligation. Arthur had a photo of Theresa that had been taken when she was in her mid-twenties, and she was lovely, like Joan, and I wished I could meet that young woman, that bright and funny, sardonic and spirited young woman and not apologize, because no one may genuinely apologize for slights and small crimes of meanness and exclusion committed in childhood; rather, I would talk to her about books, because surely she reads a lot, and I would listen, for hours and days, as long she would need to tell me everything or simply all she would care to tell, and I would promise always to listen. I'm told she became a nurse and married a guy in the army and has three kids. I'm told, by Arthur or Chris or both, that she wants desperately to avoid all contact with her past. She has a new name and is lost in America with her new family, and I wish her happiness, and hope she is writing letters and stories and poems, or simply keeping a diary, because the girl who wrote that letter to her dying mother should write all the time. In the Republic of Burma Shave, she had lived between two sets of males, older and younger, and from the time she was six or seven told everyone who would listen that she would be an archeologist when she grew up. I'm sure it sounded to her child's ears like an endeavor which would take her far away from such circumstances as those into which she'd been born. Archeologists stood above brothers and stinking laundry and silver tins of government surplus food. Surely, no archeologist would spend hours, days, weeks, months, years in the backseats of cars crunched between four boys. Surely an archeologist got lots of room and good things to eat, and was not constantly insulted. My sister, I hope that whatever you are doing, you are in your own heart an archeologist.

One might say that among those
who were caught that way the
souls who had come down from
heaven were not in a minority
because they had no experience
of evil. The majority of those
who had come up from the earth,
having suffered themselves and
seen others suffer, were in no
rush to make their choice. There
was thus an interchange of evils
and blessings for the majority
of souls. . .

Book X 619 d

In Innsbruck, Austria, teaching in my university's overseas program there, one morning while jogging along the River Inn, on the prim promenade heading toward the downtown from the north, I saw the Spirit of the Age. A well-scrubbed, ratty-haired, cherry-cheeked alcoholic woman in her sixties sat on a bench staring into the river. I'd just finished my miles, and was holding my knees, paying the woman no attention. When I did glance at her, hands on my hips, panting a little, the expression on her face commanded my attention. That is, as she gazed, she did not blink and did not move for a long moment; she was absolutely expressionless, and remained so as she held up a yellow plastic lighter, flicked it, and without changing her expression, slowly moved her palm an inch above the flame, then didn't move it at all.

I don't know how long she held her hand over the flame; I don't know because I ran away. Fifty meters up the path I paused and listened for a scream or a whimper, but heard nothing. I'd just acted like an incredible coward. I was more frightened of that woman than I'd been of any bogey I'd imagined as a child, or of any actual physical danger I'd ever confronted. For three or four seconds I'd been utterly terrified. Her power, her unconcern, her stoicism, terrified me. I was in a quaint, quintessentially pretty and prosperous Alpine city where kids' anti-Nazi graffiti on walls and bridge railings was aimed at their actual (we should presume ex-) Nazi parents and grandparents, people who had hated Jews, though few had ever even seen any, and had found rather swell the idea of persecuting them. The Tyroleans are sticky with folkish pride; old men still wear those ridiculously boyish costumes, with feathered hats spangled by little medals commemorating interesting mountain hikes. The whole culture is based upon dragging cows up mountain slopes that the flatulent bovines might shit a little agrarian prosperity into the hearty lives of those who drag them. And deep down they all, except for a few thousand of the enlightened young, hate everything that they are not.

What did that woman hate? It is too easy to say she hated herself. Perhaps she hated something inside herself, some aspect of what she had become; so, she would not douse herself with kerosene and strike a match; she would attack, torture, only the small part of herself she could not reconcile with the rest, the palm of her hand, perhaps next time a cheek, a temple, or her tongue. She committed her own private genocide, before my eyes, and it must always begin that way, self-loathing turned outward toward anything, anything at all corresponding to the torment within. Has your life been so isolated and barren as to seem absurd? Burn the absurdity, then search for that, without, which is isolated unto itself, and destroy it.

Perhaps the Spirit of the Age had simply been jilted by a lover, or abused as a child by a grandfather, or both, and more. Perhaps she has her counterpart in Central Park somewhere, or on a bench overlooking the Mississippi. But I saw her in a place where almost all the prosperous old men and women are former Nazis, or former members of the Nazi Youth, and where the same sick folkish spirit prevails as had enabled them to embrace an ideology of hate and destruction. Surely the woman's actions had not been ahistorical, strictly personal. Surely that hustling little river beyond which she'd stared so intently, without blinking, reminded her of who and what she was beyond herself, beyond collapsed particles of personal memory. The question is what loathed part of herself she was searing away.

I feel very stupid for not understanding anti-Semitism. I mean, I understand racism against people of color; I understand how some people recoil from what is so unlike themselves physically. I hate it, but I understand it. A few years ago I myself got caught in pernicious behavior. A junior colleague I'd grown to like and whom I'd mentored a little was conducting a difficult long-distance relationship with a young guy, a professional musician, she'd been involved with for quite a while. A red-blooded American citizen, he was ethnically some sort of Mid-Eastern Muslim, I don't recall which, perhaps Saudi, but whenever I inquired as to his well-being, I made some stupid joke about his name acting like I couldn't remember it—I probably wasn't acting—and saying something like How's Ala or Ali or Alababi. She eventually wrote me a note pointing out, among other things, the racism implicit in my running joke about his name, and I was devastated, because she was right; I shared mainstream white America's prejudice against Arabic peoples and for all my self-righteous breast-thumping against David Duke and the Klan and neo-Nazis and rednecks and the right wing of the Republican Party, I too had been a racist shmuck.

But anti-Semitism in America—one should say perhaps anti-Jewishness, though it sounds horrible (and not in the way it should) because Arabic peoples may also consider themselves Semitic; the designation is technically linguistic and not racial—is much more palpable than even racism against people primarily of African descent. In some cases, the one thing that neo-Nazis and some American blacks may agree upon is that Jews are bad. And those black Americans who are anti-Jewish are no better than neo-Nazis.

I get the Christian angle; it's stupid, but I get it. Yet how many anti-Jew black Americans have had any meaningful social contact with Jews? What representative of a cabal of Jews has snatched the bread out of the hand of a baby anywhere? That last question is loaded because, to some, Capitalism is a Jewish concoction, and the kooks who think so are among the most dangerous in the world. But I don't get anti-Jewishness. It seems that Jews are proportionally more successful than non-Jews in whatever society they occupy if that society allows honest competition, and they of course have thrived historically even where they'd been unabashedly oppressed, so perhaps it's jealousy, but I can't believe that jealousy was the primary motive behind the mass butchery in Europe.

I know I'm sounding incredibly stupid, and this sort of naive drivel has been said before, but I've read a lot about the Holocaust, and quite a bit about European and American history, and I have to say I don't have a clue as to why Jews have been so hated. They're the ones who got the shit stomped out of them again and again and still managed, many of them, to prosper. I understand a little how that Chosen People thing might rankle, but that dovetails into the whole Christ-Killer thing, and seems more often than not simply an excuse to strike out against the Jews for some more fundamental and visceral reason I find utterly mystifying. The whole thing can't be connected to the fact that for so long in Europe Jews were the only ones who could loan money, and that the kings and nobility would often drift into grotesquely large debts; hell, so often when that happened some king would simply kill the Jews to whom he owed money, and that was that. It's not as though those Jewish merchants had armies of thugs serving as a vast collection agency. Always, Jews existed by the good will of the established power, and there was rarely very much good will.

When Dom, Ema and I stayed in that ridiculous apartment seventy meters from Lois's and my house, several of Dom's friends from Prague visited. One was K, a young lawyer who has since become quite rich and successful in his career. He seemed, and still does seem, a decent fellow, a bit haughty but decent. Unlike Dom's best friend E, K did not avail himself of the large and vibrant gay scene in the French Quarter, but rather stuck pretty close to Dom. His English is quite good, and he's not shy, and I assume he knows how to conduct safe gay sex. He simply wasn't interested in submerging himself in a gay scene. Dom explained to me that whereas E loved to fuck indiscriminately, K liked to fall in love, mostly with boys. So, I saw much more of him than I did of E when E later visited.

One late afternoon the conversation wafted toward the general idea of social and cultural prejudices, and I casually brought up anti-Jewishness, how Jews are hated by so many people who have never even had any contact with a single Jew. K waded into a very calm and reasoned discourse centered on the observation that Americans really don't understand this aspect of European culture, and that it must have been quite vexing, for example, for many poor Catholic Poles to see how many of the factories in their country were owned by Jews, et cetera. Three or four minutes into that calm and reasoned discourse I realized I was listening to an explanation, from a "European perspective," as to why non-Jewish Europeans hated Jews. The person, the European person, making the explanation was in his late twenties, and I wondered how he could know any better than I just what the hell was going through the hearts and souls of Central European peasants who ultimately enabled the mass destruction of so many Jews. I stopped him, yelling, screaming, that he was an anti-Jewish punk, that as a young dandy, as a gay man from a society even less tolerant of homosexuality than American society, from a society where he may be what he is only by stealth, how in the name of the Crucified Jesus could he sit there and talk so matter-of-factly about what the Jews did to get themselves hated! It was the same thing homosexuals had done! I told him. Indeed, there are many striking similarities. Homosexuals like Jews often lead private lives, that is to say lives among themselves, that are very different from the private lives of those in the majority, even as in the workplace, in the marketplace, they are often indistinguishable from those in the majority. Homosexuals, like Jews, are often discriminated against by the same Christians who find in the New Testament ample justification to loathe both. Homosexuals, like Jews, are often quite successful in business, the professions, and the arts. Hell, one wonders why a band of gay Jews hasn't sashayed into the United Nations wearing pink yarmulkes and simply taken the whole goddamned world over! Allen Ginsberg for Emperor! But K wasn't convinced, except that I was a typical American liberal with no real understanding of European culture, and he spoke calmly about how Jews do possess inordinate power over Western media and financial markets, and I shot back that there were probably as many nelly lawyers moving billions or controlling the editorial agenda of major publications, but he said it wasn't the same thing, that Jews worked together, and that their interest wasn't simply to survive, but to thrive above others; their purpose was to control.

So it was out. The Jews wanted to control the world. I asked him if he'd ever played poker when more than one Jew was at the table, had he ever been in a group of people in which there was more than one Jew present during a general discussion, especially a heated one. I wondered aloud if he'd ever watched Jews interact. Hell, I said, if Jewish culture, or cultures, are determined by anything it's argumentation. They're always rhetorically at each other's throats! There I was, arguing against the notion of Jewish conspiracies using the same kind of logic asshole anti-Semites used to support the concept! I argued from anecdotal evidence that Jews were simply too contentious among themselves, too much determined by a tradition of passionate argumentation over, and constant reinterpretation of, vague ancient texts to pull together as a team to rule the world. I cheerily if fiercely swooped down my slippery slope, yelling at a bright and well-meaning, anti-Jew Czech lawyer whose idea of bliss was sucking the cocks of adolescents. He seemed so convinced of his position, his belief that Jews had brought ruin upon themselves, and that they conspire among themselves to rule the world, that I finally could only marvel at his condition, his sickness, and I wondered how many more of his generation in Central Europe, good-looking, educated, hard-working young men and women, the shining futures of their respective nations and of the European Union itself, hold similar beliefs, and I realized that probably many, many more probably believe just as K believes. Of course they believe the Holocaust was a "terrible thing" (K's words); but we must try to understand the concrete conditions which turned so many non-Jews against Jews.

I wish it were that easy; I wish there were concrete reasons for the Holocaust. Someday explaining it to my daughters will be easier if there were concrete reasons. I'll have them read Ann Frank's diary when they're able, or ready, but the point of their reading it will not be to discern reasons, concrete reasons as to why that girl was destroyed, but the point will rather be that they should marvel at her humanity, so like their own, so powerfully like their own, that they may then marvel at the prospect of anyone wanting to destroy her. Then we'll talk about power, how certain kinds of authoritarian structures may render otherwise decent people into monsters doing the evil bidding of monsters who are themselves only doing the bidding of monsters who must do as monsters above them dictate who are taking orders from the ultimate monster, above whom there is only the authority of centuries of loathing for which there are no concrete reasons, an authority which suffused the hearts of even the decent people who do the bidding of monsters, but who finally should admit, but will not, that the ultimate monster, the ultimate authority was not at the opposite end of a chain of command, but in their own folkish hearts even as they did the bidding of monsters.

During my brief stay in Innsbruck, soon after I witnessed the Spirit of the Age, I was alerted by a colleague there, a fellow teaching German, to the fact that I and other Americans teaching in the program harbored prejudice against German-speaking people. The idea at first flush seemed odd, but I soon realized that he was correct. The very sound of the language makes me recoil slightly, and my first associations with the sounds of German are goose-stepping enemies. Hollywood had performed it's wartime job of propagandizing against the Germans all too well. The very sound of the language has for most Americans of my generation, those born after World War II and who grew up awash in the "old movies" of the previous decade, the immediate association of efficient, militaristic evil. One does not think immediately of the lyric poetry of Rilke or the prose of Goethe; one does not think of the great German thinkers, or of the great German composers. One hears a few words of the language and thinks of those funky German helmets and of German soldiers snapping their heels and thrusting out their right arms in Nazi salute. So, yes, at my core I am prejudiced against the Germans, or against anyone speaking the German language. And if the truth be told so is most of non-German-speaking Europe. German tourists are considered even bigger asses than American tourists, pushier and more demanding, more insistent, implicitly more insistent that they are superior in that old goose-stepping sense, even though in some fundamental ways the German and Austrian cultures seem genuinely the most civilized and socially enlightened in the world. Germany's robust Green Party is but one indication of its society's progressive nature. Its government's official position on race and ethnicity is another, but the folkish heart cannot be officially affected. All that old German shit, alas, is still in play. I have a little German in me on my mother's side; I recall Joan's mother Bula stating that she was a quarter German; that would make me a sixteenth, just enough to appreciate a little bathroom humor once in a while—German popular culture seems obsessed with shit and where it comes from—but not enough to appreciate Wagner, that great idealizer of the German bowels. When the rest of Europe begins to round up Germans and Austrians (those who characterize Austrians as the Nazis' "first victims" should be laughed at then slapped upside their heads) and put them in camps, when the rest of Europe begins to exterminate the Germans and Austrians, I'll start rooting for the Germans and the Austrians. For now, I acknowledge the greatness of German-language culture, and that there are among the German-speaking people of Europe some of the most enlightened and humane citizens of the planet; I also observe that the sickness which resulted in the earth's greatest horror has not been cured in many, perhaps most, of those people's hearts.

Do you not think it mean and
greedy to strip a corpse? Is it
not womanish and small-minded
to regard the body as your enemy,
when the enemy himself has
flitted away and left behind only
the instrument with which he
fought? Do you think such
behavior any different from
that of dogs who are angry with
the stone that hits them and
leave the thrower alone?

Book V 469 d

Boxing is my favorite sport. I admire the courage of real professionals, and the lyric nature of even the most brutal "slugfest." I know that I should deplore boxing. I should deplore it not only because of the brutality in the ring, but because it represents yet another example of exploitation of the poor. Young men who excel in boxing often do so because it is quite simply the only path out of poverty, and because they're angry and want to beat the shit out of someone, anyone. To be successful, they have to get over wanting to hurt people and see the sport as pure process, a job, a craft. But they can never get beyond not wanting to be poor. No one does.

My first moments of political consciousness were in Mexico when I was five or barely six. I recall Dick making a big score and rolling for the border. Joan even dyed her hair blond and looked terrible. She was probably in the early stage of pregnancy. That first night across the border in Mexico, we stopped at a filthy little motel that had a restaurant attached to it. Dick, using a phrase book, ordered chicken, and we heard from behind the wall facing the back of the motel scared chickens scurrying. When the chicken finally came, Dick bit into a drumstick, and blood flowed from the steaming meat. He said that meant it was really fresh.

In Mexico City there was poverty and there was wealth. I noticed that there was either one or the other, and virtually nothing in between. I remember asking Joan about it. I said something like how come there are those big rich houses and right next to them those ugly little poor houses. I don't recall what she answered. Dick got us a good furnished apartment that even had a television, and tried to teach us Spanish from his phrase book. He taught us la pluma and el libro, and that was about it. Years later in college I would improve upon this base very little.

Once Joan and I went shopping together, and I said look, that meat is moving! We looked closer, and it was indeed moving, covered with flies. I watched bullfights on TV, and some cartoons so old they no longer aired on U.S. television, cartoons with stick figures. I liked the kind of music on the radio there, and found much that was pretty to look at, but couldn't get over how many poor people there were, people who were dirty and looked hungry, real hungry, the way I had been only a few times, when Dick had been out doing business and hadn't come back for two or three days and we had had nothing, absolutely nothing to eat in whatever motel room we waited (once, after two days away, Dick returned with a loaf of rye bread, and I shall never forget how those slices tasted, not particularly good but almost heavenly for being substantial). Some of those people I saw were beyond waiting. No daddy would suddenly appear and shower them with burgers and fries. I knew this. I was sad for them, and asked lots of questions Joan could not answer. Mexico was different, and the people in it were different. They spoke a different language and lived in a different way. From what? From us, but by then I knew that no one lived like us. But at least from where we had come I could understand the television and there weren't any poor people, not like in Mexico, anyway.

Those proud little fighters from Mexico are my favorites. I especially like the ones with records like thirty-four victories, eighteen defeats, and five draws, bantam weights who will fight anyone anywhere anytime, and do, and lose lots of close decisions in white boys' hometowns, decisions they should have won. But they don't care. They just keep fighting. They're always pressing, always moving, bobbing, flicking jabs, looking for the Big Punch. They don't get great training; in fact, most of what they learn is in actual prize fights, and the main thing they learn is that when they're finally given a decent fight, they're usually fodder for some smooth black kid or white kid from the States, and they're expected to look tough getting whipped, and they always do. Such fighters are the pure products of poverty, soul-killing, blood-sucking poverty. Often not particularly talented, they fight as though there is death and there is fighting, and they choose to fight. Put the heart of such a man in a poet or singer and hearts will get broken. Put the heart of such a man in a politician and he'll never get elected to anything. Put the heart of such a man in a mother and she will simply birth such men. I suppose it is true that such hearts should not be allowed to happen.

Intellectuals are a pain in the ass, especially the ones drunk on theory. I've read lots of social and literary theory, and I'm glad that I have, though I'll never again read anything (except memoirs, histories, or works of fiction) about the suffering masses, or about base and motherfucking superstructure, or another goddamned book by or, worse, about, Derrida, Bakhtin, or Habermas or Foucault or Deleuze or Gramsci or Lacan or Spivak, or anything by Eagleton or Jameson or their clucking minions. That stuff almost destroyed me, and I'm not even a real intellectual.

There are relatively few real intellectuals in the world, and very few of those are in the United States. There are people with valid Ph.D.'s in the social sciences and humanities who are not real intellectuals. Oh, perhaps one should distinguish between three levels of intellectuals in America. There are a few thousand real ones, that is, intellectuals of the First Order. Then there are intellectuals of the Second Order, a group I suppose I am a member of with seven or eight million other self-involved schlemiels. Then there are folks who watch *Jeopardy* and get lots of the answers correct, shouting them back at the TV before the buzzer. An intellectual of the First Order knows most of what there is to know about one thing, and lots about a lot of other things as well. She knows all or almost all there is to know about quasars or chrysanthemums or lyric poetry, and dedicates her life to understanding that knowledge and advancing it to the extent it is possible to do so. Level Two intellectuals know, relatively speaking, a lot about one or more things, and either eschew or fake understanding; they are usually followers of, which is to say parasites on Level One intellectuals. Level Three intellectuals are real good at board games. I admire Level One, that is, real intellectuals, greatly. It's just that they're a pain in the ass because they often lack wisdom. That is, they often seem not to realize that smelling a fart in a crowded elevator may have had as much to do with a sudden flash of understanding as the unremitting contemplation of certain imaginary numbers. Wisdom—and not that folkish crap—is a function of the bowels and bladder and hormonal fixations. Wisdom always brings us back to the body. I think even Plato's Socrates knew this. Christ, too, or at least his press agents. That suffering on the cross thing is all about wisdom, but it gets corrupted as religion. Prizefighters are usually quite ignorant, but very wise. Each at some time in his career hangs on a cross, gets counted out, and rises. Each visits Truth and Beauty on Queer Street. There is no more beautiful gesture than two fighters embracing after the final bell of a good, brutal prizefight. That embrace is, unambiguously, the most civilized event any human being may participate in.

There is not now, has not been
in the past, nor ever will be in
the future, a man of a character
so unusual that he has been
educated to virtue in spite of
the education he received from
the mob. . . . We must realize that
if any character is saved and
becomes what it should, in the
present state of our societies,
you would not be wrong to say
that it has been saved by a
god's intervention.

Book VI 492 e

Joan was very depressed between the time Joey gingerly dumped her and Dick got out of prison the second time. She was pregnant, and knew, I think, what Dick's response would be. Several times I crawled in bed with her and talked with her. I wanted so much to help her, to blow away the sadness, to make her smile or laugh. I asked her to sing for me, and she sang "Soft As the Voice of an Angel," and apologized for her cracking contralto, blaming the Pall Malls, the red packs of which cost a quarter. I didn't care that her voice cracked. I loved to hear her sing in the twilight. And because it was summer we were often all in bed before the arrival of total darkness, though sometimes I would stay out and play Smear the Queer or just mess around. My instinct during that interim period, however, was to stick close to Joan, and go to bed early.

I was born of the sickness which was my young parents' marriage. Surely she knew early on that he was a pathological liar. Surely he knew early on that it was her nature to go psychically limp before his will to move, constantly move, until he grew tired of moving. What is more American than the idealization of movement? Movement is progress, advancement, a peculiar achievement unto itself regardless of motive. Motiveless movement defines the Republic of Burma Shave.

Dick and Joan were born in 1932 and 1933 respectively, on March 7th and 8th respectively. Dick's father drank faithfully but did not show the effects of liquor. Joan's father drank sporadically but got stinking drunk when he did, always ending the evening with interminable choruses of "When Irish Eyes Are Smiling," in a brogue which appeared only when he drank. Dick's mother was a spunky, raunchy little dark-haired Greek. Joan's mother was a tight-assed Irish-German. Dick and Joan were both the products of sad marriages. But that fact does not explain them, does not explain Dick's compulsion to move without reason, nor Joan's acquiescence to that compulsion.

They came into puberty during the War. Joan began to bleed probably just as the War was surging to its conclusion, perhaps within days of Hiroshima, Nagasaki, and the revelations of Death Camps. I imagine Dick smoking his first cigarette. What did kids think about Death Camps when they saw them in newsreels at the movies? They thought probably pretty much what they were told to think, that the Japs were evil and had to be torched, that the krauts were evil and solely responsible for what happened to the Jews and the others. The main thing was that we were good and won the war, with a little help from the Brits et al. And then the unprecedented activity, the transformation of America into postwar America, into the vast American backyard, where fathers preside over black fiery grills flipping meat. The early '50s. Dick and Joan met in '52, got married in '53, the year I was born. I'm told Dick tried to hold on to a job; even after his father died, he tried to play it straight. But then he started bouncing checks. Then Chuck was born in Newport News. Then the movement, the motiveless movement across America. Then my memories begin sometime in 1956, in earnest in '57, and I am rolling across great expanses, every day, moving over highways, staring through glass smudged by little fingers, staring into battered books and magazines in the backseats of innumerable cars which are one familial car, trying to write letters and numbers on crinkled pieces of paper Joan would give me, asking questions, always asking questions.

As a young man I did not seek Joan out to comfort her before she died, and that will always be my greatest source of guilt, but I am not incapacitated by guilt. I remind myself often of how tiny is my life, the story of my life, and my guilt, along with everything else I am, is diminished, rendered quaint, even. My infidelities, too, are quaint. So are my passions and convictions. I am at home in my quaintness whether I am in New Orleans or Prague.

And being quaint is a hell of a lot better than being dead or destitute. There are many people who helped me not destroy myself as a young man. Glover Davis, big, beautiful Glover, my first teacher in college, the first one I took seriously and who took me seriously, seriously enough to kick me out of his classroom on the second day of the semester; Glover whose plodding grace is like a bear's in life and in his beautiful verse; Glover Davis whom I will always love like a brother, and in some ways as I would a father. Bruce H. Boston, whose humor and style, whose life's rhythms I tried so hard to imitate, to make my own, I will always love as I would a brother, and in some ways as I would a father. Robert L. Jones, who always kept faith with his idea of what a poet should be, even as he destroyed himself, I will always love as I would a brother, and in some ways as I would a father. Those three men, eight to fourteen years older than I, were what I suppose one calls role models. Our lives have drifted apart—sweet Bob Jones's away—but I will always feel great affection for them. They are three angel fuckers, true lyric poets, singers of American loneliness and beauty and wonder. They, and Ca, taught me to be an angel fucker.

The other father in my life has been Gerald Stern, one of the two or three most original voices in American poetry. His is a tragic vision, but few seem to understand that. Few see beyond the humor and the affirmations of life to the core of his poetry, which is soaked with tears of lament, tears of loss. Beneath the foliage, under the thick leaves and nodding roses, there are many corpses in Gerald Stern's garden. His expressions of joy are radical acts of faith in nothing more than life itself. I would like to cut a similar swath through life as he, though I don't know if I have the character to do so.

My mothers have been women I have loved, in my fashion, and some I have not. My stepmother, whom I love and respect but don't at all like, was a terrible mother, but perhaps precisely the kind I needed, that is, one who would not allow me to wallow in feelings of loss I hadn't earned by feeling truly. Her severity was always an insistence on truth, simplistic truth often, but a place to start. Even when she insisted I lie about my past, she spoke to the truth of Chuck's needs and her own, and forced me to question my own motives.

The woman who hired me over fifteen years ago, gave me my first and only teaching job, though she is now a political enemy, I suppose was a kind of mother. She is tough and brilliant and should be provost or chancellor or goddamned governor of Louisiana, but isn't any of those for reasons that are boring, but primarily because she probably doesn't need that kind of prestige. I am proud to have as an albeit minor enemy one of the classiest, shrewdest, most politically astute persons I've ever known.

My first surrogate mother was Esther Hale, who managed the gee-dunk on the Amphibious Base on Coronado Island. She was my boss for the four years, off and on; I worked there stacking chairs, sweeping, mopping, waxing, buffing, unstacking chairs. Esther was six-feet tall and weighed maybe a hundred and twenty pounds. Her hair was bluish white, short, neatly styled. Her uniform was a white waitress dress, the same as the women on the line behind the steam tables wore, a name tag and white shoes. She was in her late sixties and looked older, but she was tough and diligent and taught me to work. She was a clean freak, and actually on occasion inspected my work with white gloves. She arrived at the geedunk at five in the morning and left, with me, at six in the afternoon. The last couple of years she gave me rides home. The image of her thin forearm and hand, covered with the ugly blotched bruises of an active old age, reaching to lift the lock on the passenger-side door of her car, is an inexplicably lucid and powerful memory. She'd worked at the geedunk since before World War II, and had advanced to general manager. She'd given her life to a military cafeteria, which, though I genuinely cared for her, I found absurd, not yet realizing that if you don't give your life to something it's not even yours, that you give your life to something in order to have a life. But no matter how absurd I found Esther Hale's diligence and loyalty to such a squirrelly place as one where sailors and Marines congregated to drink coffee and swill deep-fried and grilled food, I respected her, and always did what she told me to do. If she told me to take a toothbrush and scrub all the corners of the large L-shaped room, I got the toothbrush, the Ajax, a pail of water, and did it. If she told me to lie on my stomach and reach beneath the long counter and wipe up the disgusting clumps of organic matter under the deep fryer, I screwed up my face, rolled my eyes and did it. There was not an inch of the entire structure I had not touched, rubbed, scrubbed. I was more tactilly intimate with that drab, chrome and tile and plastic kitsch palace than I've ever been with a woman. I hope the fucking place has burned down. Surely Esther Hale is dead, and that geedunk doesn't deserve to exist without her.

My last surrogate mother was Rayburn Miller, whom I wasn't particularly close to and yet felt a deep, formal affection for. He was brilliant and gifted. He was a dignified and private man who deeply desired to fuck and be fucked by "hunky numbers" (the phrase, and the sentiment, is from one of his poems). He had a comically huge ass, and the face of a venerable university administrator, which he was. He had a broad bald pate, an immaculate little mustache, and wise sad eyes that were small in his head. He was someone for whom considerable intelligence was a burden, and who believed the world is such that to procreate should be a criminal act. For those thus transgressed against, the living, he offered affection wrapped in contempt, and always with what seemed an arch civility. I hope there is a heaven each of us makes for herself or himself, a parallel universe among innumerable universes each of us may open onto upon expiring. Of course death is final, but I'm having a little fun here, in Rayburn's memory. Positing such a heaven, such an afterlife, I see Rayburn mooning over lovely boys in fifth-century Athens, perhaps following one around, finally winning him, and spending lazy hours talking about ideas, pure ideas, before sweaty funky homosexual fucking. Rayburn Miller was a supreme angel fucker, a wonderful, sad, underrated poet. He was kind to me, in his fashion, and was, on a couple of occasions, over the phone, motherly in his expressions of concern and affection, and in his offer of careful and wise advise. I didn't know him well enough to miss him. I simply think fondly of him, and know that he was one of the strongest talents of his generation. He was a person without hope (except when he was fucking angels) who lived with dignity.

And so many Czechs before the autumn of '89 had neither hope nor dignity, though by insisting upon the former they achieved, collectively, the latter. Those November and early December days were mostly cold and gray, in sharp contrast to the mood of the people who swelled the boulevards and squares in Prague. The city was a goofy earthly heaven. People who otherwise knew better were filled with giddy hope, hope edged with Czech irony, but unabashed all the same. The whole thing got started when a kid named Martin Šmíd, a math student, was thought to have been beaten to death by the riot police. It seems some cheeky students, emboldened by recent events in East Germany and throughout Central Europe, decided to have a memorial march for some kid snuffed by the Nazis. Of course, the Party thugs couldn't say anything about that, except that it was clear the students were also memorializing Jan Palach, the kid who torched himself to protest the Soviet invasion of '68. This latter, of course, the thugs had a hell of a lot to say about, and they said it with police batons. Some of the confrontation was videotaped. One sees the grainy figure of a young woman holding out a flower to the line of blue-hatted police, and then a flurry of movement and some batons waving up and down, one would suppose striking people. I was not there when the police beat up the kids, though I knew quite a few people who were, all of whom had had the good sense to run like hell. The next day, though, Dom and I walked the short distance from her Rybna apartment to the site of the beatings and even as we stood there, people started sticking candles to a corner of the sidewalk someone said was where Šmíd had been "killed." The rumor was flying that a math student named Šmíd had been murdered by the police, beaten to death. I recall one old guy, nicely dressed in a suit with a thick tweed overcoat and a tweed hat, screwing up his face in anger as he stood on that corner staring at the candles, and I recall how he joined in jeering at a police car that passed, and his anger was the spontaneous anger of most of the city. A kid was dead, everyone thought, just because some Party thugs didn't like his politics. Those first hours were wonderful. Folks were fuming; old women, babickas who would nudge and elbow ahead of you in a queue for bananas, were walking around with clenched fists. They were pissed. The students of course were pissed. The generation of '68 was particularly pissed, probably as much at themselves as at the thugs who had humiliated them. Everybody seemed to have a healthy anger glowing within, and the first mass demonstration in Wenceslas Square seemed from my wholly ignorant perspective wholly spontaneous. I followed Dom onto the Square, and nothing much happened. There wasn't even a sound system with which the huge crowd could be addressed! That level of organization wouldn't occur for a couple of days. That first demonstration was pure presence. People mulled about, tens of thousands strong, and the thugs couldn't do a goddamned thing about it.

It didn't matter that Šmíd was alive. The rumor of his death had filled the Square that first day, and that first demonstration was the real victory from which all the changes flowed. The Czechs killed their bad daddies that first day they poured onto the Square with no leadership to speak of, except that of collective will. The corpses wheezed for a little while longer in the halls of power, but the rest was carnival.

"Throw me something, Mister!" is one of the chants of Mardi Gras. It's what you yell to those Wannabe Rich Boys who pay to wear masks and throw trinkets to hoi polloi from the kitschiest floats ever designed.

Actually, I don't have anything against those Wannabe Rich Boys (some of them may actually be rich, but not so rich that people really notice, and so they wannabe *that* rich); indeed, I actually like and respect some of them, and have to admit that more and more I admire the civility, the ethos of friendliness, that is at the heart of New Orleans social life. I find it boring and stifling, but admirable for its fiercely provincial insistence upon the singularity of its purpose: to be exactly what it is, whatever that is, until the end of history, or the world, whichever comes first. "Throw me something, Mister!" hoi polloi chant, and the Wannabe Rich Boys, the doctors and lawyers and owners of stuff, chuck trinkets to those they disdain, their customers, that is, the scum who get sick, slip and fall and cheerfully sue, and buy stuff.

The year David Duke ran for state senator from that bastion of White Flight, Metairie, Louisiana, a pristine suburb of predominantly black New Orleans, I stood on St. Charles, somewhere east of the middle, chanting with the eight-deep crowd, "Throw me something, Mister!" I reached for a long strand of fat white beads, a real prize, and caught one end as someone caught the other. I ripped it from his hand, then turned to glance at whom I had defeated. It was George Bush Jr.! I knew it was George Bush Jr. because, well, it was fucking George Bush Jr.! The President's boy, whom I recalled owned part of one of the Texas baseball teams and who, according to some TV pundits, had political ambitions.

He was a nice guy. I told him I hated everything he stood for, or everything I thought he stood for, and he responded like a mensch. He told me—and he talked to me as though I represented my demographic niche, and as though therefore everything he said would be duly disseminated through that niche—he was down to help whomever the dummy was opposing Duke. He bad-mouthed Duke, over the roars and chants of that Bacchus crowd on St. Charles, for several minutes. I nodded, then said the Republican Party had empowered the nasty little schmuck, and that I was giddy at the spectacle of Country-Club Republicans swooning on the altar of Duke's successes. Bush's twangy response was sunny and stupid, media-savvy inarticulate, but as he spoke I couldn't help but like him and of course I was pissed at myself for liking him, because the guy was obviously playing me.

George Bush Jr. (George W. Bush, but how can one not think of him as Junior?) truly seemed a decent guy. He's now governor of Texas, and the leading candidate to be the Republican Party's nominee for president in 2000. We'll see where that goes. Maybe he beats his wife and fucks farm animals (or the reverse, which in some parts of Texas would probably be considered more reprehensible), but I doubt it. My brief, silly encounter with him is perhaps for me little more than an opportunity for name-dropping. All the Wannabe Rich Boys who ride in Bacchus probably love him, though he may be too far to the left for some of them.

David Duke scared a lot of people across the American political spectrum. The scariest thing about him was that he chanted perfectly legitimate conservative themes and ideas. Indeed, he was ahead of the discursive curve on welfare reform, and looked like a legitimate conservative candidate at a time when conservative ideology was in the ascendancy. If only he didn't religiously celebrate Hitler's birthday. If only he hadn't been a Bullgoose dickhead of the KKK. If only he didn't have a reprehensible past, that nose job might have been his ticket to the governor's mansion.

Horseshit. The twit got as far as he did precisely because of his past. David Duke was simply the slit from which the disgusting pus issued, the infected pus. It bubbled below the surface a long time, and then the swollen limb got slit. Duke was the slit. The disease had been evident, of course, a long time, and leaking the pus hasn't necessarily had any curative value, and lest I drag this ugly trope to an ugly and convoluted conclusion, I'll say simply that the fears Duke played upon run deeper than most people, who are not black, imagine.

A few years ago we lived four months in Prague and eight in New Orleans each year, and four years ago we rented a smallish place in that Culture Free Zone, New Orleans East, in a "gated community" to which otal Fitness was attached. All of us were middle- to lower-middle class in our little gated, tree-pretty village, and most of us were black, the rest white and other. Ema's tree, that is, the little Japanese Plum directly in front of our living room window, got clotted with kids the moment school was out. I've photographs of my little fair-haired darling entwined with the blithe dark bodies of her playmates in the strong though haggard limbs of that tree, and I find those images quite moving, for I am sentimental that way, and living in what was until recently the Murder Capital of America, where almost all the murders were, and still are, mostly black kids killing black kids and any sign of racial harmony, no matter how small and goofy, will choke me up. For I believe black kids kill black kids because they are deeply, even pathologically, shy.

An epidemic of murders blamed on shyness? Yes, among other things, for a pathological shyness is one symptom of what racism had done to children of color, at least in the South. They are soaked in Euro-American commercial culture from the time they are born; they are presented with a cultural norm that in so many ways has nothing to do with who and what they are as social beings; they see and hear white people in media, in the streets, probably in their dreams, yet they have, many of them, no opportunity to interact with those ubiquitous pale creatures except as Other. No kid wants to be Other, and that's not a Black thing; it's a kid thing.

And most black children have a natural, healthy curiosity about white people, a curiosity they are made to feel guilty about by both white and black social conventions. I have smiled and said hello to black kids who have shot glances at me and said nothing. Part of that may be that their parents have told them not to speak to strangers, but it's also more than that. They don't know what to say. It's not the sort of salutation they're used to, so they're immediately taken aback. But there's something else, too. They recoil out of a shyness so profound it is a defining feature of their psyches. Their sense of being Other, which racism creates and by numerous vicious means exacerbates from womb to grave, is further confounded by a pathological shyness imposed upon them. To kill otherness is what every black kid of the "underclass" as well as middle class wants to do.

In Ema's tree the kids were fine. Everybody was fine. Everybody was tangled up in the branches and trying to reach the little knobs of fruit. All the kids ran in and out of the house asking for stuff to eat and drink, and they all called me Tata, because they'd heard Ema call me that and they didn't know in means Daddy in Czech. It was an in-house joke that Ema particularly delighted in, and so she didn't tell them what Tata means. One seven year-old—(Lord, now he's almost twelve; I hope he's well) Joshua—was always in and out. He'd yell, "Tata!" through the mailslot, and I'd tell him to wait until Ema got back from shopping with her mother, but he kept messing with the slot and making noises at the door until I acknowledged his presence, and I always did, letting him in to hang out, eat and drink something. I once heard him bragging to his friend Nicholas, "I can go into that house anytime I want to!" At least for the kids who climbed Ema's tree, three particular white people were no forbidding mystery. With us they didn't have to feel shy. The world they live in day to day is still racist, and they will do well to be wary of white people generally. But maybe they, especially Joshua, won't have to feel quite as shy, quite as Other. It isn't much. It's sentimental, and not much. But David Duke wants to kill black children. He's never said it, officially, but it's implicit in his life, the verifiable details of his life; it's even implicit in his nose job. Lots of white people want to kill black children. They want to obliterate them, erase them. The children know this. They feel it. And they erase themselves.

I once had as a student a cop taking night classes to improve himself. He was a decent, upstanding fellow who openly professed religious convictions and had a gentle nature and strong sense of fairness. He announced one night during a rambling class discussion about Gun Control or Affirmative Action or maybe even Abortion—it doesn't matter; to those all-white night classes they're all one issue—that the New Orleans police pretty much like that drug dealers are all killing each other, and that there's no way any of those murders ever gets followed up by the NOPD.

By "drug dealers" he meant black kids from the projects. By "New Orleans police" he meant white cops, though, maybe some of the black cops have gone blind and numb, too. The black politicians certainly have. Too many of them are as sleazy and corrupt, as self-serving and pompous and mean-spirited as their white colleagues. Many of the New Orleans black politicians are Don Kings without the funny hair and quick wit. Like so many black politicians everywhere, they talk talk talk that preacher rap, that boring high-flown rhetoric absolutely void of sense or substance, and the kids keep dying. Most of those politicians would rather be Dr. King than Don King, and they might as well want to be Jesus Christ or Steven Spielberg. Black politicians all over America should stop that preacher crap. Black children need representation, not rhetoric, dead, scabbed over, boring rhetoric.

America needs a Marshall Plan, or at least a G.I. Bill, for its innercities, something big, radical, and dignified, and centered on education. And that's something black politicians will have to take the lead on efficiently and, in the beginning, quietly. Even after the Colleges of Educations are boarded up or redeployed, it's got to go beyond that Empowerment Zone crap. Commerce will take care of itself. The future of American education, indeed of America, is the computer chip and the good mind of a black child. Put state-of-the-art computers at the disposal of every inner-city kid in America, and a creative energy almost unfathomable would be unleashed. Don't mess with them. Just show them how to use the things, and give them access, lots of access, and all those racist clichés about rhythm and potency will collapse upon themselves, and new and exciting cultural and social contingencies will shine forth, and new American art forms will dazzle the world, and Jesus Christ I'm sounding like Jessie Jackson.

Fatherless kids, black and white and other, who are poor don't need bombastic surrogate fathers. They need food, security, and access to the same technologies the rich have.

Often a poor man, spare and suntanned,
stands in battle next to a rich man who
is pale for lack of sun with much
superfluous flesh, and sees him panting
and at a loss. Do you not think that he
would consider that it is through the
cowardice of the poor that people like
that are rich, and one poor man would
say to the other as they met privately:
"These men are at our mercy; they are
no good."

Book VIII 556 d

Poets are famously stupid about politics, and social issues generally. I certainly am. I'll cheerfully opine about anything, and sound pretty good doing it, for about a minute and a half. Then the ranting starts, and that's the poetry part, because that's one important aspect of what poetry is, formal ranting, a sanctioned occasion for ranting (Gerald Stern says something like this in one of his wonderful poems). Even when I'm not writing poetry, I rant after about ninety seconds of discoursing on any subject. I can't help it. It's a genetic thing. Whatever mangled genetic code compelled me to have a mystical experience while taking the garbage out under the stars also compels me to rant. For example, above I ranted about David Duke, black politicians, and giving black kids computers. What the hell do I know about any of that? A little more than squat. A Marshall Plan for inner cities? On what Sunday morning news show did I hear that? Black children dying of shyness? Well, that's original, and profoundly silly, though I half believe it. I half believe a lot of things. Indeed, I half believe everything I believe. The only thing I fully believe is that I love my children with all my heart. After that, I'm full of halves. I half believe there is no God and death is final. I half believe that almost everything that Freud proposed was true. I half believe that in the long run something like global socialism is humanity's only chance for survival, and I half believe that in the short run of, oh, the next century or so post-industrial, global capitalism must run its course. I half believe that art is relevant, and that I'm capable of making a little of it. I half believe cultural pluralism does not necessarily lead to racial hatred and genocide. I half believe that feminism is the most important intellectual/social development since the invention of writing, that it is the most significant paradigm shift in all of human civilization since the emergence of monotheism. I half believe that Ali's second fight with Liston was not fixed. I half believe that UFOs are evidence only of how incredibly stupid and gullible most people are. I half believe Oswald acted alone. I half believe that Shakespeare was Shakespeare. I half believe that MTV is evil. I half believe that the human heart is only healed in the act of forgiving.

People full of half beliefs may rant just fine, but they rarely make good zealots. Most racists—not just dullwits incapable of seeing beyond stereotypes, which are most of us at least some of the time are zealots like Duke, and I sometimes wonder if my penchant for half believing is a matter of nature or nurture; that is, I wonder under what conditions I may have been a True Believer of anything, even a racist vision of reality. What would I have been like if I'd been fed a lot of racist poison as a kid? Dick is certainly a racist, but one didn't see many black fellow travelers in the Republic of Burma Shave, so race was never a topic of conversation, unless Dick was reminiscing about his boyhood, and recalled with sentimental affection Vastigh (pronounced vast/eye; I actually have no idea how to spell it), the black maid who pretty much raised the kids and took care of the house.

Joan was simply enlightened on the issue of race, and I have no idea how she got that way. A few weeks after we'd gotten to Elizabeth City, I called a new friend, a white kid, a nigger. I was so ignorant I wasn't even sure how to use the word. I only vaguely knew it was a word for the folks who lived in all the houses after ours, but I wasn't certain if that was its only designation. Joan heard me, ran out, and told me I was never, under any circumstances, to say that word. She told me it was evil.

I was impressed. I'd never heard her call anything evil before. And I understood, viscerally, from her expression of seriousness, her wholly unironical demeanor, what she meant. How could a young woman from the South, a vaguely Catholic beauty who'd dropped out of school in the eleventh grade, who'd been stupid enough to marry, birth five children by, and follow faithfully a raging, pathologically lying racist lunatic like Dick, how could such a person have achieved enlightenment?

I'd like to think that before she met Dick she'd had a black lover. I doubt it, though, only because it would have been logistically too difficult back then in Norfolk, Virginia. But somehow she knew that racism is evil, that it was important to tell her kids that it is evil, and that the language of racism is evil.

Under what circumstances could I have been a David Duke-type racist? I don't know, but I'm certainly capable of vague loathings. For example, as a waiter I hated Europeans generally because they acted like they didn't understand tipping customs in the United States. I especially hated the French. I wanted to kick the shit out of every Frog who came into the French Quarter restaurants I worked in. Each was rude, demanding, and petty, and reminded me of that evil prick who screamed at me in French when I went to first grade for two weeks in Montreal. And they never tipped! After I'd worked doggedly and elegantly for one Frog and his blowzy American date, lighting cigarettes as soon as they reached their lips, getting the food out with perfect timing and impeccable presentational technique, after doing everything but slowly licking both of them into mutual and protracted orgasm, the pretentious little twit stiffed me. When I returned to the table after dropping the check, over two hundred dollars, amid the small clutter of crumpled napkins, corks, and glasses, was the signed credit card slip with no tip added, and three one-dollar bills.

I ran, literally, out onto the street in my tuxedo, spotted them wedging through a cluster of tourists, ran up behind him, put my hand on his shoulder and spun him around. Then I stuffed the three dollars into his jacket pocket and told him if he ever stepped foot into that restaurant again I'd kick his ass at the door. The woman babbled What's wrong What's wrong and he knew quite well I knew he knew that the gratuity had not been added to the bill, so he said nothing, just stared at me contemptuously, and I screamed at him about the Maginot line, that only the fucking French could have come up with such a cowardly stupid-ass thing as the Maginot line, and that the whole goddamned country should take a fucking shower, then I walked back into the restaurant.

So maybe given a different mother (not genetically but ideologically different), a different life, this biological essence which I am could have developed a social consciousness amenable to the most virulent forms of hatred, or to embracing the most dubious cultural forms. Under no circumstances, however, could I have been persuaded to love the French. Well, maybe Catherine Deneuve. And Madam Bovary and that cheesy little genius who loved her into existence. And there was a little French prize fighter in the '60s and '70s whose name I forget. And the food. And the wines. And Sartre. And Camus. And Rimbaud. And Baudelaire. And that wretched little genius Céline. And Richard Wilbur's Molière. And tongue kisses. And the sound of the language. Christ, if the beautiful bastards would only learn to tip.

The French are probably the earth's most cultured people, and I wish I understood what makes cultured people such assholes. In fact, I wish I understood why assholedness swells in direct proportion to how cultured one is. My brother-in-law, who helped bring the Stones to Prague in early '90 and now owns a successful law practice and spends his summers in the Giant Mountains (anything but) on the northern border of Czecho, told me of a fellow he hired to do some labor around the cottage. The fellow was of hearty Bohemian-agrarian stock, worked hard if a trifle slowly, consumed prodigious quantities of beer while he worked (like most Czech laborers), and when asked after the first ten-hour day of labor how much money he was owed, shyly stated that three hundred crowns, about ten dollars, would more than suffice. At around noon the next day he was asked if he would like some goulash, which he accepted. Then, when offered a knife and fork, he refused politely, asking instead for a spoon, because "I am no intellectual!"

Here was a fellow proud not to be an "intellectual," and who assumed the brazen use of all utensils other than spoons to be the reprehensible behavior of one. At least, however, he had a conception of what an intellectual is, and frankly I don't think he was too far off.

Culture, the code which is meant to set the sensitive/knowing/sophisticated off from the rest of raggedy-ass humanity, is that which is worshipped primarily by second-level intellectuals, and probably begins with eating utensils.

I don't give myself credit for much, but I am proud that from the time I was a kid I have not feigned being cultured; I have not felt the need to. I loved ideas, loved to read, and read broadly and voraciously; doing so I certainly was trying to put distance between my life and the circumstances in which it burned, but not because I wanted to be "one of them," one of the cultured, the sophisticated, perhaps only because I had no models. I certainly put on airs, condescended to people who hadn't read as much as I, but not because I believed that by virtue of reading and thinking—such as the juvenile machinations of mind I squinted or grunted through were thought—I had earned entrance onto some blessed order of Platonic social engineering. The whole thing was deeply personal. I didn't want to be an intellectual, nor in any sense did I seek to be "cultured" if only because I didn't know what that meant. I wasn't trying to join a club; I didn't know such a club existed. I just wanted to be different from everyone around me; I wanted to set myself apart from them even as I was one of them. I wanted to eat goulash with a spoon and read Plato.

A quite gifted, wise, and bright former graduate student of mine, a youthful woman in her fifties, spoke offhandedly once of how her father, a Harvard archeology professor, encouraged conversation about books and ideas every night at the dinner table. I mentioned that I hadn't sat at the same dinner table with my entire family more than two or three times during my entire childhood in the Republic of Burma Shave. That is, I don't recall a single time we all sat down at a dinner table, all seven of us, to partake of a meal one or both of my parents had prepared. We'd crowded together at numerous seedy diners and cafes, but there had been little formality otherwise to our meals. Food was usually something which arrived in a bag that got distributed from the front seat to the back seat. It wasn't until I started working in restaurants that I came to appreciate the formality of eating. In fact, it wasn't until I started working in restaurants that I began to appreciate the formality of anything, the sense in which artifice is as necessary an aspect of life as sustenance itself. I came to realize that holy places through time have been simply where the need for artifice and the holy terror of death have pressed palm to palm. Fine restaurants, great libraries and museums are where the need for artifice disengages a while from the holy terror of death. Engrossing conversation—never gossip, never, never gossip—over a fine dinner with fine wines which all participants consume using appropriate utensils is the height of civility, of civilization, of culture. There is no greater degree of social artifice, of beautiful fakery, or sumptuous highbrow horseshit.

Some nights after all the beautiful faking, my faking it as a truly profes-
sional waiter and my customers faking it as cultured human beings, a
bevy of Arab princes would come in to one particular restaurant where I
worked for over a year. They would always come after all the other cus-
tomers had cleared out, and F, our fat and charmingly polyglot maitre d',
would stick them in one of the banquet rooms, the one nearest the
kitchen. And then the fun began.

They always brought high-priced hookers, two for each of the five of
them, and we were ordered to keep the Dom Perignon rolling. They'd go
through cases of the stuff, at a hundred bucks a bottle, and though those
of us who stayed to help F were weary and sore from the night's work, we
were more than glad to hang around until four or five in the morning for
an extra couple of hundred apiece. Of course F probably walked with a
grand or so, and didn't do much, except talk to them in Arabic, one of his
seven languages. F had gone to no more than a few years of school, but
had gotten great training in France and Italy, and simply had a knack for
languages. He was one of those sexy fat men who looked great in a tux,
and would charm middle-aged women until their drawers got gooey. He
robbed us all of a significant percentage of our tips. But I kind of liked
him. He was refreshingly frank. He insulted us to our faces, and robbed
us likewise.

Those Arab princes poured the Dom Perignon all over each other
and the hookers and even us; we ended up drinking several bottles and
charging them. M, out brilliant, haughty chef, would also hang around for
his cut. The Arab princes would order huge silver platters of French fries,
and M the nervous genius, M whose ice carvings were among the most
dazzling anywhere, whose confection was delicate and exquisite, whose
original dishes were subtle and sumptuous and brilliant, would peel the
fucking potatoes himself, cut them and fry them, and present them with
a flourish, and each platter cost three hundred dollars, of which M got
two. Those Arab princes, those handsome swarthy boys spending their
stern daddies' cash, those men otherwise convinced of their own culture's
moral superiority, a superiority born of women wearing veils and having
no rights to speak of, a superiority born of strict prohibitions on alcohol
and social fraternization between the sexes, were among the crassest,
most dishonest little twits I've ever observed, but God—or Allah—were
they loaded! Each time they came in they dropped the equivalent of the
cost of a mid-range American automobile.

Into the morning hours they railed drunkenly, with actual good
humor, against American society. They laughed at what shits America is
comprised of. We kept pouring and drinking their expensive champagne;
we kept gouging them outrageously and as we did we agreed what shits
we all were, all except F and M, who were European, and therefore slight-
ly superior to the Americans, but the rest of us smiled and nodded and
poured and served; one of the waiters even got a blow job in the pantry
from one of the hookers, but I wouldn't have anything to do with the

women that way. I kind of liked them, though, and appreciated their professionalism, not unlike our own. We were all well-dressed over-priced sluts into the early hours of the morning, prostitutes going through the motions of granting pleasures, motions which were a kind of grotesque artifice, a mockery of the beautiful lie fine dining is supposed to be.

It seems that if a man who in his
cleverness can become many persons
and imitate all things should arrive
in our city and want to give a performance
of his poems, we should bow down before
him as being holy, wondrous and sweet,
but we should tell him that there is no
such man in our city and that it is not
lawful that there should. We would
pour myrrh on his head and crown him
with wreaths, and send him away to
another city.

Book III 398 a

I've over the years heard bright and otherwise well-read folks casually refer to Plato's ejection of the poet from his Republic, but that's not at all what Plato's Socrates proposes. Over the course of Socrates's discussion of art and artists and their relation to his ideal of social order, Socrates simply posits what kind of art and artists would be appropriate, would best encourage the public good as he has argued it. It is not unlike a tenure decision: you have two poets up for tenure, and only one tenure position. One is wildly talented, but by his or her demeanor and the iconoclastic nature of her or his verse, encourages albeit mild disruption. Students under this person's influence tend to be more raucous in other classes, and are quick to dismiss most claims to authority. The other is mildly talented, but encourages in his charges a respect for the institution and its authority. His acolytes get their papers in on time in other classes, and have memorized the MLA style book.

It's never that clear-cut, and actually the former candidate would probably win out maybe not in most, but many cases. We've become more sophisticated in our understanding of human communities and of organizations within those communities. Disruption, a little chaos, must be factored into any consideration, if only because we understand that the Second Law of Thermodynamics is indeed applicable to all systems, not just physical ones. Social forms ceaselessly break down and reconstitute themselves; I mean every minute, every second. We rarely consider how fragile our organizations are, and how resilient. Every company division or university department, no matter how stable it may seem, careens towards extinction every moment it is operating, and almost but not quite simultaneously is reconstituting itself into something stronger or weaker than what it was. Every successful organization needs a quota of Company Men/Women, and needs as well a few, at least one Official

Yahoo, one Designated Wild Thing, a court jester with an actual portfolio.

The Wild Thing does her or his work, is probably even gifted, but by his demeanor, the nature and quality of his presence, is a constant reminder that the social construct is no less an artifice than a musical or poetic formula; the Wild Thing is a double dactyl in the middle of an otherwise pristine Spenserian sonnet. Perhaps tomorrow, or in twenty minutes she'll be an off rhyme in the closing couplet of an Elizabethan sonnet, but she is creative disruption in either case, tending the whole toward chaos, and also, potentially, reinvigorating it, pressing it toward an acceptance of greater and greater diversity within, always within, the structure. Perhaps organizations that are most successful are those in which everyone, at one time or another, gets tapped to be the Designated Wild Thing.

And to the extent that the Wild Thing is institutionalized, hope is, as well, because the Wild Thing is also That Which Doesn't Belong But Is Allowed To Be, and represents a system taking into itself a tiny bit of precisely that which it exists in spite of, and must ultimately be obliterated by.

We're all doomed and we know it. Even before the sun collapses, and the planet rolls into the black hole our White Dwarf will become, the earth will be a toxic dump few of us would want to occupy. I pray to Nothing it happens after my daughters' long and relatively happy lives are over; I pray too that humanity can accomplish numerous more swell and wondrous things before the long slide back into the First Light, but that we're already sitting in the chute waiting for the Big Push is pretty obvious.

Poetry is irrational hope. The contagion magic all poetry came out of is just that, hope against the grain of history, human and cosmic. A Neanderthal—not an interior lineman with a single-digit SAT score, but an actual prehuman—saw lightning strike a mountain peak while he was defecating, and then a herd of furry things broke from a stand of trees; of course, he assumed that an interaction between the lightning and his own feces caused the good hunting fortune, and literally the lightning had scared the herd; but of course our extinct relative assumed a more dynamic causal connection between the three events—shitting, lightning, scurrying herd—and cheerily thereafter grunted on his haunches out in thunderstorms, until a bolt split open his skull. His cousin, Homosapien, painted pictures of the ancient bovines on a cave wall, put on the hollowed-out stinking head of one of the things, played around in the bones scattered about on the cave floor, made sounds like those the furry food made when lolling in the grasslands. He, the imitator, was the more successful poet in the family, though both cousins proceeded on similar assumptions, that they could affect their world positively with sounds and movements, and by interpreting experience. All of those prehuman humans were poets. And those of us calling ourselves poets today are just as stupid as they were. The first humans were all angel fuckers, in unutterable awe of their obviously futile circumstances, assuming divinity a thick dispersal of sorrow and luck, of miraculous connections revealed in the raw facts of simultaneity. Each being, folded into a clan, or alone in a sense no one any longer is capable of understanding, looked up at the stars, and with pungent scents of life filling her head, with the smell of her own feces filling her head, did not imagine, I believe they did not imagine Big Mamas and Big Daddies as the First Cause, but wondered perhaps if they were not in the belly of one hell of a shaggy mammoth, or if in fact one extremely tall fellow didn't hook those tiny fires to the darkness. They must have assumed themselves little gods, of sorts, little gods among big and little hairy gods, and gods that swooped in the air, and buzzed over the piles of shit that were probably everywhere. And the rocks and trees and stones were gods, too, and so were the mushrooms, the ones that killed you and the ones that did not. Nothing was mere. They must have felt a little sorry for the sky, the pitiless sky, often blank, sometimes crowded with clouds or stars, but the very essence of loneliness. They hadn't learned to stick all the world's divinity in the sky, they hadn't learned to suck it out of everything but stupid little altars to be guarded from joy, and screw it into the sky.

Poets are the prototype for the Designated Wild Thing. They are fools, necessary fools. Even wretched poetry is necessary, and very little of it isn't wretched. Just as Plato's puppet Socrates could not conceive of poetry apart from poets, text apart from performance, so the subversiveness of poetry is the subversiveness of poets, which is nothing less than the subversiveness of hope. Even Plato knew he couldn't eighty-six the poet, so he just booted out the really good one. He knew that if you eighty-six entirely the singer of tales, in a few years your republic is death row in Attica or Angola, and your lawyer hates you.

The Republic of Burma Shave was drenched in hope, stupid, sometimes insane hope. We drove from where hope wasn't to where it might be, which, as far as we knew, could be anywhere, and it was therefore everywhere, throbbing, the spongy, indefatigable heart of contingency. My beautiful, insane young father and mother heard it in their heads, that throbbing, and so do I.

> When a wrongdoer is discovered
> in petty cases, he is punished
> and faces great opprobrium, for the
> perpetrators of these petty crimes
> are called temple robbers, kidnappers,
> housebreakers, robbers, and thieves,
> but when a man, besides appropriating
> the possessions of the citizens, manages
> to enslave the owners as well, then, instead
> of those ugly names he is called happy and
> blessed. . .
>
> Book I 344 b-c

My last contact with Chris and Dick was indirect. Dominika was back in Prague on business and I was single-parenting Ema and Anna for a fortnight with a little help from Jarka, a sweet late-twenties Czech on hiatus from the Ph.D. grind at Charles University, in New Orleans working on her English and picking up a little money slaving in a family bakery in Slidell. Jarka, who was helping out the first couple of days of each of the two weeks, was still asleep in Ema's room; Ema and Anna were just rousing from my bed when I heard a banging at the screen door of the front porch. I'd been preparing to enter the shower, so wrapped a towel around my waist, and still crusty-eyed I checked it out.

Three Aryan-looking fellows, casually well-dressed, unsmiling, stood shoulder to shoulder, and one, short but powerfully built, told me to put my hands where he could see them as he flashed a badge and announced that they were federal marshals. I was holding the ends of the towel together behind my back, and I told him that to show him my right hand would require my exhibiting parts of my anatomy he and his colleagues may prefer not to witness; clearly taken aback, he flicked a glance at the well-groomed sourpuss at his elbow, and asked to be let in. I unlatched the screen door with my left hand, and backed up through the front door because the towel did not reach all the way around, and my exposed rear I assumed would be no more interesting to my guests than my front.

I asked permission to put on pants, and felt ridiculous doing so. These assholes were in my house, and I was clean clean clean, not even outstanding parking tickets did I have, and as I jumped into some running shorts, my girls stirred, and Jarka opened the door to the other bedroom. Annie squealed and Jarka scooped her up; I told Jarka, half in pidgin Czech, that these men were police but not to worry; they'd be gone in a minute, and to keep Annie in the bedroom for awhile.

What had I done? I couldn't think of a single illegal act I'd commit-ted in many years. It had been years since I'd ingested any illegal drugs. I'd certainly not stolen anything; the time I ripped off Barbara notwith-standing, I'd never been inclined to steal. Even as a kid the few times I'd stolen, mostly comic books, had made me feel terrible. Only stealing food when I was extremely hungry had not piqued my conscience. I supposed that there were a couple of people who, if found murdered, especially if they'd been beaten to death, would cause investigators eventually to con-sider me a suspect, and that's what I thought as I half-naked entered my kitchen to interact with those three scrubbed and dour white boys with big badges in their wallets. Had someone offed the movie-critic associate dean I'd been battling for years? Or the sweet, profoundly self-deluded thirty year-old ex-expatriate I'd wrenched the Prague program away from? Or—sweet Jesus let it not be—what if Lois. . .

I offered to make them coffee, and felt like an idiot doing so. They declined, obviously uncomfortable; surely they sensed, as those in their profession must in such circumstances, that I was innocent.

And I am, have always been. I can imagine doing evil, but have never committed an evil act. Petty, nasty, insincere, but never evil. The marshals, who looked like Sears Catalogue models and certainly dressed like such soulless creatures, asked to see some ID which I scrambled to show them, and then they asked about Chris, if I'd seen him or heard from Dick, and I sighed, chuckled. I told them that if I were to see Dick and Chris, my strongest impulse would be to kick their asses, that I intensely disliked both my father and youngest brother, and that neither under any circum-stances would ever assume my house to be any kind of safe haven from law-enforcement authorities. I asked what they'd done, and the powerful-ly built little one—I figured he could bench three-fifty—shrugged and said nothing big, just a perjury charge in Virginia, and I didn't quite believe him, at least not the part about its not being a big deal. He asked about Lois, whether she might know anything, and I assured him she wouldn't but he read her address out loud for me to confirm, which I did, and he left his card with a couple of local numbers jotted in pencil. I promised that if I heard anything I'd phone him.

After they left I wished I'd asked a couple of other questions, like what did Dick have to do with any of this? Were they after both Chris and Dick? Surely Dick was too old for his old tricks; surely technology had rendered a petty check kiter like him obsolete. Whatever Chris had done was a felony or the Sears triplets wouldn't have been sniffing after him. Perjury he'd said. In a trial? A deposition? Something regarding Dick?

I stopped wondering. Ema, who'd stood in the hall listening, was a little shaken. I explained to her that my brother and father are bad men, and the police just wanted to know if I'd heard from them. Why are they bad? I don't know. But isn't there some reason? Yes, well, I think my brother's a little bad because he's just imitating our bad father. Why don't I also imitate him, since I'm the oldest? Because I got lucky and found other men to imitate. Like who? Like Ernest Hemingway, Walt Whitman, Gerald Stern, Bruce Boston, Glover Davis, and Bob Jones. Who are they? They're poets, except for the first guy, though he really was a poet. Are they famous? Some are, some aren't. The main thing is they tell the truth, except for Hemingway, sometimes, and never steal anything, except ideas; they steal ideas. Isn't it bad to steal ideas, even? Not if you make something beautiful and true out of them. So if you steal a bunch of stuff from the store and make something beautiful out of it, it's okay? I want to say yes, but to do so would be irresponsible parenting, so I say no, it's not the same thing, because ideas, real ideas, don't really belong to anyone, anyway. When you steal an idea to make art it just means that somebody had used that idea before you, but in fact somebody had used it before him, and somebody before her, on backbackback to prehistoric times, before things got written down, recorded. How many ideas are there? Not very many, maybe five or six. What are they? Well, there's Someday You're Going To Die, So Live Well Right Now; and there's You'd Better Try To Understand Your Own Heart, Because Not To Means Your Life Isn't Worth Much; and there's Nature Is Beautiful And Mysterious And You'd Better Be Good To It And Try Not To Cheat It If You Want To Be Happy; and there's Heroes Always Have Something Wrong With Them That Makes Them Mess Up Their Lives But They Always Keep Their Dignity Even After Messing Up; and of course there's Life Is Full Of Sorrow And The Only Happiness Is The Absence Of Pain; and then there's All The People In Power Are Corrupt And They're Hurting Us So Let's Change Who's In Power. Is that it? Well, I think those are the main ones. Why is my tata so bad? He's confused. About what? About who he is. Kind of like the second one? What do you mean? Kind of like the one about knowing your heart? Yeah, that's it; he didn't try to know his heart, so he was confused and did some bad things. Do I know my own heart? Well, that's kind of why I write. I stole that idea from my favorite poets and friends, that a poem is a way of knowing your own heart. Even if nobody ever reads it, at least it told the truth and helped me know myself a little better, and that's real important. Do you have to write poems to know yourself? Goodness no! The wisest people are often the ones who don't say anything and so don't get noticed. People who make art to know themselves just aren't wise enough to do it quietly.

Annie, who's just begun to walk, waddles in and grabs my leg more to keep from falling than out of affection, though while she's there she hugs it and bites it till I shout in pain and she giggles. Jarka, shy and very bright, comes in and asks nothing but I explain to her—a Czech old enough that three plainclothes federal officers banging on a door in the early morning have a particularly odious resonance—that I have relatives who've gotten into trouble, and that I've done nothing wrong; the marshals were only here for information. She's probably curious, but doesn't press.

When one is forty-five, all the excuses of youth are long gone, though one may still not have shaken the habit of thinking of oneself as young and therefore forgivable, forgivable as only the young are. What does a terrible infant become? A ridiculous middle-aged man or woman, or much quieter. Or ridiculous at his worst, and at her best very quiet.

In my earliest memories, the police were bad. We hid from them. We ducked down in the backseat to confound their headcounts. In my earliest memories I felt I was an outlaw; I couldn't have said so because I didn't understand the concept, but certainly there was an Order, and we, the four, five, six, then seven of us didn't fit into that Order. There were the People Who Lived In One Place, one house in one town or city or out in the country or on a mountain, and then there was Us, in one car after another, passing by all those people and the Order they comprised. When Dick was in prison, we were waiting for him to get out, and that condition of waiting defined our existence, especially Joan's and mine. In our waiting state we were still outside the Order, because we weren't living, we were waiting.

When Chuck and I were adopted we entered the Order, and I have occupied it, uneasily, ever since. But I can't entirely shake the feeling of being an outlaw, though I am a law-abiding citizen. In other words, I have been in the Order for over thirty years but feel more afloat at its murky edges than lodged in its clear and stable center.

Because I run, with Dominika and a very decent guy and good poet named Bill Lavender, a program called the Prague Summer Seminars, I've heard many Czech writers talk about the differences between being an artist under the old regime and being one now. By now, most of them are quite bored with their own stories, their own past heroism, that is, their good-faith exploits against Commie oppression. Each year they lecture a little less enthusiastically, though the Americans grow no less excited to hear them. Almost ten years after the Velvet Revolution, they are even bored discussing how ironically nostalgic they are for the Bad Old Days when at least they were "relevant." Klíma, Vaculík, Stránský, Kriseová, Pekárková— to name but a few— have all pushed on into the New Reality, and though they seem no less miserable than their writings of the '60s and '70s and '80s suggest they had been, they seem to find the new misery preferable to the old.

Whatever socialist ideals I once fancied, my decade-long intermittent residency in Prague has not shattered but buried, maybe forever, maybe not. So many hours of my young adulthood were spent pouring over Lefty philosophy and social and literary theory that the paradigms of Leftist sentiments and modes of perception are scorched somewhere behind my eyes, as indelible as the bogus after-image on the Shroud of Turin.

And yet in the deepest chambers of what I am, where a boy still ducks down when he sees a police car, I am an outlaw, someone temperamentally incompatible with ideological structures in which the individual must give himself over to the wisdom of the collective. I'm actually better suited to functioning in top-down authoritarian structures (not that I've ever actually experienced one outside of organized sports and innumerable jobs in restaurants) than in goosey collectives in which there are cheerful honkings of egalitarian bliss, but which are no less repressively hierarchical than daddy-centered systems. I'd probably have been a better Fascist than Commie, but of course history shows that there wasn't a spit of difference between them, except, perhaps, that which was purely ethnic. Communism became Slavic Fascism. It turned out not to have a hell of a lot to do with Marx, who was a poet, an angel fucker, and an intellectual to the bone, and would have wept if he'd been exhumed and revived and propped up to chat with Brezhnev for ten minutes. He'd have wept to view a Moscow May Day Parade circa 1973, especially if he'd had to stand around and shoot the breeze, on the ridiculous raised stage overlooking Red Square, with those bushy-browed fat-fuck alcoholic automatons who ran the show with ol' Bregie. All indications are they were semiliterate, myopic and profoundly ruthless, and wouldn't have known what to do with a real idea if they'd stepped in one. What would Marx have thought of Premier Lenin, who was just hitting puberty when Marx died? They'd probably have gotten along fine for a couple of hours, but two guys who want to be Jesus can't occupy the same space for long. What would Marx have thought of Stalin? Jesus and the Perfect Asshole can't occupy the same space, breathe the same air, for ten seconds, because the Perfect Asshole, being perfect, is unredeemable. What would Marx think of what has come of his ideas? His and Engels' and all the other beautiful Nineteenth Century Lefties'?

A couple of years ago I was standing by the window of a restaurant overlooking "Long Street" in Prague 1, chatting with Arnošt Lustig. We were sipping our beers, waiting for the rest of that year's faculty to arrive for dinner. Arnošt is a beautiful, foxy, sexy geezer whose smile is unkillable, and who is witty and funny and nasty and deeply human. Arnošt, after the train carrying him and many others from Auschwitz to Buchenwald— where they were to die immediately— got bombed by an American plane that mistook it for a troop transport, escaped into woods, made it back to Prague and joined the Resistance. He became a communist, joined the Party early on, and began to fall out with the authorities only because of his vocal support for Israel. Arnošt, flashing his beautiful, nasty smile, stood with me by the window chatting about recent developments in the Czech Republic. I complained about the ashen-faced oldsters who still haunted the counters of hotels and stores, still waited tables and generally still were the gatekeepers of most public services. They were the proud "workers" of the Old Order, and surely now are pissed that their status has diminished even as their tasks— mostly irrelevant make-work— have not changed. One such fellow, a petulant scawler who manned the desk of the university-owned hotel where some of our faculty were staying, had been so rude to two of our people they'd begged to be moved. As I told this to Arnošt, he shook his head and chuckled, looked away. He'd spent twenty years in exile in America, teaching and continuing to write his woeful and beautiful fiction about life in the camps. But he knew what I was talking about. His eyes got a little sad as he gazed into the street where dazed tourists gawked and hustled among poker-faced Slavs, and he said, almost in a whisper, "They fucked up a beautiful idea for a hundred years."

"They" were the assholes who turned Communism into a religion, and by so doing repeated the errors of all religions of all time; they were the men who never read Marx and Engels except through the filter of Lenin (it is amazing how few Czechs have read even Marx's major works). Poetry and science are the enemy of orthodoxy, and Marx--I'm not qualified to say if he succeeded; probably not—desired profoundly to make both a science and an art of living. The Party, by its very nature, could only exist relative to orthodoxy, and so a beautiful liquid idea got frozen.

The establishing of temples, sacrifices,
and other forms of service to the gods,
spirits, and heroes; then again the burials
of the dead and the services which ensure
their favour. We have no knowledge of these
things and in establishing our city we shall
not, if we are wise, acccept any other advice
or use any other than our ancestral guide.

Book IV 427 b

I can't remember Joan's face or voice. I was thirteen when I last saw her.
I should be able to recall everything about her, but when I conjure her
the visual image is not so blurred as abstracted. Her reality, in my
memory, is the idea of her; it loops back upon itself such that all of its
minute particulars get dragged into a gentle drift of generality.

There are four of her. The young, beautiful woman who laughed a
lot, whom I could make laugh, whom I worked hard to entertain. There
was the woman who wept convulsively on whatever bed was near. There
was the dark head I stared at from the back seats of dozens and dozens of
stolen automobiles. Then there was the dying person who occupied the
very heart of despair. What might she have been? What other life might
she have fashioned before the disease got her?

She dropped out of high school in the eleventh grade, after receiving
an F in an English class. I recall her telling me that she'd loved reading,
loved English classes, and failing that one crushed her and she dropped
out of school.

Could it be that some heartless bastard of an English teacher tipped
the first domino, that Joan stood before many rows of black blocks, and
that one or two even meant success at something, a little happiness, and
that some prick of an English teacher fucked her, figuratively, and by so
doing engendered, in a manner of speaking, an English teacher? The
irony is too thick, too hilarious, too ugly. But I do recall, or seem to, that
the teacher was male, that she referred to him as a stern, mean man.

In Elizabeth City and in Norfolk Joan read voluminously. She got
stacks of books from the library, and after she'd put us all down read into
the pre-dawn. Only now am I realizing that she was so distracted in the
mornings, so out of it, so lethargic, such a bad manager of our lives
because she was sleepy all day, especially in the mornings, and that she
lived for the evenings when she could read. And I don't think she read
trash, but I don't recall what she read, just that the books were thick and
there were several and she exchanged them weekly.

A generation later, looser standards would have meant that she'd not have flunked eleventh-grade English and would have graduated. She'd probably have been encouraged to go to college, and would have been able to get student loans and major in English, for surely she would have taken literature courses and not gotten pregnant when she was nineteen, and again when she was twenty-one, again when was twenty-three, again when she was twenty-four, and again when she was twenty-six. By the time she was twenty-six, she'd have been well on her way to finishing graduate school. She wrote literally thousands of pages of letters to Dick when he was in prison. All that reading, all that writing—in terms of the time and effort—were no less than what a person does for a graduate degree. She had no mentor, no direction, no fellowship with people who shared similar interests. But Joan was a reader, a writer. She was a terrible mother, that is, a terrible manager of children, but was a great friend for a boy she made grow up too fast, whom she fashioned into the Telemachus, her Oldest Son, her surrogate male companion when Dick was in prison.

I should have gone to her in the early '70s; upon returning from Japan I should have found her—it would have been easy—and stayed with her until she died. I'd be a better human being now if as a young man I'd had the courage to find her and read to her and help tend to her unto death. I should have been with her when she died. But I was fucking and taking drugs and reading books and attending classes that were irrelevant and writing wretched poems. Barbara made me feel that my having any contact with Joan would have been somehow an insult to her, Barbara, but I can't blame Barbara for my young-man's narcissism, my self-absorption, my cowardice. Barbara's agenda was one of dominance and humiliation, a fairly easy one to ignore, subvert, simply by staying away.

I didn't know Joan would die so soon. I'd heard that people with the disease even got better sometimes. Why didn't I at least try to find her, phone her? I suppose that though I didn't want to deny my past, nor did I wish to reconnect with it, begin living it again. I'd become comfortable with the idea that my life divided between two family configurations, one past and one present, and though my present family was contrived and cool, my past family was too much hunger and despair.

I know that I laughed a lot as a child, that I knew wonder and affection and excitement, but what I recall most clearly is leaden unhappiness, and endless gray sky and us rolling endlessly beneath it. I never had any sense that we were going anywhere but to the next city, and when we got there I was soon restless to roll on to the next. By the age of four I was conditioned to "duck down" whenever I saw a highway trooper because one of the indications that we were who we were was the number of children in the car at any given time. To most who saw us we were a beautiful if ragged family on vacation, or in transit to a new job and new life. Joan was beautiful, Dick was handsome and smooth and we kids were, no doubt, darling.

Perhaps I came to hate Joan as much as I hated Dick for the weird life they'd given me. Surely she was as much to blame. Perhaps as a young man I simply wanted all that pain, all that familial despair to remain in a manageable past, manageable in the sense that memory is an organizing agent, a process that shapes the constellations comprising us, the beautiful fuzzy lights in all their meaningless patterns, even as we are comprised as well of Dark Matter, all the redundant passing seconds linking uncountable sighs and glances, farts and nudges.

But I never hated her any more than I hated Dick. I loved them both, and as a middle-aged man now see them in their youth and wish I could reach back and somehow protect them, help them.

How did they manage such a life with so many kids? Taking brief trips with my two is harrowing; I could never live on the road with them; I simply couldn't pull it off. The details, the details of child care are overwhelming if you do it right. Of course my parents simply did it wrong. We'd go days without bathing, sometimes days without eating much. We, especially I, got beaten abusively and learned to shut up when told to. But even bad parenting is hard work when two, three, four, five children are involved. Dick drove eight, twelve, twenty hours at a stretch, and when he wasn't driving worked his scams. Joan never, never got a break from us, was never not with us. What horror those two beautiful and glib, incredibly naive and emotionally stupid, young people brought upon themselves. What horror and wonder I am heir to.

My new family was Normalcy. No matter how much Barbara pissed me off, no matter how oddly pathological she became in verbal abusiveness, her meanness, she was my link to Normalcy, and she discouraged me from even talking about my abnormal past. In a sense she gave me a kind of permission to ignore Joan, to act and feel as though Joan were already dead.

I suppose because she figured we could use whatever structure we could get, marshalling insitutional Normalcy, Barbara forced Chuck and me to attend the Baptist church on Coronado for that year and a half or so after we returned from Sasebo and before I turned eighteen. Barbara and Ray and their three kids never attended, not once, but Chuck and I were compelled, with no explanation, to go. Joan had sent us to Baptist summer day camps because they fed us, though sometimes only cookies and Kool Aid. Relatives in Elizabeth City sometimes dragged us off to church on Sundays. At the Baptist church on Coronado they fed us Kentucky Fried Chicken after the service, and I squirmed impatiently through the fire and brimstone to get to the breasts and thighs, my favorite parts of the chicken, and what parts of the tender daughters of the pious parishioners I glanced at twitchingly as the preacher roared and almost wept.

I tried to believe, even when I was sixteen and seventeen, but couldn't quite push my load of compulsions to the peak of my fear that it could coast down the other side by that momentum called faith. Just couldn't do it, couldn't do the faith thing, couldn't give myself over to a beautiful idea radiating prohibitions and fantastic promises, the latter but functions of the former. I stared at that image, a guy hanging on a cross, and felt only twinges of fear I'd known as a child when Christ had tried to eat my face in a lucid dream. The preacher, a large fortyish blond doughy fellow with a nasty little translucent 'stache, a Lieutenant Commander on the North Island Naval Air Station, worked himself each week into such a state he scared me a little, but everybody seemed to love him; the old women shook their heads yes unceasingly during his performance and smiled so big they seemed agents of such a bliss as only a God who had suffered for them would allow. And suffering quavered in every word spoken by the preacher, and every word sung, mumbled or lip-synched by the small congregation that packed the tiny church each Sunday. The idea of Christ's suffering got rammed home every eight seconds, about the same duration as that between my thoughts of pussy, and sometimes in those eight seconds I wondered how bad it really was, that dying on a cross thing.

Not that I thought it wasn't horribly painful, a really ugly way to go up the ol' Pipe; I just figured it wasn't any worse for Him than for all the other poor schmucks who got turned into advertisements, living (briefly) billboards for human viciousness, public service announcements communicating succinctly and most effectively that one must not fuck with the State. How did that guy go from being just another Don't Fuck With Caesar billboard to being the Ultimate Sufferer and Border Guard to Eternal Orgasm?

Good PR of course, and in the spirit of If The World Hands You a Lemon, etc., when the little rabbi got splayed, that After Three Days thing got concocted, and abracadabra, redemption was born.

I love the idea of redemption, and in that sense I'm a Christian. It was the one idea I got out of all those stupid, pathological preachers I had to listen to as a kid, that everybody gets second chances (sometimes several) and each Second Chance is bought with Forgiveness.

I'm a better Christian than most faith-brimming mean-spirited assholes—like Dick and the vast White Trash Klan of semiliterate half-humans he has joined—will ever be, because I forgive deeply and fundamentally individuals I'd enjoy slapping senseless, like Dick and his ilk, like Newt Gingrich and his ilk, like Nancy Reagan and her ilk, like the entire Louisiana State Legislature and their ilk, like David Duke and his ilk, like Rupert Murdock and his ilk, like Henry Kissinger and his ilk, like the entire nations of France and Germany and their ilk. In one grand sweep of my hand, I forgive them all, and wish them no harm, except for a quick smack upside the head which I would gladly administer.

I (half) believe that the genius of Christianity is the forgiveness/redemption equation. It seems that some deep truth of the human organism gets touched by that equation. The whole process of self-revelation which is the soul of Freud—my patron saint—is a process of redemption, and I think that for all his harking back to the Greeks it was primarily in the footsteps of another Jew that Freud proceeded.

Forgiveness seems necessary indeed on an organismic, hardly a "spiritual," level. Every time we catch cold or get an earache or develop cancer our bodies beg forgiveness, and in healing are redeemed, reborn into healthfulness, or into painless sleep or death. Each time we are filled with sorrow or rage the weeping or howling is a movement towards forgiveness, notwithstanding vengeful acts, passionate acts of revenge which are simply failures to forgive, the heart's bad timing.

Surely, I said, once our city gets
a good start, it would go on growing
in a circle. Good education and
upbringing, if preserved, will
lead to men of a better nature,
and these in turn, if they cling
to their education, will improve
with each generation both in
other respects and also in their
children, just like other animals.

Book IV 424 a

R ight before Chuck and I were adopted, a few weeks after leaving
Joan and the "little kids" in Norfolk, I spoke with Joan on the
phone, and after thirty-two years I'm just recalling that I did. She
wanted us to come back, but was willing to give permission for the adop-
tions. She wanted to know what I wanted.

I recall now the sadness in her voice, the flatness of it, though I can't
recall her voice or how she said what she said precisely. I was reading Ian
Fleming's *On Her Majesty's Secret Service* and eating better than I ever had,
and living in a house like none I'd ever occupied, and kissing frequently
two girls in that palm-lined neighborhood in San Diego, and I certainly
didn't want to go back to that school in Norfolk where a large fellow was
waiting to hurt me, and where the band teacher was probably furious
about the new trumpets Dick had hocked somewhere in the Deep South
for gas money. Raymond had told us we'd be moving to Sasebo, Japan in
a few months, and that seemed just fine to me.

I told her I was happy where I was. I think she wept, and I think I
did, but I can't really recall if either of us did. I was to choose between a
sick and profoundly sad and impoverished mother and one I hardly knew
but who seemed healthy and rich and who fed me great food and often. I
was to choose between misery and hope, and even then realized that that
wasn't much of a choice, because at that age I felt only the slightest sense
of familial duty, and as I look back now impose unfairly a mature sense of
familial duty on that boy who just wanted to be normal, and in America,
in the America I had seen, most people were rich, that is, they lived in
nice houses and there was a father who worked at a good job and people
dressed well and didn't lie, and kids didn't have to duck down in cars. In
the America I had seen most were prosperous; even in the projects the
insides of people's apartments were much better than ours, with nice pic-
tures on the walls and clean floors and furniture that wasn't ripped up.

Wherever we would be, from the time Chris was two, he would need a yaya (both a's flat) to go to sleep, a pinch of gray cotton from the rips in the arms of chairs and couches. Whenever we received from clucking relatives a "new" piece of furniture, it was understood that Chris, the baby, would now have a fresh source of yayas. The nightly ritual was that Chris would waddle to one of the ripped patches and choose the perfect puff of soft fiber. The rest of us, including Joan, rooted him on in the selection process. When he'd chosen, he'd hold the cotton to his cheek, rub his cheek with the cotton as he hustled off to bed, where he'd rub his cheek with that pinch of cotton unto sleep. In the morning he'd throw it away. For some reason each yaya was good but once.

Couch arms would be plucked down to the wood in a few weeks, and it was accepted that when all the yayas had been harvested from one arm, Chris would start working on another. Over the course of a year the entire living room in our second house in Elizabeth City was destroyed. Wood was exposed in both arms of the couch and in both arms of the two chairs, large lakes of wood in the dark upholstery, and that was just fine with Joan, because her baby needed yayas to sleep.

What choice did I have? Barbara's house was so nice, so normal. Joan was sick and needed help with almost everything.

I wish I could recall that last conversation. I wish I could recall if we wept, or if I felt anything but relief at the opportunity to be normal.

Sometime in the mid-'70s, Robert L. Jones housesat for Glover Davis while he, Glover, was on sabbatical from State. Inasmuch as I at the time was for all intents and purposes homeless—bouncing between several women's apartments—I was happy to apartment-sit for Bob. I now realize that he didn't particularly need me there, and asked me to "take care of" his place purely as an act of kindness to me. He knew how I was living.

Bob was eight years older than I, which at the time seemed like a lot. He seemed to have known all the poets whose works I admired, and introduced me to the works of dozens more. Bob was my teacher and I didn't even know it. In his little studio apartment he had three ceiling-high bookcases packed with first editions of contemporary poetry books. I've never seen a finer collection in any library, and only Dave Smith's rivals it. I'm sure there are hundreds of collections just as fine, but that one was mine for most of a year, and I read all of it, every single volume of the hundreds there, the more than a thousand books of the best verse that had been published from 1960 to 1975. Every night I ignored my course work, or half-assed got through it, and then knocked off three, four, five volumes from Bob's collection.

Then I'd get together with Bob, or Bob and Bruce Boston, or Bob and Bruce and an odd fellow named Jay, or with Ca or Barbara Cully—dear Barbara, my wise and brilliant sister poet—and talk about books, about poems, about ideas. Bruce and Marsha Boston and Bob Jones, old friends from Fresno and then UC-Irvine where Bruce and Bob did their graduate work, tolerated me with much, at times wary, affection. Bruce Boston was my teacher, too, and much more ostentatiously so than Bob. Bruce

Boston, one of the smartest and funniest and most gifted men I've ever known, is a born teacher, someone for whom teaching is an art, and had he not been so blessed with teacherly talent his writerly talent, which is considerable, would have shined so brightly he'd have surely been one of the major voices of his generation (God, how hollow such designations sound), on the same plane with Bob's and Bruce's dear friend Larry Levis. Bob, too, had enormous talent, but rather than having the light of one talent outshine the light of another, as has been true for Bruce, Bob was just slow, slow as rust, a watched pot, a sloth. Bob was so predictably slow friends would make their dates with him considerably earlier than he was actually required. He worked constantly but slowly, very, very slowly. He turned out one lovely collection of verse in addition to a chapbook, and numerous splendid translations of Mexico's leading poets. His Spanish was better than fluent, and he was deeply admired by a wide range of Mexican artists and intellectuals. Bruce and Bob were like older brothers to me, one mercurial and intellectually exciting and the other gentle and wise. Temperamentally, I was more like Bruce, and I took him as a role model, imitating as best I could the beautiful music of his voice, his commanding physical posture, his Californian fuck-you-and-kiss-me attitude toward the world of others. Much of what is "original" in my early work, and surely what is is only conditionally so, is not what I got from the hundreds of books I was reading, the thousands of poems, but from the music of Bruce Boston's speaking voice, one which, back then at least, was too rarely pressed into the service of his own sweet art.

But it was Bob who taught me the most by taking me more seriously than I deserved to be taken, by listening to me and correcting me, but so subtly I didn't know I was being corrected. It was Bob who would talk with me endlessly about books, poems, ideas, in his kitchen as he stirred an eternal pot of pinto beans, or in his little living room where he drank, constantly and oh so slowly, talked and drank each hour more slowly—always coherently—until finally he ceased, his voice just quit, and he sat upright, asleep, a glass in his hand.

Sometimes I took the glass out of his hand and let myself out, or gently pushed him over and covered him up and let myself out. Bob patched together gigs at several junior colleges and universities, living for years close to the ol' soup bone, but decently. After I left San Diego, I came back only rarely to give readings and visit. When I saw Bob, he always seemed fine, a little puffier, but fine. I'd heard he'd gone deeper into the bottle, the eternal fifth of the cheapest vodka he kept in the freezer, was even homeless for awhile. I heard that friends—organized by the beautiful Elise Miller, beautiful in the most enduring sense—pitched in to give Bob a monthly stipend while he was living in his car. I heard that he became, for awhile anyway, unemployable.

But then he pulled his life together, got and kept a job, I presume got some kind of control over his drinking, and began to write and translate in earnest. I heard that one day a letter arrived in his mailbox announcing that he'd been selected to receive a relatively large sum of money to live in Mexico and translate Mexican poetry, enough money, considering how modestly he was able to live, to sustain himself for years. That letter was in his mailbox when he dropped dead on his sidewalk, I'm told, a few yards from his door.

Bob's apartment, the one he let me stay in while he took care of Glover Davis's German shepherds, was in Hillcrest directly in the flight path of one of the main runways of the San Diego airport. Every morning at exactly 6:48 or 6:51 or 7:02 or whatever it was, the passenger jets started coming in, clearing the roof by no more, literally, than a hundred feet. It was a throaty, mumbling racket one could not grow used to, but to which one could resign oneself and having done so, perversely enjoy. They came in base-register waves of seven, eight, or nine, one screech-wrapped-in-a-bowel-scraping-rumble after another. They were why Bob had gotten the place so cheaply, and why he'd leapt at the opportunity to spend some months in Glover and Sandy Davis's quiet little house overlooking an empty canyon. Those planes plucked at my liver every morning as I lay strapped to Bob's rock-hard bed, and whatever the world was doing with the fire I'd given it, my torment seemed extreme. But those glass-rattling, bone-jarring tons were actually just the price I paid for Bob's remarkable poetry collection, and to have a place to bring women rather than always having to stay with them, though regulars learned that sleeping over was unwise, and so that nerve-shattering traffic at least served to insure I'd be alone in the mornings, which was as I wished.

The greatest blessing of that time in my life was the brutal honesty of Glover Davis, Bruce Boston, Bob Jones, Barbara Cully, and Ca regarding my bad poems. In fact, brutal honesty was at the core of the ethos of that community of poets, an import from Fresno, where all but Ca, Barb and I had originated. Everyone seemed genuinely to desire that everyone else write good, emotionally honest poems, and took it personally when someone didn't. It was a quite wonderful little community of poets for awhile, angel fuckers taking themselves and each other just seriously enough. Ca was the star, and didn't get along with Glover Davis, her colleague at State, but she was very close to Bruce and Marsha and Bob and Barb, and we constituted an odd family of sorts. Everyone tolerated my boyishness, a quality I'd maintained beyond its chronological appropriateness, though one which I realize now was a compensation for having had to grow up so fast, for having had to be so serious, so sad for so long as a child. My twenties were a protracted adolescence, a quite joyful time I cannot regret. And those dear people who tolerated me, instructed me and took me on my own boyish terms, I'll always recall with the deepest affection, especially—in addition to the ones I've mentioned—the sweet and bright Larry McCaffery, Cinda Gregory, and Elise Miller.

I lived on city buses between the San Diego State campus and wherever that week I was sleeping, sometimes in Coronado, though as the '70s proceeded and especially after I returned from my first summer in New

Orleans and at Breadloaf, less frequently. I worked in restaurants and on campus and I taught karate and somehow, somehow, made enough money to eat everyday. I also sold dope, though not much and not for long, and constantly met women who would have sex with me. And probably not because I was a particularly good lay, but because I was, as Barbara Cully once referred to me to our friends, a "professional waif." Someone told me this years later when the sting of it would be mild, and it's a perfect characterization. I was tall, thin, and a little pretty. I had long thick hair and walked barefoot through the streets of San Diego. Because of my karate training, I was quick and physically confident, and didn't mind chancing a fistfight with just about anyone, but mainly lived for poetry and sex, and advertised that fact brazenly by how I lived and carried myself, and women probably took me for the fool I was, but a safe one, a sweet and safe fool, a tough but boyish, even girlish, fuck, one who should not be depended on for anything but a little fantasy, a little false intimacy. What a harmless little prick I was, what a boyish pleasure seeker, a professional waif. And of course heckling that sweet kid in Prague I was heckling that childish man I'd been.

In 1969 a young man, a boy, really, named Jan Palach set himself on fire to protest the Soviet invasion of Czechoslovakia. In snapshots he has a sweet face, full of Slavic resignation, full of sighs. I've seen so many kids who look like him on the streets of Prague, especially coming and going around the street and building bearing his name, the building that houses the Charles University Faculty of Philosophy and Arts.

Lyric poetry is a function of youth, and when one continues making poems into midlife and beyond, it is always in relation to one's youth; Yeats's late great stuff said Fuck You I'm Old But I'm Still Singing, as though to do so were a little naughty, and it was, gloriously so. The lyric impulse past a certain age is a kind of spiritual Viagra, so naughty, sweet and nasty. Perhaps this is because the symbolic order of which lyric poetry partakes resides wholly in the body's own creative impulse, for women no less than for men, and is primarily a function of youth.

That boy thought about it a long time. As I recall the story, he and some friends had formed a horrible little club. And they were all going to burn themselves in public, one after another, to protest the invasion. They drew lots or something, and Palach won, getting to go first. He didn't die immediately. He lived a few days in what was surely hellish pain before dying in the hospital.

He became a symbol. Buildings and streets got his name after the Velvet Revolution, and indeed the Velvet Revolution itself on some psychical-cultural level was inspired by him.

I imagine that kid the moment he set himself ablaze; I imagine the moment all that symbolic beauty which motivated him turned into nothing but the most excruciating pain imaginable. All poetry turns to shit in that moment, and everyone who would fuck angels in that moment becomes something more despicable than the most loathsome pedophile.

For that boy was the perfect lyric poet, and every adolescent who commits suicide for love or an idea is a perfect lyric poet, a perfect angel fucker. For a moment they become living symbols; for a moment each gets generalized, departicularized with emotional generality. For a moment, Love, Freedom, or even Meaninglessness, not acne, blue balls, or a sense of particular awkwardness among particular peers or a sense of humiliation at the figurative or literal hands of a caretaking adult, defines the shiny symbolic act of self-destruction, though surely that moment is followed hard by the truth, the horrible truth of the organism's dread of extinction. Surely Palach's symbolism, to himself, as he cooked, became irrelevant. Surely within moments of the act there was only horror, and his body's desire to escape the pain and be whole again.

What wretched pornography is our love of ideas and principles when young people, who love purely, are moved to sacrifice, the profoundest lyric expression in the universe, and the greatest lie.

I started thinking of myself as a poet immediately after the mystical experience I had while taking out the garbage when I was eleven. But I really didn't have a word for what I knew I'd become. I connected my life-changing experience to the odd little texts I was producing in vague religious terms. The words "poem" and "poet," though they occupied the nether reaches of my vocabulary, never occurred to me as a designation for the products of my new activity and for what I'd become by engaging in that activity. But Mrs. Tunstle soon told me what I'd become.

I'd not attended much of the fourth grade because Dick got out of prison early in the autumn of that year and we hit the road. Luckily, he was busted less than a year later, and I was able to attend all of the fifth grade while we lived in the projects in Norfolk. I suppose they tested me and I performed well enough to go into the chronologically appropriate grade, as did Chuck, Terry and Art. We'd missed almost an entire year of school, but somehow got into our appropriate grades. I'd missed, practically speaking, most of the first grade as well. At that point, I'd attended two full years of school in Elizabeth City, and that was really about it. I'd sat in a few classrooms, learning virtually nothing, when I was of the age to attend first grade. I attended a few weeks of fourth grade in Elizabeth City, and then sat in classrooms God-knows where, somewhere in Arizona, I think, and a week or two in California, Sacramento, maybe.

Anyway, I entered fifth grade with roughly twenty months of schooling under my cracked and peeling Salvation-Army belt (all of our clothes were from the Salvation Army) rather than the thirty-six everyone else came in with, but I did fine; the lovely old woman with long white hair tightly coiled on her head seemed to love her job. There was one extremely smart girl in the class; she had curly blond hair and buck teeth and was pretty much boss of the room. There were several other kids who seemed generally brighter than I, but I was commended often for my vocabulary, was told that I seemed to know more words than the other kids (one day I muddled through a definition of "obituary," and I really thought I was just guessing, but somehow I nailed it, much to the old woman's delight).

But my obsession in fifth grade was who I would get for sixth grade, and along with everyone else I feared, deeply, with a biblical intensity, that I would end up in Mrs. Tunstle's sixth-grade class.

She was gaunt, tall, severe, efficient, demanding, and no motherer. Every teacher I'd had mothered a little, especially my fifth-grade teacher who, when kids came to school too hungry to learn, which I recall happened with some frequency, she took them to the coat room and gave them milk and crackers; we'd wait until they finished before the class began. My fifth-grade teacher hugged us all, a lot. She was wonderful, and I can't remember her name.

But Mrs. Tunstle. . . she didn't hug. She was no one's surrogate mother. In fifth grade I'd see her monitoring her charges during recess and get chills. She failed kids, held them back, a lot of them. She could make kids cry simply by staring at them. Surely she was the witch who, since I could remember, haunted my hours before sleep. Surely she was evil.

And when she walked into the classroom that first day chills enveloped me, and surely everyone else in the room. We'd dreaded that moment for the entire previous year; some kids dreaded that moment all the way back in first grade, for Mrs. Tunstle's reputation had dark, mythical resonances that could be evoked almost anywhere. "Jesus, you got *her*? Your ass is cooked, boy," a neighbor's mother chortled to me as she hung clothes. Even Rudy, fifteen years-old in the sixth grade—a "special" class—and who was big as a man and kicked the shit out of everybody but me; Rudy who saved me from getting beat up by three white kids who chased me through the woods for no reason I can recall; Rudy who was dull and angry and probably seriously dangerous but who for some reason kind of liked me, even Rudy feared Mrs. Tunstle. In fact, when Rudy rampaged it was she, not the "special" teacher, who handled the situation, staring up into his face and speaking to him with a calm that dripped power. No one, not even God, fucked with Mrs. Tunstle.

So when she walked into the room, when my deepest terror was suddenly confirmed, I dropped my head and prayed that Dick would come tonight and drive me away from that doom.

She was wonderful, the first strong woman I was to know who didn't derive her authority from some vague maternal imperative. She drilled us in math, and there was a black kid named Edward who was very good with numbers. His clothes were worse even than mine, torn up and filthy, and he didn't care for much else that went on at school, but he loved messing with numbers, and she pushed him, pushed him harder than she pushed anyone else in math, and as I recall that's how she related to each of us; she found out what each of us—black, white, or Asian—was good at and pushed. Tony, a tall Filipino boy, was good at drawing and so in addition to what everyone else did she made him draw a lot. Freckled Susan was good at spelling, and so on. I was horrible at everything, or I was going through a phase when I couldn't remain focused on anything.

I was thinking a lot about Dick being in prison, and Joan was getting sick though she didn't know from what, and she was beginning to spend time with that odd man we called Mr. Terry, and I was reading books to keep from thinking about how sad I was, mostly science fiction, and D.C. and Marvel comics, and then one night taking the garbage out I looked at the stars and didn't think of heaven or spaceships or anything but the darkness and the little lights strewn through it, and I was filled with a joy I am still drawing on, and wrote down how I felt, and didn't know what to call it, so I showed it to Mrs. Tunstle, and she told me it was a poem, and she smiled at me, and all her severity, her power to terrify, melted away.

She had us write a play about ancient Egypt. She stood at the board and we dictated the story and the dialogue. She told us that Egyptians were Africans, dark-skinned people who created the first great civilization, a point not lost on the two thirds of the class who were black. We wrote the play, made the costumes and gave two very successful performances. I was a high priest and wore much tinfoil around my arms and neck and on my head. Having contributed to the writing of much of the play, I took an author's pride in the rousing applause we received.

She should have flunked me. Though I'd participated with vigor in the writing and production of the play, and continued to write poem after poem and show them to her, I didn't do much else, except play in the band.

One day she asked if any of us wanted to try out for the band, and about ten of us did. She lined us up and marched us to the auditorium where the hopefuls of several other classes were waiting. The band teacher held up a clarinet and asked who wanted to learn to play it, and I threw up my hand and fluttered it. He walked through the crowd studying mouths, picked several and told them to stand on the stage. Then he held up a trumpet, and with everyone else I threw up my hand, both hands, and fluttered them. Again he passed among us studying mouths, and picked several and told them to stand on the stage. Then he held up a French horn. . .

Everyone was on the stage, staring down at me and the band teacher, a chunky little white guy still in his twenties, though to us he was just a Grown-up, who looked somberly into my eyes and asked my name. On the table around which the clarinet, the trumpet, the trombone, the snare and bass drums, and the French horn lay in frozen orbit, stood—and yes, as the others lay prostrate it stood tall on its battered bell among them— a gray and dented b-flat upright bass, the tuba.

The pudgy little guy told me the tuba was the "backbone of the band," probably the single most important instrument, and he wanted me to learn to play it, to be the backbone of the band.

I was honored. It was bigger than all the others; it was glorious. Surely the fact that at that age my face seemed little more than a support system for a pair of lips influenced the band teacher's decision to honor me thus, but I didn't stare up at my fellow soon-to-be musicians, most of whom were black, and scrutinize their mouths. I had no idea why I was being honored, and asked no questions. I lugged that battered horn home almost every night and Joan let me fill the house with teeth-rattling blasts of farting scales, up and down, down and up, for almost an hour, or until the other kids were weeping in misery. I wrote poems, read comic books, played tuba, got into fights, and otherwise was sad and distracted. Mrs. Tunstle should have flunked me, but one day near the end of the school year she caught me yet again staring off instead of doing whatever scholastic task she'd assigned, and grabbed my hand and half dragged me into the hall, holding her grade book with the other hand. She opened the book to the back and ran her finger down a column of numbers. She told me to look at a number; it was by my name, and she pointed out that it was the highest number in the column. She said it was the result of some standardized tests we'd taken earlier in the year. She explained to me that I'd scored the highest of anyone, and that she was sending me to a special school over the summer, one for gifted students and that they'd pay me for going there and give me a big breakfast every morning and then a lunch, and that all the kids there would be the smartest from their schools and that we'd all be encouraged to do what we were good at. I asked her if that meant she wasn't going to flunk me, and she said she would not keep me in the sixth grade.

That summer school—they didn't really pay me to go, but paid for my transportation by city bus to get there—wasn't particularly memorable, except that the teacher gave me poems to read and let me sit and read and write all morning. And the food was good. In my school in the projects, I'd been a white ticket, which meant I only had to pay ten cents a day for lunch; blue tickets, those whose families weren't on welfare, paid considerably more, a quarter, I think. I lived for lunch, though the white ticket I had to hand the cashier embarrassed me a little, especially if on a particular day I stood in line among blue tickets. At the summer school, we didn't have to mess with tickets, and the food was much better, and they let me have seconds. I believe I was the only white kid there, or one of only a few, and during one day of unstructured reading I came across a picture in a magazine of a man who looked like my Uncle Mac, Joan's older brother who was a Merchant Marine and whom I'd not seen very often. I showed my teacher, who was black, and she pointed out that the man in the picture was black. I stared at the picture awhile. I knew I was part Greek, part Irish, and even had a little German. The teacher, very sweetly, suggested that perhaps I had an ancestor from Africa.

When I got home, I told Joan the story, and asked if indeed I was part African. I hadn't seen her laugh in a long time. She was growing progressively sicker, and the doctors hadn't yet discovered what was wrong. She cracked up, slapped the table laughing, and as the laughs turned to chuckles she sucked into a teary smile, she just shrugged and said she wasn't sure, but probably not.

It was about this time I had my first experience of being hated. Across from our backdoor was the backdoor of a single woman with two red-haired sons, one my age and the other three years older. I became casual friends with the one who was my age, Skip I think his name was, and got along okay with his older brother whose name I can't remember but whom I'll call Larry.

I don't remember the exact circumstances, but one day Larry and I got into it, and I beat him up on the grass between our two yards, pummeled him, busted up his mouth, made him weep in humiliation for having been skinned by someone his brother's age and almost a foot shorter.

Skip and I remained friends, but for the entire year Larry spoke not a word to me. He ignored me absolutely, profoundly. And after a couple of months it was killing me. I'd walk beside him for blocks chattering like a real buddy, and he would not in any sense acknowledge my existence. After six, eight months I was sincerely begging him to talk to me; I offered gifts, my best marbles, my *Daredevil* one through twelve (Christ, how I wish I'd kept my collection; it would be worth a small fortune), but he didn't blink in my direction; I was a ghost whose haunting came to nothing. I told him I'd let him punch me in the stomach as hard as he could, twice, but expressionless as a god he walked on. He'd obliterated me. For him, I was dead, or never existed. His loathing of me was pure and ran to the depths of his being, and obliterated the me that was inside him. I was in awe of him. He became a kind of hero to me, exhibiting behavior I was wholly incapable of, and which gave him power, a power over me, I didn't resent so much as envy. He was skinny, nearly six feet tall, and like his brother was covered with freckles and had flaming hair. He was in ninth grade, and sometimes his friends would hang out with him at the apartment, and when I visited Skip at such times Larry's friends would treat me normally, goofing on and condescending to Skip and me, and did not seem ever to notice that Larry never acknowledged my existence, even when I spoke directly to him which I did often. The guy was beautiful. I've no doubt that wherever he is, he's rich and powerful.

That the man who has tasted human
flesh, a single piece of it cut up
among the pieces from other sacrificial
victims, must inevitably become a
wolf. Have you not heard that story?

Book VIII 565 d

I am, I suppose, a rather competitive person, and unconsciously assume a fighter's attitude in any confrontational situation. I won most of my fights as a kid and through the time I studied karate won most of my tournament fights. But I do know what it feels like to lose, to be matched against someone physically superior, or whose rage that moment is more powerful. In karate, I learned to control my rage, and to some extent the rage of my opponent. As a kid, though, the rage was all. The kid who went absolutely nuts, with rare exception, won. Once I fought a kid who became a monster, who indeed distracted me with the sheer intensity of his anger. My own anger dissipated; as I fought him I became fascinated by his rage, a pure singularity of emotion, and suddenly he was sitting on my chest pounding me in the face.

I have never spanked Ema, and of course not Anna. I've swatted Ema on the fanny, but according to the definition we, Ema and I, have agreed on, a spanking is multiple swats. But even swats, administered more often by her mother than by me, are wrong I think, though oh so difficult to avoid administering. They don't really hurt, aren't much as punitive punishment goes, but quite simply send the signal that violence is an option in the settling of disputes. Of course, Ema can spend hours discoursing on the subject of why she should not at a particular moment be compelled to clean her closet or start her homework or pick up the towel from the bathroom floor. I can begin with a gentle voice, and repeat a command several times up the vocal scale until my booming voice, which people tell me can be quite imposing, is rattling glass and charging the air with threats of retribution, and Ema, if she is in her stubborn mood, will be wholly unaffected. She fears me not at all. Dominika tells me my anger sometimes frightens her, but Ema fears nothing about me, ever. On some level, I'm her pet, protecting her and serving her and loving her. For a standard psychological test that all kids in the Czech Republic take, when asked to draw a picture of her home life, or something to that effect, she drew a very happy picture of me lying on a bed reading a book and her standing by me with a big smile, and the school shrink commented on how comfortable Ema is with her tata, her father, her big pet bear who reads to her, tells her stories, and talktalktalks to her.

And she is so much like me, dreamy, easily distracted, good-hearted, driven by an impulse to tell the truth, though I have learned to lie in the ways one must to live among others, and she will too. We possess similar intelligences, make similar kinds of intuitive leaps and notice similar kinds of things as we pass through the world. Dominika is much more practical, and analytical, more grounded in details. Ema and I skim along the surface of life's details. We drive Dom crazy, but she loves us, and compensates for our driftiness, our dreaminess, our penchant for living within ourselves inattentive to the details, for us the sometimes inscrutable details, of daily domestic existence.

I am a good partner because I'm only truly happy when I'm with my family, and I do try to carry my share of the domestic load. However, I'm not one to play Mr. Fixit, and figure that one aspect of feminism benefiting my selfish interests is that which admonishes against a too-strict adherence to gender roles relative to work. I have no problem letting a broken something-or-other remain non-functional until Dominka, exasperated, pulls out the tools and fixes it herself. I'll wash dishes, mow lawns, sweep and mop, cheerfully change Annie's soiled diapers, give baths, hang clothes, haul furniture, do daily shopping, but I'll fix nothing. For that Dom must rely on her own acumen, or, as we half-joke, "find a real man," like her brother. If Ema ends up with a life partner like me, being so much like me herself, she'll be in a hell of a fix domestically speaking. Luckily, I'm raising a family with a woman who compensates nicely for my weaknesses, and besides being beautiful and smart and wonderfully stubborn, possesses a great sense of humor. Dom, Ema and I, and even little Annie, laugh a lot. Our home is full of emotion, great swings of feeling and loud expressions of it. You'd think we were Italian. Dominika stomps around in the morning getting things going. As she begins the arduous work of bringing order to our lives for that particular day, she flips between Czech and English, imploring Ema to get up and get ready for school and me to attend to Annie. I sleep three or four fewer hours than she most nights because I get up to write and read, so am not quite as focused in the morning. Ema, Anna and Dom become at times a banshee chorus, a shrill rippling of commands, shrieks and loud pouting all of which can shift in a second to giggles and laughter.

And so it is throughout the day as we come and go, in New Orleans or Prague, together and apart and in different combinations. The delicious noise of my family, its uninhibited expressions of feelings, its unabashed responses to the world and each other, fills my life.

Er said that it was a spectacle
worth seeing how the souls each
chose their lives. It was pitiful,
ridiculous, and surprising. For
the most part their choice depended
upon the character of the previous
life. He said that he saw the soul
which had once been that of Orpheus
choosing the life of a swan in his
hatred of women; because of his
death at their hands he did not
want to be born of a woman.

Book X 620 a

In the projects in Norfolk I was playing baseball, or one of those sand-lot spin-offs, like "Five Hundred"—one guy throws the ball up and hits it and if one of the guys in the field catches it on the fly he, the one who caught it, gets a hundred points, after one bounce seventy-five, et cetera—and just as I hit the ball, exactly at the moment I hit it, a loud thump exploded on the street. We ran to see.

The retarded kid, the eight-year old village idiot, I think his name was Mark, lay in the street, his head soaked in blood. The driver stood over him, stunned, mumbling that the kid had run out in the middle of the street. I don't recall what happened after that, except that that evening, at least for the twilight part of it, I and the others of my family stayed in one of the apartments across the way. For some reason we were waiting for news about the retarded kid with one of our neighbors and her two kids. Finally news came. It circulated from apartment to apartment, kids carrying the information from slapping screen door to slapping screen door. The retarded kid was dead.

He hadn't been particularly loved, even liked much. But he'd always been around. He'd been good for shagging balls that sailed into the wooded lot across from our little horseshoe of dingy brick apartments, and when he'd gotten bothersome he'd been easy to shoo away. I wish I could say sweet things about the poor, grinning idiot. But I have no sweet memories. All I may really say is that he'd always been around, that he'd not been much trouble, and that for a few weeks his absence was conspicuous. Those first several nights, especially the first one, were full of dread. Death was squatting on our lives, and it messed up our sleep, our dreams. But then time scabbed over, and we continued our routines of play and mischief. The retarded kid's absence became less and less conspicuous, until even his absence was gone.

An admiral's son named Mitch drove a motorcycle off a cliff in Sasebo. The story was that he got really drunk up on Dragon Heights where all the brass lived, and just aimed the thing for the cliff. He was kind of a handsome guy, with a lantern jaw, who wore glasses. I'd been in Sasebo about a year when he arrived there, and got along with him fine. He found a girlfriend real fast, a good-looking one, and was a good bowler, which was a big deal in Sasebo where a one hundred and eighty-six average in league garnered considerable prestige. I think he even played with G and me on the basketball team. He was liked. He drank, like the rest of us, and may have gotten his hands on other stuff as well. I recall that he did get a bit wacky when he drank, but nothing over the several months he was in Sasebo prepared anyone for his suicide, much less in the manner he achieved it. G and Leo and I went to the hospital to check on Mitch, and the head of the hospital, a tall and skinny old four-striper whose daughter we went to school with, told us to pray for our friend. We realized that pretty much meant he'd soon be dead.

And he was. We were nostalgic a while, talked about things we'd done with him, like renting motorboats from Special Services and racing out to the cluster of tiny islands known as Ninety-nine Islands, and hol-ing up in cemented caves where Japanese anti-aircraft guns had been sta-tioned. We'd drink Akadama port wine and speculate as to what the graf-fiti, in kanji of course, meant.

Lying in bed that evening I recalled the time we all went on a field trip to the "Atrocity Museum" at ground zero in Nagasaki. We'd walked around glancing at the mangled clocks, the actual shadows of humans whose limbs were akimbo like in cartoons. And we'd paraded in front of photographs, the images of horrors. I think I'd read Hersey's *Hiroshima*, and at the age of sixteen was beginning to try to fathom the horrors of the world. I recalled the Japanese kids walking around among us, seeming as abstracted from the documented horror as the American kids were. I recalled Mitch cracked a couple of jokes under his breath about French-fried Japs and such, and though I'd not been mature enough to be out-raged, nor had I been able to laugh. I recalled, though, getting chills when among the school kids, Japanese and American, I'd seen an ancient tiny woman in full-dress kimono. As I lay in bed recalling her, I again got chills, for surely she'd lived through it. With no concrete evidence, I was certain that she'd lived through it. And I still believe she was a survivor of that conflagration, that as old as she was, as formally dressed as she was in such a place as that, she could only have been someone who had sur-vived what she gazed upon, and I recalled she had gazed placidly, tight-lipped, her head always up, unblinking. As I lay there that evening of the death of a casual friend, one I'd liked okay, but not well enough really to mourn, I thought about that ancient tiny woman, and about how she'd gazed upon the horrors she herself had surely survived, and my friend's absence, his conspicuous absence began immediately to fade, and I knew that in only a few weeks or even days, in the hearts of his peers his absence would itself disappear.

All over Prague are memorials; on many buildings are encased old photographs of wartime martyrs and people whose names and images their loved ones simply wanted not to fade. In New Orleans, when one of the old jazz men or women, and certain individuals who were simply cool in life, die, they get jazz funerals. Brass bands play peppy numbers with lots of soulful distortion, and mourners dance under frilly umbrellas behind the caskets. Everything tends toward absence, and then the absences disappear.

Like my birds. I'd get them from the Bird Rehab at the zoo, raise them, mostly mockers and jays, in my House of the Rising Sun apartment, feeding them moist cat food by hand until they were fledglings, then I'd help them learn to fly in my apartment, cleaning up their shit, constantly cleaning up their shit, until they were almost grown, when I would let them go batch by batch, and batch by batch they would return as grown birds, for weeks, to be hand-fed, one by one, lined up comically on the railing of my rear balcony overlooking the courtyard, and then after gulping their two or three pinches pulsate away. Then, eaten by cats or simply acclimated, they'd stop coming.

In a tiny apartment overlooking that same courtyard, at the far end of which was a nineteenth century voodoo shrine covered with decades-old chalked X's, my neighbor, a tiny Filipino ex-sailor in his late seventies, went completely nuts. A victim of sudden dementia, he stacked all his furniture in front of his two doors and screamed that ghosts were after him. He howled for days, off and on, and after a while the silent times were the scariest. I phoned the owner of the building, a ninetyish retired judge we called Judge Levy, but his mid-fortyish wife, the physically imposing and politically powerful Darlene Jacobs, was the one who really ran things. For all of Jacob's aggressiveness—there was a sweet gruffness about her, and she obviously feared no man, especially if he was another lawyer— she seemed a kind person, and the judge himself, still lucid and active, seemed also kind. They'd rented the place quite cheaply to the little Filipino ex-sailor out of compassion, and when they learned of his condition responded likewise with compassion, finding a V.A. hospital that would process him in and take care of him. But it took a while, and for several days I awoke to my birds squawking for breakfast, Bob the Filipino ex-sailor screaming at ghosts, and the guy who lived above me, Ed, talking, literally, to his gun.

Ed, it seemed, didn't like homosexuals, and therefore had made a very unwise choice as to where to live considering that the Quarter was brimming with queens of every flavor. Each morning, for a while, he sat in a chair on his rear balcony, which was just above mine, and cleaned, loaded and unloaded, polished and talked to his gun about how much he hated homosexuals. One morning, as I fed my squawking birds, pinch by moist pinch of Fancy Feast, and Bob screamed at the top of his feeble lungs in three languages, sometimes it seemed all at once, I heard Ed's gun click twice.

I didn't know if he'd pointed it at the sky, at Bob's barricaded doors, the floor of his balcony and therefore at me, or at his own temple or neck. But he'd definitely taken a couple of practice shots without bullets. It was an exhilarating moment, actually. I suddenly realized that except for a very narrow range of experiences all linked to familial love and work, life has absolutely nothing to recommend it. Greek tragedy came suddenly into focus. The Greeks' gods, except for Dionysius who sneaked in from the East, were simply aristocrats who lived forever and had supernatural powers. One didn't pray to such beings, not in the way even we today in the West understand prayer; one simply appeased them, hoping not to get messed with. They might pitch in and assist this or that hero, but they might just as soon tell the great mortal to kiss their immortal asses and turn away, dramatizing the gulf between gods and people. The Greeks had no conception of redemption; that was something folks on the other side of the lake, in the so-called Holy Land, were slowly concocting, and which of course Christianity parlayed into one of the world's great products, right up there with petroleum. The heroic, which is meaningless if supernatural redemption is an option, is therefore likewise meaningless except as a function of a tragic sense of life. I believe in heroism; that we all seek it— though we're ashamed to think of it that way— even in our little jobs and circles of friends, and it seems the only source of meaning beyond the love of children.

I go through life daily experiencing two powerful, simple and contrary impulses. I want by turns to brutalize everyone who gets in my way, and to embrace everything, everyone, to take care of everyone. I don't believe in supernatural redemption, but in this very real and doomed world I have seen, and felt, blessings, blessings that are fleeting, like things with wings, and like words on small signs at the side of the road.

> . . . when all had gone through, they
> all went to the plain of forgetfulness
> in burning, choking, terrible heat,
> for it was empty of trees and of the
> plants that grow from the earth.
> There they camped, as it was now
> evening, by the stream of Oblivion
> whose water no vessel can hold.

Book X 621 a

J oan, I don't know who you were. I recall when, in Elizabeth City, living above the goat people, we had a tabby cat, or, as the cliché goes, she had us, and you made me watch her give birth to four kittens in a nest of filthy clothes in your closet. I was scared to watch but you made me. Later, the Tabby left dead birds under and in your bed, for weeks, and you said they were gifts, that they were all she had to give.

Every weeping woman has been you. Every laughing woman has been you. Every moaning, sighing, screaming, scolding, talking, singing woman has been you, and I don't know who you were, and so I cannot know who they have been, who they are.

Now you are nothing. Or everything, depending on how it works, how death works. As in language, we're told, the relation between signifier and signified is random, is in and of itself meaningless, surely the relation between the living body and its life, its "soul," is likewise. That which signifies may be erased, by existing invites erasure, and so too the living body, no less mutable, though that which is signified is tenacious, protean and fierce in its projection along innumerable simultaneous trajectories in memory.

There is a man in New Orleans, not exactly a friend but someone I have always liked and admired, who has without knowing it done my soul a great service. His name is Charlie Bishop, and he was my colleague, a specialist in Victorian literature, before he retired. Charlie Bishop calls himself a performance artist now, and he is very funny, very witty, quite entertaining when he does what he calls art. I'm not sure that what he does is art, but that's my problem, not his, and to be amused for a few minutes by that which may not be art is almost always better than to have done to you what I think art does when it is not amusing.

But whatever Charlie Bishop is doing when he is making, or doing, what he calls art matters to me because at the end of each of his performances he scatters a little of his mother's ashes and bone chips near where he has just performed. That is how he ends what he calls his art. Whatever it is, it ends with a scattering of what is left of the body of the woman from whom his body issued, and even as he depletes with each scattering that which, to me, gives powerful resonance to whatever it is he calls his art, he is signifying powerfully and wordlessly something essential about what I call art: Whatever it is about it is about loss and therefore mourning, and the first loss for every person, male and female, is the mother's body. We begin our mourning in the first speech act, and it is usually a sound that refers to the mother's living body, and we utter it first and most often thereafter in a despair of separation from that body.

When you were a very young woman and I was three or four, there was a period when we were staying in a small apartment, and you made me lie down with you every afternoon to nap. I don't remember there being any other kids around, but surely Chuck, at least, was somewhere. Perhaps you made both of us nap with you and he, so small, lay on the other side such that I did not see him. Perhaps Theresa was in a crib somewhere. The feel I have for the occasion, though, is that we, you and I, were alone.

You slept and I, restless as always, could not. I played sometimes under the sheet. I liked the way the light filtered so brightly through the white fabric, and I played at squinting and trying to see through the fabric, which with my eyes pressed against it I could a little. I could see the outline of the high window through which the light poured, and I could see the shadows of little-leafed branches nodding.

I studied your body under that bright tent. It was my mother's body. I liked it. I liked the way it smelled. I poked at you a little and you didn't wake and I wanted you to because I was getting bored. So I poked you some more and you still didn't even twitch. You slept soundly on your side facing away from me. Your slip—you seemed always back then to sleep in white slips—was hiked up over your ass, so I poked you there, and then lower.

Down lower you were wet, and I smelled my fingers where I'd touched the wet and it was not a pretty smell and yet I loved it immediately. I touched you a few more times there and smelled my fingers. And for a couple of days running I did the same thing during the naps, until finally you awoke and screamed at me, and Dick came running in, and you told him what I'd done, and he beat me and beat me and beat me, until I couldn't cry, until I could make no noise, until lights were exploding in my head and you were screaming from far away for him to stop but he kept pounding me with his fist.

Then, later, he gave me a black sock filled with pennies, and wept, and then I slept alone in the late afternoon, bruised, my nose and mouth crusted with blood, battered all over my body, and dreamed of clowns.

I will never forget the odor of your young woman's body. I have smelled approximations, but no odor exactly like it. That memory is worth that beating.

7970

About the author

In addition to *The Republic of Burma Shave*, Richard Katrovas is the author of five books of poems, most recently, *Dithyrambs: Choral Lyrics* (Carnegie Mellon University Press 1998), and a book of short stories. He teaches in the MFA Program at the University of New Orleans and is director of the Prague Summer Seminars, the preeminent study-abroad program in writing, arts and humanities.

7270